The Problem of Self-Love in St. Augustine

THE PROBLEM OF
SELF-LOVE IN ST. AUGUSTINE

OLIVER O'DONOVAN

NEW HAVEN AND LONDON
YALE UNIVERSITY PRESS

Published with assistance from the foundation
established in memory of Amos Stone Mather
of the Class of 1907, Yale College

BV
4639
.038
1980

Designed by James J. Johnson
and set in IBM Press Roman type.
Printed in the United States of America by
Edwards Brothers, Inc.,
Ann Arbor, Michigan

Library of Congress Cataloging in Publication Data

O'Donovan, Oliver.
    The problem of self-love in St. Augustine.

    Bibliography: p.
    Includes indexes.
    1. Self-love (Theology)—History of doctrines—
Early church, ca. 30–600.   2. Christian ethics—
Early church, ca. 30–600.   3. Augustinius, Aurelius,
Saint, Bp. of Hippo.—Ethics.   I. Title.
BV4639.038   241' .4   80–5397
ISBN 0-300-02468-1

171.193
Au45Yo

10 9 8 7 6 5 4 3 2 1   81033015

CONTENTS

PREFACE

When an author bids godspeed to work which has occupied him for a decade, he does so with mingled feelings of relief and nostalgia. The debts he has accumulated in that time are too numerous to recount in full; but a few stand out like landmarks which help him trace the course of the path he has traveled. This study was begun in 1970 when I was for a brief time a student in the Department of Religion at Princeton University—a privilege I owed to a grant from the Advisory Council for the Church's Ministry, a benevolent arm of the Church of England. The stimulation I received there from Gene Outka will be evident to readers of this book; my debt to Paul Ramsey for his initial and continuing encouragement is less apparent but no less real. I continued my work in Oxford with the indulgent support of the Principal of Wycliffe Hall, whom I was supposedly serving as a full-time tutor, and it became the matter of the thesis which I presented to the University of Oxford for the degree of Doctor of Philosophy in 1975. Those who have had the good fortune to work with a kindly and wise supervisor will understand the extent of my debt to Henry Chadwick, at that time Dean of Christ Church. My most recent obligation is to the staff of the Yale University Press for their care and courtesy in dealing with the manuscript.

The delay in publication has been a blessing in two respects. I have been able to take advantage of P.-P. Verbraken's *Etudes Critiques sur les Sermons Authentiques de Saint Augustin,* and so bring some order to what was once the very chaotic business of referring to Augustine's sermons. I also feel that I have been able to handle the philosophical issues more deftly in 1979 than I could in 1975, and if that is so, the credit is certainly due to my wife, Joan. But the final version will not now be read by someone with whom I was twice privileged to have discussions at an earlier stage, John Burnaby, who passed from *desiderium* to *delectatio* earlier this year, saluted by grateful Augustinians everywhere.

And if our eye outlooks that mark, to whom should I express my thanks more readily than to Augustine himself? To live with him intermittently for ten years, to think, to pray, to preach, to teach under his tutelage, has been a life-shaping experience of which, I fear, the reader of this study will gain barely an idea. There can be few thinkers, Christian or not, who have so much that they can give to a careful student. And yet he gives it always with a caution: *Expectationem vestram Deus impleat ex ore nostro. Amastis enim ut veniretis: sed amastis, quid? Si nos, et hoc bene: nam volumus amari a vobis, sed nolumus in nobis. Quia ergo in Christo vos amamus, in Christo nos redamate, et amor noster pro invicem gemat ad Deum.*

September 1979
Toronto

INTRODUCTION:
THE PROBLEM OF SELF-LOVE

"The primal destruction of man was self-love." "There is no one who does not love himself; but one must search for the right love and avoid the warped." "Indeed you did not love yourself when you did not love the God who made you." These three sentences set side by side show why the idea of self-love in St. Augustine of Hippo constitutes a problem. Self-love is loving God; it is also hating God. Self-love is common to all men; it is restricted to those who love God. Mutually incompatible assertions about self-love jostle one another and demand to be reconciled. And Augustine himself refuses to undertake this task for us. There is no "theory of self-love" articulated in his pages. He rarely tells us what he means by the phrase, and when he does he is misleading.

Yet the problem has a far greater fascination than if it were merely a matter of sighing over terminological loose ends in the work of a single theologian. For the notion of self-love has never been long absent from Christian theology, and whenever it has returned it has brought its sheaves of paradox with it. Two texts from the synoptic Gospels have kept it in view. One of them, the second member of the twofold love-command, "You shall love your neighbor as yourself," was fundamental to Western Christian moral thinking. The other, while not actually using the expression "self-love," was definitive for the paradox: "Whoever would save his life will lose it; and whoever loses his life for my sake and the gospel's will save it."[1] This biblical foundation served to support bewilderingly complex and conflicting ways of speaking. We find Calvin describing self-love as a "noxious pest" and Joseph Butler lamenting that men have not enough regard to their own good. We hear Kierkegaard enigmatically

instructing us to "love yourself in the same way as you love your
neighbour when you love him as yourself." St. Thomas Aquinas
warns us of the multiple meanings of the phrase and cautions us
against confusion. Generalizing broadly, we may say with Thomas
that there are three different evaluations of self-love possible within the Christian theological tradition: friendly, hostile, and neutral.[2] But many writers have slipped, consciously or unconsciously,
from one to another of these. The truth is that despite Thomas's
cautions the idea of self-love has rarely been thoroughly examined.
In a manner quite appropriate to the texts of Scripture which
started it all, self-love has been the object of a thousand passing
allusions.

     If we look for a well-defined and limited area of study in which
to attempt some clarification, the writings of St. Augustine immediately recommend themselves. He is the first of the Latin Fathers to
make any serious use of the expression *amor sui* and the first of any
of the Fathers to offer an account of the scriptural phrase "as yourself" in this connection. He uses the phrase over the whole of its
evaluative range, positive, negative, and neutral, and so represents the
wider problem rather well.[3] And his use of it is associated with the
eudaemonist theory of ethics, central to his theological and metaphysical convictions, so that we have access to the question in a context
where the predominant theological pressures may easily be traced.
Certainly "self-love" is not a great Augustinian theological artifact;
yet it has been significantly fashioned by Augustine's theology, and
there are many such artifacts in the middle ground and background
of the picture.

     The history of "self-love" before Augustine can be summarized
briefly. There exists in Greek a word, *philautia*, the natural tone of
which is negative.[4] With this tone it makes its one appearance in the
New Testament (2 Tim. 3:2), and with this tone it is found in the
works of Philo of Alexandria, who regards it as the central impiety
from which other vices flow.[5] In the Greek Christian writers the influence of Philo can be felt: Clement of Alexandria makes a number

of references to *philautia*, Origen a few, the Cappadocian Fathers and their dependents a number. Outside this mystical company we find a scattering of isolated occurrences, some of them comments on the scriptural text, all of them negative in tone. Before Maximus Confessor in the seventh century A.D. it appears that no Greek Christian thought of *philautia* as something possibly commendable.[6]

There was, however, an inclination in pre-Christian Greek philosophy to speak of *philautia* in a different way. In Plato's *Laws* we first encounter the saying, apparently traditional, that "every man is naturally his own friend." This idea was to provide Aristotle with a developed theory of friendship. In the *Eudemian Ethics* he elaborates the theory that friendship is formed on the basis of self-esteem by the recognition in the friend of that rational nature which one has learned to value in himself; in the *Nicomachean Ethics* the word *philautia* is brought in to express this positive self-evaluation. In introducing the word, Aristotle acknowledges that common usage is against its carrying anything but a negative tone; but common usage, he thinks, is wrong. It is not, of course, the universality of this Aristotelian self-love which breaks with customary modes of speech, for anyone in a moment of disillusion may say that all men are selfish, but its neutral, or even positive, moral tone.[7]

In Latin the situation is not at all so clear, and, without the assistance of a study as thorough as that which Hausherr devoted to the Greek expression, we must be content with some tentative generalizations.[8] There appear to be three ways of speaking about *amor sui* (or *dilectio sui*), not consciously distinguished and often flowing into one another. First there is what we take to be the common, popular idea of self-love as a widespread but not very praiseworthy attitude. Often *love* seems to carry an evaluative sense in this context: self-love is having a high opinion of yourself, being blind to your own limitations.[9] Secondly, there is the Latin equivalent of Aristotle's *philautia*, the self-estimative basis of friendship. This use is in evidence in that treatise which, at one or two removes, seems to be strongly dependent on Aristotle's *Ethics*, Cicero's *Laelius*. (And inasmuch as

Cicero is more insistent than Aristotle that only virtuous men can form true friendships, "self-love" in this work takes on a more positive aspect even than it had in the source.)[10] Thirdly, there is a use of *amor sui* that is characteristic of the Stoics and relates to their doctrine of *oikeiosis*. Self-love is a natural dynamism in animal life which operates to protect and defend the integrity of the subject. Its tone is basically neutral but can fluctuate between positive and negative. Positively, it appears in both a lower and a higher form, as life according to animal nature in the infant and as life according to reason in the philosopher; philosophic conversion is the transformation of self-love from the one form to the other. Negatively, it is the reason why even adults with philosophical aspirations will retain their fear of death.[11]

The phrase *se ipsum diligere* was employed by Rufinus to translate Basil's *philautia*; but we cannot say that the expression in this or one of the other senses played any significant part in Latin theology before Augustine. Indeed, it is surprising how little attention is paid to the "summary of the law," the "two commands" of love-of-God and love-of-neighbor, in either the Western or the Eastern Fathers. Clement of Alexandria and Origen both comment on the summary and argue that the "neighbor" whom we are to love second to God is Christ; Gregory of Nyssa mentions it, and adds as a third command love of one's wife. "Barnabas" tactfully glosses the phrase "as yourself" to mean "more than your own life."[12] Until more detailed research proves otherwise, we must make the supposition that Augustine is responsible not only for the currency of "self-love" in the theology of the West but also for the predominance of the "summary" in Western Christian ethics.

THE PHILOSOPHY OF SELF-LOVE

The philosophical analysis of self-love is altogether more complicated than even the subtle St. Thomas admitted. Having differentiated the senses in which the three contrasting evaluations are made, we face extensive work ahead of us. First, we must ask what concepts of love and of self are appealed to in the various uses of the phrase. What models can we use for the act or attitude of loving? We may, perhaps, think of love as a way of human relating, a behavior pattern involving more than one person, rather like dancing a pas de deux. In this case self-love must appear, as it has appeared to many theologians down the centuries, inescapably paradoxical, and the same will be true if we take the seeking or acquisitive pattern as characteristic of love. Conceptual purism may then suggest that all thought of loving oneself had better be abandoned altogether.[13] Alternatively, we may search for a proper use for the paradox. Some reflexive expressions have a negating sense: if a man "talks to himself," for example, he need not literally address himself as "you," but may just talk into the air, to nobody; or if a man is "self-deceived" it does not mean he is so by any ruse or trick but simply that he acts on false assumptions, as he would if someone had deceived him, though in fact nobody has done so. In just the same way, it could be held, self-love is a kind of nonlove; and this could be taken either negatively as a failure to love or positively as an attitude of confidence such as might have sprung, though it did not, from the consciousness of being loved.[14]

There are other ways of understanding love which offer a better prospect for the reflexive use. Psychologists sometimes speak of self-love to mean what they express more technically as autoerotism.[15] In this context, where love is nothing more than receiving erotic stimulation, love of oneself would seem to be analogous to love of someone else. More sophisticatedly, some recent philosophical studies analyze love as a synthesis of value judgment and emotional attraction, and again, on certain readings of this thesis, there would seem to be no reason why self-love should not be treated as a literal expression. It is as easy to form value judgments about oneself as it is to form them about other people, though whether the emotional aspect is as simply accommodated will depend on how the emotions are conceived of as operating.[16] What if love is interpreted as benevolence, that is, planning and acting to promote someone's welfare? Here, too, one may love oneself in just the same way as one may love others. When we condemn "selfishness," we normally mean "thinking of oneself" in just this sense, with the unspoken assumption that "thinking of others" is something one ought to do as well, or instead. And the possibilities are still not exhausted. Within the Thomist tradition love has been used with a wide metaphysical sense to mean a movement toward, or a force maintaining, cohesion and unity, whether of the universe at one extreme or of the individual personality at the other. This will tend to yield an idea of self-love as a kind of personal ontological integrity, an "identity with ourselves, an adherence to ourselves," as Gilleman describes it. In this case love-of-self, so far from being the surd among loves, becomes the archetype of them all, a presupposition of all further loving relationships, which will, given the interrelatedness of all agents, necessarily lead on to other loving relationships if only it is itself complete.[17]

Of such a kind are the ambiguities of the word *love*. It would hardly seem possible that so inoffensive an item as the reflexive pronoun could complicate things much more, and yet here too there is room for disagreement. To certain thinkers it comes naturally to conceive of "divisions" of the psyche; to others it appears obvious that the psyche must be something unitary. Contemporary Christian theologians are somewhat jealous of their monist anthropology, and though no doubt they will accept a demand for compromise more readily from Freud than from Plato, they are still hardly likely to be enthusiastic. We must grant Christian monists the point that divisions of the soul, whether Platonic or Freudian, have a most obscure metaphysical status. Freud occasionally appears to argue for them on no more sophisticated ground than the mere fact of reflexive operations, thus begging the whole question of whether or not the operation in question can *naturally* be conceived of as reflexive or not.[18] The matter is confused still further when psychologists of the so-called dynamic school introduce their own new category of the self, defined by one representative as "the body and mind . . . as they are observed and reacted to by the individual." Here, one would have thought, there could be no suggestion of ontological independence, for the "self" is by definition a creation of the "ego," nothing more than an idea in the subject's mind; yet such a consideration does not seem to limit the ease with which this "self" is commonly hypostatized. In principle the self should be as endlessly susceptible of division as the ideas of the mind are susceptible of multiplication, any new selection of features constituting at any moment a new idea of oneself. But psychologists of this school detect sufficient consistency in the way people view themselves to generalize the possibilities into two, an empirical and an ideal self, a "self as conceived" and a "self to be realised."[19]

Once the conceptual possibilities have been reviewed, we are faced with a series of questions in the realm of metaethics. How may an idea of justifiable self-regard be fitted into a theory of morality? One possibility would be to restrict it to a subordinate place in the hierarchy of principles. There are indeed, one might say, duties that a moral agent has with regard to himself, but they arise only because they serve some higher moral principle which is not self-regarding. The father of a family, for example, should take care not to destroy his own health by overwork; but the reason he ought not to do so is simply that he owes it to his family to be well. It is not necessary that the higher principle served by such self-referring obligations should be the principle of other-regard. Self-regard and other-regard might both alike be subordinated to some more abstract and generalized principle such as justice. A second possibility would be the ethical theory of "egoism," in which all other moral obligations are held to flow from an ultimate obligation of personal fulfillment. A third theory, more difficult to pin down but highly characteristic of Christian theologians, is that self-regard and some other non-self-referring principle ultimately coincide; so that while nothing can be justified on other grounds which could not also be justified on grounds of self-regard, equally, nothing could be truly self-regarding if it was not demonstrably right on other grounds.

Within the formal framework of these three possibilities ethical theories could be multiplied almost indefinitely, not only by varying the alternatives to self-regard (justice, other-regard, love of God, etc.) but by shifting the epistemological weight from one part of the hierarchy to another. It is not necessary in any ethical theory that the principle of ultimate justification should also be the heuristic rule for discovering what is right and what is wrong. A good example of the contrary case is the theory called "Rule Utilitarianism," which (to summarize rather crudely) declares that the greatest happiness of the greatest number is the formal ultimate justification of all moral obligations, but then refers us to rules of a quite different kind, themselves justified by their utility, for daily practical guidance. A Christian theory which was formally "egoist" might nevertheless insist that only in the revealed moral law could we learn what kind of behavior served our own best interests. This point becomes of great significance for interpreting the third kind of theory, that in which two different moral principles are said to coincide. We often find Christians saying something slightly paradoxical, that virtue is indeed rewarding but that the blessing must not be "something which the agent himself intended." Thus one modern writer remarks that "Heaven is full of people who are not particularly concerned with being there." This paradox arises from an ethical theory which allows an equal but not exclusive *justifying* role to the principle of self-interest, but no *epistemological* role at all. As soon as the agent begins thinking about his own satisfaction, he is no longer on the way to achieving it. Virtue is good because it fulfills humanity. But humanity cannot pursue virtue by pursuing fulfillment.[20]

When the foothills of philosophical investigation have been crossed, there open up to us yet higher and more massive ranges. The issues now are largely theological. Why should a *Christian* choose one kind of theory rather than another? The arbitration among ethical theories is normally thought to be a task of philosophy, to be settled on grounds of coherence and consistency. Should not the theologian remain indifferent to the outcome and accept whatever theory his philosophical colleague tells him is the best? In fact, however, theologians do choose theories of morality by criteria drawn from their own discipline; they find that one rather than another is convenient for expressing what they have to say about original sin or about the moral law and divine grace or about created theology and the eschaton. The nature of this transition from theological to philosophical principle is difficult to identify, but that there really is a connection theological history alone would lead us to conclude with some certainty. It is in the last degree implausible that Catholics have stoutly defended self-love down the ages and Protestants castigated them for it solely because of a foolish misunderstanding about what each meant by the phrase. An enquiry which begins as a simple attempt to sort out the different senses of self-love is bound to end by arbitrating major theological causes.[21]

But the wider philosophical and theological issues must wait their turn until our last chapter. For the most part our study will be concerned to report and analyze the treatment they receive from St. Augustine.

CHAPTER ONE

FOUR ASPECTS OF LOVE

An essential preliminary to our study is a survey of Augustine's thoughts about "love" itself. But here we have to pick our way across the field of a major interpretative battle on which the smoke still hangs heavy—that battle, of course, which was provoked by Anders Nygren's presentation of Augustinian *caritas* as a synthesis of self-sacrificing *agape* and self-seeking *eros*. To the merits of Nygren's critique of Augustine (for that is what it is) we shall pay more serious attention in the final chapter. Our purpose for the present is to take as quick a path through the conflict as we may, observing only what will assist us in reaching our own interpretation. This will involve one or two general comments about Nygren's approach, followed by a glance at the discussion it has provoked among Swedish scholars, a discussion into which our own view of the question fits most naturally.[1]

It is inevitable that any account of love in Augustine's thought will have to distinguish different strands within it. Perhaps it is unnecessary to labor the point at this stage that such distinctions cannot be made simply on the basis of vocabulary alone. Nygren's popularizers have sometimes imagined that they could read off philosophy from the lexicon, as when one well-known writer argues, with reference to the famous "Love and do as you will" saying, that the use of *diligere* in preference to *amare* indicates the meaning "love with care" and not "love with desire." Nygren himself is not so thoughtless, and yet his astonishing assertion that Augustine was disingenuous in claiming synonymity for the words *amor, dilectio* and *caritas* betrays the same sort of confusion.[2] It may be convenient for modern thinkers to label certain motifs by the Latin or Greek words which they think incapsulate them, but they should not then suppose that they have discovered a lexicographical statute to which ancient writers can be held. The ancients spoke the language and we do not speak it. The modern reader does not always discern the many pressures which control their choice of vocabulary, and even when it is plain that one word carries nuances which another does not, he needs to be very sure of himself before asserting that those nuances must be important in any particular instance.[3]

We do not lack guidance from Augustine about the nuances of the three central words for "love." *Dilectio* and *caritas* are words more suited than *amor* to express a love directed to worthy objects, a love which may be approved and encouraged.[4] *Caritas,* furthermore, has a religious flavor; it is properly used with either God or the soul as its object, it is love for the eternal or for that which can itself love the eternal, it is the love of man for God and for his neighbor.[5] Yet on other occasions Augustine has a different account and is prepared to say that the three are synonymous.[6] His actual usage is neither as discriminating as the one theory nor as indiscriminate as the other. The rule about *caritas* is consistently observed: there is no *caritas* of evil or of worldly things, but only *cupiditas.*[7] The fact that Scripture uses *caritas* to express the nature of God (1 John 4:8,16, constantly quoted by Augustine) seems to impart an air of sanctity to the word. Between *dilectio* and *amor,* however, Augustine shows no very clear resolve to distinguish. He uses either of them indifferently to express the love of man for God, the love of God for man, and the love of man for lower objects; both, he insists, are used by Holy Scripture in good and bad senses.[8] Yet we can easily observe that in the homiletic works he finds it easier to use *amor* than elsewhere. This surely suggests that considerations of style rather than of theological content are predominant.

What are these different "motifs" that we will have to distinguish in Augustine's thought about love? Are they different kinds of love, which can and perhaps must occur separately in life? Or are they just different ways of looking at one and the same phenomenon? Nygren is quite clear that *agape* and *eros* are distinct not only in

thought but in reality. He calls them "different general attitudes to
life." He calls the Augustinian idea of love a "synthesis," yielding a
"tertium quid."[9]

Some of Nygren's critics have apparently been content to accept
the postulate of an objective plurality of loves, contending only that
the different loves so identified can and should coexist in one subject,
perhaps even in one relationship.[10] And clearly, if we have a certain
range of phenomena to study, this is a compelling approach. Consider
the difference between a man's love for his wife, his love for his son,
his love for his childhood friend, and his love for his parents. We need
to say that these are different kinds of love, species within the genus.
They are different to the one who experiences them, they are different to one who observes them. If this had been the kind of distinction
that Nygren was making, it would have been sufficient to reply that
though different these loves are not different attitudes to life. They
are meant to exist in combination. To be the subject of a number of
them is to be a whole and balanced personality.

But neither Augustine nor Nygren generally had this wide scope
of particular affections, each with its different psychological structure,
in view. Their discussion turns on the universal moral attitudes which
Christ commands as the sum of moral and religious duty, love-of-God
and love-of-neighbor. And to attempt to distinguish different kinds
of love within either of these would appear to be artificially precise.
How could one love God with the wrong kind of love? One can love
him too little; one can love Mammon in his place. But the love of God
is simply the love of God, not an attitude in need of further specifi-
cation before we can discern what it is that is required of us. The same
can be said for love of neighbor, provided that it is still the universal
attitude and not the particularized relationships that is in question.[11]

When we find ourselves distinguishing different strands of thought
about love-of-God and love-of-neighbor, then, it is not that there are
several different loves, immanently distinguished, but that the loving
subject stands in a complex and variable relation to the reality which
his love confronts. Pluriformity is imposed upon his love from out-

side by the pluriform structure of reality; or, in Augustine's favorite phrase, his love is "ordered." He may find himself dependent or depended upon, equal or unequal, commanding or under command; but these are not things that he controls, and his love must still be love in whatever relation to its object it may find itself. Thus we do well to speak of "aspects" of love rather than of "kinds" and to remember as we differentiate them that we have to do not only with subjectivity but with the complex order of reality that is love's object. *Subjectively*, love-of-neighbor is one thing. Augustine himself will even be prepared to say that it is one thing with love-of-God, for in either case the ontological ground of love is the Holy Spirit shed abroad in our hearts.

Nygren contrasted his eros and agape especially in terms of their differing grounds, objective and subjective, for finding an object valuable. Eros "recognizes" value in the object of love, agape "creates" value in it.[12] A love which presupposes a subject–object polarity between itself and the value in which it rejoices is, for Nygren, "thirsty" and so self-seeking. Only when value is posited in the object by the subject is there self-giving love. If we measure Augustine's view of love by this criterion, it is clear that only God's love for man can be agape, for that alone is without presupposition. Man's love for God rests in the absolute value which is intrinsic to God's being, while man's love for man presupposes the value which God, as Creator and Redeemer, has already set upon the object before the subject stumbles upon him. No man could claim to have conferred the value that he finds in his neighbor. On the other hand, Augustine's defenders have put a question mark against Nygren's equation of delight-in-objective-value with self-seeking. Why must it be that a lover who finds value objectively given in the object of his love should wish to appropriate that value to himself? Can the subject–object relationship not be understood in quite a different way?

Joseph Mausbach's foundational work *Die Ethik des Heiligen Augustinus* (1909) had already drawn attention to the significant con- concept of order in Augustine's thought about love. Nygren's first major Swedish critic, Gunnar Hultgren, made important use of this notion in pitting Mausbach's "ontological" conception of order against Nygren's "psychological" conception.[13] "Order," in either case, is a teleological notion. The subject–object polarity between love and value does not have to mean that the subject imposes his own teleological order upon the objective value he finds. He does not have to love it for himself, subordinating it to his privately conceived goal of happiness. It can equally well mean that he discovers, with the value, a teleological order that is already implicit in it, and that in loving it he bows in obedient conformity to the order he finds. For Nygren, objective value could only be loved by the subject's imposing an order upon it; for Mausbach the order was given objectively with the value.

Hultgren used Mausbach to correct Nygren's account of Augustine; and yet he conceded that there was a psychological order present in Augustine's thought as well as an ontological, and that there was a certain untidiness in the overlap of the two. No such concession was made by Rudolf Johannesson or by the latest in the distinguished series of Swedish contributors to the debate, Ragnar Holte.[14] For Holte every feature of Augustine's moral discourse is to be understood in terms of an ontological cosmic order. In particular, the "happy life" (*beata vita*) is not something which man posits as a goal for himself, but is, quite literally, God himself. The desire for happiness is a spontaneous movement of the soul released by the Idea (Platonically conceived) of the Good. Thus Holte's presentation of Augustine sets him diametrically at the opposite extreme from Nygren. Everything is given in the object, so much so that the very reality of the subject as free agent becomes problematic.[15]

It is striking that neither Hultgren nor Holte, both of whom concentrated their studies upon Augustine's earlier writings, made any use of a passage from *City of God* in which Augustine, almost in so many words, confronts the difference between positive and objective order:

Now among those things which exist in any mode of being, and are distinct from God who made them, living things are ranked above inanimate objects; those which have the power of reproduction, or even the urge towards it, are superior to those who lack that impulse. Among living things, the sentient rank above the insensitive, and animals above trees. Among the sentient, the intelligent take precedence over the unthinking—men over cattle. Among the intelligent, immortal beings are higher than mortals, angels being higher than men.

This is the scale according to the order of nature; but there is another way of valuing things, based on the use that each individual has for them [*pro suo cuiusque usu*]. By this we would put some inanimate things above some creatures of sense—so much so that if we had the power, we should be ready to remove these creatures from the world of nature, whether in ignorance of the place they occupy in it, or, though knowing that, still subordinating them to our convenience. For instance, would not anyone prefer to have food in his house, rather than mice, or money rather than fleas? There is nothing surprising in this; for we find the same criterion operating in the value we place on human beings, for all the undoubted worth of a human creature. A higher price is often paid for a horse than for a slave, for a jewel than for a maidservant.

Thus there is a very wide difference between a rational consideration, in its free judgement, and the constraint of need, or the attraction of desire. Rational consideration decides on the position of each thing in the scale of importance, on its own merits. whereas need thinks in terms of means to ends [*quid propter quid expetat*]. Reason looks for the truth as it is revealed to enlightened intelligence; desire has an eye for what allures by the promise of sensual enjoyment.[16]

Certain things are left obscure in this passage; in particular, what relation does the order of use have to the evil wills of the rebellious angels and to the "law of justice" which prefers good men to evil angels?[17] But the general message is clear. Augustine distinguishes the ordering imposed upon things by individuals pursuing their private ends from the order that things have in themselves. But this, of course, is the late Augustine. Early Augustine did not make this distinction but worked with a very simple rule of order: "Whatever is for something else is of less value than the thing it is for."[18] Yet he needed the distinction; and the lack of it sometimes led him into absurdity, as when he persuaded himself that professional singers, because they perform "for money" or "for fame," know nothing about music since they imagine music to be of a lower ontological status than money and fame.[19] As we shall see, it is significant that Augustine had not yet discovered the distinction at the time he wrote the first book of *De doctrina Christiana*.

This ambiguity affects Augustine's handling of the classical tradition of thought about the *finis bonorum*.

A tradition originating in the opening pages of Aristotle's *Nicomachean Ethics* and continuing in the Peripatetic and Academic streams of philosophy down to Cicero interpreted morality as the pursuit of a "final good" (in Latin, *finis bonorum*) or "supreme good" (*summum bonum*). This offered an account both of the homogeneity of the moral enterprise in all its forms as the pursuit of a common goal, and of the wide variety of conflicting moral beliefs as differences of opinion about the identification of the goal. In the form in which Augustine first encountered this tradition and in which it had the profoundest of influences upon him—the form in which he met it as a young man reading Cicero's *Hortensius*—the final good was assumed to be identified with "happiness," and the variety of opinions were all concerned with what happiness consisted in. It was "eudaemonist."[20]

But this tradition was susceptible both of a more realist and of a more positivist interpretation. On the realist side one could stress that there was at least this single goal toward which all rational beings moved, thereby minimizing the extent, if not the importance, of disagreements. On the positivist side one could regard the concept of final good simply as a convenient point of comparison, so that for each school the "final good" was what it chose to make it.[21]

There was much in Augustine's Neoplatonic inheritance that inclined him to a realist interpretation of the teleological tradition. Especially if we concentrate on the concepts of "happiness" (*beata vita, beatitudo, beatitas*) and "supreme good" (*summum bonum*) in his thought, we are bound to say, as a generalization at least, that his preference was to characterize the *telos* objectively, in terms of the order of beings. There is an argument to which he returns constantly throughout his life, demonstrating that, since the supreme good could hardly be something "below" man and is unlikely to be something of an equality with him, it must be looked for "above" him.[22] But we cannot go all the way with Ragnar Holte and conclude that the positivist strain in the tradition exercised no influence upon Augustine. For the very same apologetic concern that led him to identify the "final good" of classical philosophy with the transcendent God of Christianity required him to criticize non-Christian philosophies not simply as mistaken in their description of the human situation but as morally perverse in the goals that they set for themselves. And so it is that Augustine continues to speak of "positing an end" (*finem ponere, finem constituere*), especially when he is engaged in systematic criticism of the classical options. While *summum bonum* is an expression to which he usually gives a realist interpretation, *finis bonorum*, though ostensibly a synonym, more often introduces a positivist note.[23]

Intersecting with this ambiguity we may discern another. The Peripatetic tradition supposed that the finis bonorum was a function of the subject himself, an activity or state of being. Augustine, again under Neoplatonic influence and again with a Christian apologetic concern, objectified this into a transcendent object of worship and delight, God himself. Thus the classical tradition of morality as seeking one's own true well-being became transformed into the Christian command that one should love God as *summmum bonum*. Frequently Augustine refers to God himself as the true *beata vita*, a strikingly paradoxical identification which puts the axe to the root of the subjectivism in the classical eudaemonist tradition. On the other hand Augustine found that this identification left him with a problem: how was he to maintain a sufficient *opacity* about the identification of God and the happy life? Once again, Christian apologetics required him to criticize the pagan options, and this he could hardly do if they all amounted ipso facto to the love of God. And so we find a marked withdrawal in his later writings toward a description of the final good once again in terms of a state of the subject, as "peace in life eternal" or "fellowship in the enjoyment of God."[24]

Clearly the debate between advocates of a "psychological" and advocates of an "ontological" account of love in Augustine will turn on the relative significance assigned to the Academic and Ciceronian strain in his thinking on the one hand and to the Neoplatonic on the other. Nevertheless, it is important that the debate should not become polarized. In between the extremes of *cosmic love* and *positive love*, as we shall call them, the cosmological force in which the subject is hardly let to be subject at all, and the self-direction of the subject toward the end which he has chosen for his happiness, there are intermediate possibilities which became increasingly important to Augustine as he continued his search for an "ordered" love in which the subject was neither victim nor master. He can represent love as an admiring appreciation of good, in which the subject recognizes a teleology which he has not himself imposed but from which he can maintain an observer's independence. This we refer to as *rational love*. And Augustine also conceives that the subject, having recognized the objective order of things, may freely affirm it, thus giving the weight of his agency to support an order which he did not devise. This we describe as *benevolent love*. In tracing these four aspects of love in Augustine's thought we will show how he may have been moved from one to the other in order to do justice to the command of love that Christ gave to his disciples.

COSMIC LOVE

Clearly Augustine believed that love is firmly grounded in the fundamental realities of the cosmos. The three Stoic divisions of philosophy
are included in the two precepts upon which the Law and the Prophets hang: "Here is our natural philosophy! Here is our moral philosophy! . . . Here is our logic!"[25] That the command to love God and
neighbor should be regarded, even in rhetorical exaggeration, as a
datum of natural philosophy is likely to surprise a modern man accustomed to making a rather sharp distinction between moral and physical necessity. But Augustine stands in a tradition of classical
cosmology which was used to explaining the motions of the heavens
by the attraction of like to like, an attraction described as *philia* or
eros, and he sees the love of man for God as a special case of the same
attraction. Because all things *do* move to their goal, their final cause,
therefore man ought to.[26]

    This view of love as a natural law of the universe is well illustrated
from the passage in *City of God* XIX where Augustine examines the
"love of peace" and finds it expressed in a wide variety of events.
"Just as nobody is reluctant to be glad," he claims, "so nobody is reluctant to have peace." Even warriors fight in order to establish a
peace which will suit them. Those who disturb an existing political
peace do so not to abolish peace but to exchange one form of it for
another. This thesis he defends with a series of extreme examples
which imply an a fortiori argument. Bandits depend upon "peace
among comrades," the mythical half-human wild man Cacus slays and
kills to maintain peace with his own body, the wildest birds and animals preserve their own kind in a sort of peace, and finally, the most
grotesque example, a man suspended upside down, so that the natural
"peace" between soul and body is inevitably brought to an end, will
nevertheless achieve a certain "peace" as his body decomposes, pro-
viding food for the creatures which breed in its putrefaction.[27]

    The significance of this argument for our purposes lies in Augus-
tine's readiness to subsume a number of differing phenomena under

one all-embracing natural law which is a kind of love. A physical phenomenon, that matter in flux seeks an equilibrium, is compared with a political phenomenon, that men form communities even in the course of overthrowing others, and both are compared with the anthropological phenomenon that men do not want to die and will fight to preserve their lives. Behind all of them is discerned the universal tendency toward *pax*, a word which we might translate as "stability" or "equilibrium" were it not that it must also do justice to the perfect bliss of the City of God. Man cannot love *no* peace, for that would be to erase the last features of nature, but he may love an *unrighteous* peace, a kind of stability which falls short of perfect peace in the presence of God. The fact that he must love some peace is the ground of the argument that he ought to love that peace. And so we see that the distinction between natural necessity and moral obligation is not completely eroded, but that the one is used to give strong reinforcement to the other.

If a natural law such as this is to be the basis of human morality, its application must be differentiated. Each item of the natural universe loves the kind of peace which is appropriate to it. The peace to which farmyard animals are drawn is the peace of the carnal life; it is their appropriate good. The tree, which cannot love anything with sentient motion, seeks to grow more fertile and fruitful. The stone, the river, the wind, and the flame, with no sense of life at all, still tend toward their proper places of rest. "For the movements of gravity are, as it were, the 'loves' of bodies, whether they strive downwards or upwards as heavy or light objects. As the mind is carried by its love, so is the body by its weight, each to its own place."[28] Such analogies are a favorite theme with Augustine. "Weight does not fall to the bottom simply, but to its own place. Fire goes up, a stone comes down. . . . Oil . . . floats on water. . . . My weight is my love; by it I move wherever I move."[29] Thus the love of God is interpreted metaphysically as the proper movement of the human will toward its final cause. It has its own "force," so that "love cannot be idle in the soul. It must necessarily cause movement."[30]

In accounting for love in this way Augustine faces the major difficulty that human love is free to direct itself to an improper object. The cosmic account seems to prove too much; disobedient and unnatural motions are left without satisfactory explanation. In a passage of *De libero arbitrio* Augustine addressed the problem by comparing in some detail the movement of a stone falling to earth and that of a will inclining to sin, clarifying what the two phenomena have in common and where they differ. The difference is expressed like this: The movement of the stone is "natural" while the movement of the human will is "voluntary" and therefore susceptible of praise and blame. It would be monstrous to blame the stone for falling because it does not have it in its power to restrain its downward motion. How are the two movements alike? "The movement of the soul is like the movement of the stone in this respect: just as the one is the *proper* movement of the stone, so the other is the *proper* movement of the will."[31] Translation is difficult. If we say, "It is the stone's own movement," we render the assertion trivial, for it conveys nothing to declare that a moving will is like a moving stone in that it is the will or the stone which moves in either case and not something else. But neither can we render *proprius* by "characteristic," for this would be to make Augustine say something he does not believe; it is the destiny of the human will to cleave to God, and any movement away from him toward sin is, in an important sense, out of character. Rather, the movement of the stone and of the will are each "proper" in that they occur without any exterior propulsive force intervening as an *efficient* cause. It is not a "proper" movement of a stone when it is thrown upward into the air, but only when it falls again and is drawn downward by its *final* cause.

Love accounts not only for natural motion in the universe but also for natural cohesion. If we were not convinced that timber and stone held together, bound into loving union, we would never dare to step inside even a church building![32] There is a corresponding series of expressions in which the Christian soul's love for God is pictured as rest in God and as unification with God, whether proleptically of spiritual experience in this life or in an eschatological context. "Cleaving" to God, *adhaesio* or *inhaesio*, is a common expression, particularly under the influence of the text Psalm 72 (73): 28, "It is good for me to cleave unto God," a verse which Augustine quotes often. The perfected soul "rests" in God, sharing the sabbath rest which he has eternally in his own being.[33] By cleaving to the Lord the believer is "one spirit" with him, drawn into his life, "glued together with him through immortality."[34]

The premise from which the metaphysical notion of love proceeds is the derived status of man as a creature. Insufficient of himself for himself because he does not have true being in himself, man is drawn back toward the source of being with a love which expresses his dependence, needy and thirsty like Plato's *eros* in one of its aspects, full of the longing which affects us for things to which we naturally belong but from which we are separated, *desiderium*.[35] And yet the Christian doctrine of creation-from-nothing has imposed its own distinctive shape upon a cosmic teleology which is in other ways similar to the Neoplatonic conceptions of Plotinus. Whereas for the pagan philosopher each degree of existence, body soul and mind, had its own inherent good, form life and intelligence respectively, related in each case to the degree above it, soul mind and God, as effect to cause; in Augustine's Christian Platonism the good of each degree is actually identified with the degree above it. Thus love-of-the-good does not operate self-containedly upon the different levels of the derived order, but reaches up in each case to the higher level upon which the subject depends for its existence. The result must inevitably be that the highest of all goods, God himself, exercises a totalitarian claim upon the love of man.[36]

Here we meet a major problem for Augustine's ethics and indeed for any ethics which makes serious claim to be Christian. Augustine was aware (what theologian ever more so?) that the Bible sums up the Christian ethic in *two* love-commands with *two* objects of love, God and neighbor. To these he is constantly alluding; they are the very heart of the meaning of Scripture, they are the two wings on

which we must mount, they are the two feet on which we approach
God, the two pence paid by the Samaritan at the inn, and even the
twin lambs borne by all the flock in the Song of Songs.[37] And yet, as
metaphysician, Augustine was impelled to the conclusion that only
one object of love was permissible: "It is a simple love by which the
multiplicity of loves is overcome! One love is needful to overcome the
many! One good love ranged against all the evil ones!" Any love was
perverse unless it was totally directed to God, for "he loves thee less
who loves ought beside thee."[38] This is not, as is sometimes suggested,
a mere vagary of Augustine's Neoplatonic youth. The totalitarian
claim is persistent because it is implied in the very idea of a single *summum bonum*, and that implication is drawn out, rather than concealed, by the modifications which Plotinian teleology underwent at
Augustine's hands. The problem is succinctly stated in the early commentary on Galatians: "Contemplation of the truth is founded on the
love of God alone; good morals are founded on the love of God and
neighbour." It is plain that unless some formula can be found for saying at once that God alone is to be loved and that our neighbor is to
be loved at the same time, the demands of the spiritual enterprise will
be left hopelessly at variance with the demands of the moral law.[39]

In the *Soliloquia* we see Augustine already conscious of the difficulty and attempting to resolve it. The famous formula of the early
dialogues, "God and the soul," is to be understood as an attempt to
reach a resolution on traditionally Platonist lines. In this phrase the
exclusive claim of the spiritual world to our love seems to be honored
since the soul of man, like God, is spiritual and not material. At the
same time it allows us to love other men, in that they too are souls
and so included in the legitimate object of our love.[40] As a solution,
however, it falls down at two points. One of them was apparent to
Augustine from the beginning: there was no real basis of unity between God and the soul, no guarantee that love of God will not pull
one way and the demands of our friends the other way. God and the
soul are not, as they may seem, one single object of knowledge and
love.[41] The second difficulty emerged more clearly later in his devel-

opment: the formula "God and the soul" concedes nothing to biblical materialism. Whatever solution is found to the problem of the totalitarian claim, it must allow for love of our neighbors as material bodies and not only as souls.[42]

The solution had to lie in the idea of an "order" of love. But this proved difficult for Augustine to work out. The concept of love as cosmic necessity allowed him no room for it; and so he turned to supplement it from the other side of the classical tradition and establish an order of love in the free choice of the subject. Thus it came about that he took the false step of which his critics accuse him and of which Holte attempted to excuse him. Certainly he took it but equally certainly he recovered from it. The mistake was to see the ordering of the two loves in terms of an imposed subordination of means to an end.

POSITIVE LOVE

Man's relation to the good, in the eudaemonist tradition that Augustine learned from Cicero, was usually expressed by the verbs *desire* or *pursue* on the one hand, *gain* and *achieve* on the other. In Augustine's vocabulary we find a range of verbs of this kind, especially *petere* and its compounds *expetere* and *appetere, optare, sequi,* for pursuit, and for achievement, *adipisci, habere,* and *invenire.*[43] Augustine innovates on the tradition, however, by using the verb *love* as a synonym for the verbs of pursuit. This at once gives the idea of love a new significance as the quest for a subjectively conceived good and at the same time marries this positivist teleology to the cosmological Plotinian teleology as its obverse and complement.[44] Love takes on new positive connotations without losing the old cosmic ones. Naturally this identification of love with the pursuit of subjective goals has been helped by the other modification Augustine made to the tradition, the transformation of the *finis bonorum* from being a state of the subject to being a transcendent object of attention, God himself.

The eudaemonist tradition offered Augustine a way to formulate an "order" of love. It spoke of the difference between what we have come to call "ends" and "means," more clumsily, things which are pursued for themselves and things which are pursued for the sake of something else. In Augustine's vocabulary this idea is expressed by the preposition *propter*, "for the sake of," and by the verb *referre*, which is used of the subject's "directing" his interest in some object to the pursuit of a further goal.[45] But Augustine also employed the more general verb *uti*, to "use," which from the beginning to the end of his literary career was his favorite term to describe the Christian pilgrim's attitude to worldly goods, things which must be subordinated to his heavenly goal. Yet, whereas "love" is early used as a synonym for the pursuit of a goal, even of a false goal, Augustine does not for some time bring himself to employ it as a synonym for "use," the pursuit of a means to the goal. Indeed, "use" is the opposite of love. It is a way of "ordering" that which one does *not* love toward the goal of achieving that which one does.[46]

For quite a brief period in the 390s Augustine departed from this practice, believing that he had found in the concept of "use" a good way to accommodate the second love which Christ commanded, love of the neighbor, within the unitary love of God that Christian metaphysics demanded. The steps toward the experiment are quite clear. First, into the general category of "objects of use" Augustine introduced the particular relations that bind us to other human beings, so that we are said to "use" our friends for kindness, our enemies for patience, etc.[47] Then the term *use* was brought together with its partner *enjoyment* (*fruitio*), which is love in possession of the supreme good; these two, which had been quite independent in the writings of the 380s, would frequently appear as a pair thereafter.[48] Thirdly, Augustine took the decisive step of including human beings among the proper objects of "use."[49] And finally, in the first book of *De doctrina Christiana* (397), he characterized "use" as a kind of love, so that the use-enjoyment pair corresponded to the twofold command of love to God and neighbor.

This book has well deserved the considerable attention it has received both from mediaeval and modern readers. But its very popularity may obscure the experimental and finally inconclusive character of its solution to the problem of the order of love. It begins with a distinction, important for the subsequent direction of the later books, which are about language, between "things" and "signs"; "things," which are to be the subject of the first book, are then categorized into "objects of enjoyment" and "objects of use." In the initial characterization of this distinction, "enjoyment," but not "use," is described as "love": "To enjoy something is to cleave to it in love for its own sake, to use something is to direct (*referre*) the object of use to obtaining that which one loves" (4.4). These terms are then left on one side for the first half of the book, which is devoted to a review of the Christian doctrines of God and salvation; this, however, is still intended to support the contention that "only eternal and unchanging things are to be enjoyed, and others to be used with a view to achieving the enjoyment of those." Returning to the pair halfway through, he asks whether men should "enjoy" or should "use" each other and adds: "We are commanded to love one another; the question is whether man is to be loved by man for his own sake or for the sake of something else." Tentatively Augustine replies: for the sake of something else (22.20).

This is the first occasion on which he has spoken of "use" as a kind of love, and the novelty of the idea seems to call for some defense. No one, he insists, has a right to resent our loving him for God's sake, since that is how we love ourselves too. God alone is to be enjoyed. Any other object of love that occurs to us should be "carried off in the direction in which the whole stream of our love is flowing" (22.21). However, he will concede a qualification. Not all "use" of temporal things is "love." "Love" is appropriate only to four kinds of object: God, self, neighbor, and (an exceptional addition to the usual three) our own bodies. One of these four is above us, one is ourselves, one beside us, and one beneath us (23.22). At some length (23.23–26.27) he proceeds to reconcile this list of four with the twofold command of love for God and neighbor by arguing that love of self and love of one's body can be taken for granted. On this we shall have more to say at a later stage.[50]

We should notice in passing where his need to qualify the use-enjoyment scheme has led our author. He has appealed to an overtly ontological order of things, a hierarchy of reality for which the subject's devising of end and means is not responsible. For a moment he lingers about this alternative approach, anticipating his mature thoughts on the order of love: "Holy and just living means being a sound judge of things. Such a one has an ordered love, neither loving that which should not be loved nor failing to love what should be loved, nor loving more what should be loved less, nor equally what should be less or more" (27.28). Here for a moment we see an order of love which is imposed upon the subject's judgment by the order of things, not imposed upon things by his pursuit of his own ends. Love is "ordered," not "ordering."

Meanwhile, however, Augustine is stuck with defending the contrast of use and enjoyment, and when, after a digression about proximate relations, he returns to it, he quickly gets into difficulties. Of what kind is God's love for us? It is unthinkable that we should call it "enjoyment," which would suggest that God was in need of our goodness, and so we must call it "use," "for if he neither enjoys us nor uses us, I do not know what kind of love he could have for us" (31.34). But then again there are problems in thinking of his using us: we "direct" our use-love of men to our enjoyment of God, and so God must "direct" his love for us to his own goodness; but as our existence depends upon this goodness, it is not his welfare, but ours, that is served by it. So that God's "use" of men has a double "direction" or "reference," to their welfare and to his own goodness. And as though this was not confusing enough Augustine points out that man's own love of his neighbor has the same kind of double reference, being intended in the first instance for his neighbor's welfare, though it carries with it as a consequence that it will serve his own (32.35).

Here once again we see Augustine tempted to abandon the means-end order and account for the subject's ultimate welfare as an unintended consequence of his love of the neighbor. And at this point, when he has conceded that the neighbor is the term at least of the subject's benevolent intentions, he lets slip a phrase which is new, speaking of mankind's "enjoying one another in God" (*nobis invicem in ipso perfruamur*). But how is this expression to be reconciled with the judgment that we "enjoy" only God and "use" men? It is to be understood, replies Augustine, as a loose expression, authorized by St. Paul's address to Philemon (Philem. 20). To enjoy someone in God is quite different from enjoying him in himself, for it is really God in that case and not man that one enjoys. He closes his discussion with a stern reiteration of his rule: "To pass through the pleasure one takes in an object of love, and to refer it to that end where one wishes to remain, this is 'use,' and can only loosely be called 'enjoyment'; while to stay in it and remain with it, making it the end (*finem ponens*) of one's joy, that is what 'enjoyment' properly means, and that we must never do except with that Trinity which is the highest and unchangeable good" (33.37).

These words belong entirely to the tradition of classical eudaemonism. The end is something one "posits": there is a right end and a wrong end, but right or wrong one posits it where one will. "Enjoyment" and "use" are determined entirely by the subject's attitude and not by the object—and that despite the fact that in the past Augustine has sometimes been unwilling to speak directly of the "use" and "enjoyment" of improper objects.[51] It would appear that in the first book of *De doctrina Christiana* positive love has prevailed. And yet, as we have seen, Augustine was already feeling for a different conception of order in love. He has shown himself ready to fall back on the ontological order when he feels pressed to defend the positive order. He has hinted at the distinction between the intentional, posited term of an action and its implicit ontological term. And above all he has conceded a "loose" way of speaking which avoids the scandalous formula that we must "use" our friends.

As we have observed, the book has often been taken too seriously as representing Augustine's final thoughts on teleology.[52] In fact, it was a false step. True, Augustine did not repudiate it in the *Retractationes*, but his subsequent behavior speaks for itself. There is no single instance in any later writing of the verb *uti* being used of the love of men for other men.[53] The pair "use" and "enjoyment" continues to be a familiar mark on the landscape, but whenever Augustine wishes to accommodate love-of-neighbor into this contrast, he does so by means of the phrase "enjoy in the Lord"—and quite without further apology for its looseness or impropriety. The "use" of means is never again a form of love. The only positive love that remains is that by which a man pursues his final goal, his *finis bonorum*.

RATIONAL LOVE

"Holy and just living means being a sound judge of things (*rerum integer aestimator*)," Augustine ventured to say, even while attempting to work out the order of love on a positive basis. This introduces an idea which is consistently present in his mature thought. The subject stands at an observer's distance from the good, as one might stand at a distance from a painting to admire it. His reason is engaged with the object's goodness; but this engagement is not a force drawing him toward it nor a hand reached out to possess it but a relation which allows the contemplative distance to remain. Love is neither "appetite" nor "movement" but estimation, appreciation, and approval.[54]

Such synonyms for love are plentiful in Augustine's writings: "Let us admire them! Let us praise them! Let us love them!"[55] Especially prominent are the expressions *adprobare, aestimare, magni pendere*. The lover's response to the object of his admiration is *delectatio*: "Nothing can be the object of love which does not afford *delight*."[56] But the basis of this delight is rational. The more the object is known, the more it is loved; one could not delight in something one understood to be evil, since it is precisely the knowledge of its value that permits one to love it.[57] But neither is this rational delight purely passive, since it evokes conformity in the subject to the good which is the object of his love. "The more you love someone," he remarks in passing, "the more you take him as a model for your actions."[58]

On the face of it there is no place left for love of the wicked, a conclusion which is obviously going to be unacceptable to anyone who believes in God's love for sinners and the Christian's duty to love his enemies. Augustine has a way of avoiding this conclusion. He can continue to speak of rational love for the unworthy by allowing the possibility of loving a certain aspect of a person. This also permits him to distinguish right and wrong love of the worthy: If we love that which is admirable in our friends, their faithfulness, benevolence, and their love of God, we love them rightly, while if we love their injustice, concupiscence, error, and stupidity our love is not well directed.[59] But what does Augustine find to be lovable in the wicked? Two things: by virtue of his creation each man has a good "nature" which is quite distinct from his empirical wickedness, and by virtue of God's redemptive work he has the possibility of being saved. What we love in our enemy is what he is essentially and what he yet may be. An impressive indication of the prominence of the rational idea of love in Augustine's thought is his constant appeal to these justifications for love of the wicked. We love our enemies "because they have a share in goodness."[60] We hate their iniquities and love what God has made.[61] There are two distinct words, "enemy" and "man." We love "what God created, the man and not the error."[62] We love "the fact that they have rational souls, true even of brigands."[63] Even in his wife a man is to love merely "the fact that she is mankind."[64] And God, too, is said to love "what he wished to make, not what he found in us." The verse Genesis 1:31, "God saw everything that he had made, and behold it was very good," is taken as the basis for God's love: "God loved them all, in their different grades of excellence, because he saw that they were good since they were brought to being by his word."[65] The love of a person's future possibility is expressed somewhat paradoxically in essentially the same way. The doctor "loves the healthy, not the sick"; it is the patient's capacity for health which demands the doctor's interest and constructive attention.[66] The Christian ought "to regard each one as though he were what he wants him to be." Love is claimed by human nature "whether yet to be perfected or already perfect."[67]

The objectivity of rational love offers Augustine a way forward to a flexible and coherent statement of the "order" of love. What he needed was an account in which every proper love of creature implied the love of its Creator, while from every improper love this implication was missing. The order of use and enjoyment knew only two grades of dignity, the end of the subject's choice and the means that he directed to that end. Rational love, on the other hand, could accept as complex an order as it discovered to be present in the universe, since love was at the same time an understanding which comprehended the object's place in the scheme of things. Love's order is given by its comprehending conformity to the order of reality. This is the significance of the text from the Song of Songs (2:4) which Augustine began to use at the end of the 390s, "Order love within me!" Love accepts and does not impose its ordering.[68] It has to be appropriate to its object: "That love may itself be an object of ordered love, wherewith we love well love's proper object, that within us there may be the virtue of living well. It seems to me that a concise and accurate definition of virtue is 'ordered love.' Which is why in the Song of Songs Christ's bride, the City of God, sings, 'Order love within me!'"[69]

And so we may be allowed and encouraged to love things which are not themselves the supreme good, provided that we do not mistake them for the supreme good, the source of blessedness. "Woe unto your love if it takes any object to be more beautiful than He is!" It had been Augustine's mistake as a youth, when reduced to despair once at the death of a friend, not to love "humanly." There was an element of pretence in that bitter grief, a self-deception which hid the plain truth about himself and his friend, that they were both men and not gods.[70] Correct rational love perceives that God is the supreme source of value and being, and loves him "*as* God." Correct rational love discriminates that which is of real value in an evil man and loves him not "*as* sinner" but "*as* man."[71] And within any man correct rational love can discern that the soul is of greater value than the body: "It is beyond question that the inner man is more loved than the outer man," an evaluation confirmed even by the behavior of those who are accustomed perversely to subject their souls to their bodies and yet at the moment of choice prefer to live.[72]

In revising his understanding of the order of love Augustine revised with it his use of the preposition *propter*, which continues in use as the most usual expression for the subordination of one object of love to another. To love someone "for God" (*propter Deum*) is equivalent to loving him "in God" and to loving "God in him."[73] Its opposite is to love him "more than God," or "in himself." To explain the logic of these expressions we need to state the true or false understanding that is implied in each love. To love man "in himself" is to admit the false belief that he is a self-standing, independent being. It is to see him as though he were his own source of value and so to set him in the place of the one who is in fact his source of value. To love him "in God" is to recognize that his real nature can be grasped only by reference to his Creator, while love "in Christ" implies that he is what he is by virtue of membership in Christ's body.[74] To love "Christ in him" or "God in him" is to make precisely the same assertion, identifying as the beloved's most valuable feature that which relates him to God. To put the *propter* language in this context is to free it from the embarrassment of seeming to commend a kind of friendship which has an ulterior motive. Augustine may now say, without any sense of contradiction, what he first attempted to say in *De doctrina Christiana* I, that we seek the welfare of a friend for its own sake (*propter se*) while we love him "for God."[75]

BENEVOLENT LOVE

The order of things which rational love acknowledges is a teleological order, which is to say that each object has not merely a place within the structure but a destiny, a *telos*, to fulfill within it. Apart from

God, whose *telos* is his own being and who is therefore always at rest,
all beings are in motion toward their final cause. Just as we ourselves
are drawn by the pull of the supreme good, so is all that we observe;
and we cannot understand the place in which a fellow creature stands
unless we also know the place to which he is being drawn. As we have
seen already with love-of-the-enemy, to love someone is to love his
possibility. Thus it is that the objective order evokes more than delight from the contemplating subject. That which is lower than God,
that which still has to fulfill its destiny, demands also the subject's
willing assent to its fulfillment. This is what Augustine means by
benevolentia. It is the will that something which has its existence
from God should fulfill its existence for God.

Benevolent love is a possibility only between creature and creature, for God has no fulfillment to which he strives. But because
benevolence is still concerned with an order that is independent of
the subject, it cannot be appropriate either for inferior beings whose
telos is to be of use to man. An entertaining passage of the *Tractates
on 1 John* makes the point rather clearly:

> All love contains an element of good-will towards those who
> are its object. For our love for mankind ought not to be (in-
> deed, could not be) . . . like the love which gourmands express
> when they say, "I love *grives*." You ask, "What does this love
> mean?" It means killing and eating. He says that he loves them,
> and his love means their extinction and destruction . . . Is that
> what we mean when we say we must love mankind? That we
> must swallow them up? No, there is such a thing as friendship
> based on good-will, a tendency to support those we love when
> necessary. It does not matter if there is no occasion for actual
> support, for the good-will alone makes the love. We should not
> wish our friends trouble so that we can have the opportunity of
> giving aid! . . . It is better to love someone in prosperity when
> there is no need for support.[76]

But if benevolence cannot be shown to God and cannot be shown to objects of man's use, it is, as the same passage makes clear, a feature of *all* relations of love between man and man. It is not one kind of human love but a partial analysis of the whole of human love. Hence the importance of freeing it from empirical conditions such as actual deeds of kindness and of distinguishing, as Augustine sometimes does, between the attitude, *benevolentia*, and the act, *beneficentia*.[77] This again emphasizes the independence of the beloved from the lover. I must will the fulfillment of my brother's existence even though that fulfillment is not in myself and will very probably make no call upon my agency. Otherwise I shall be loving him falsely, as a lower being dependent upon me, not as my neighbor who is beside me.

Certainly in this way of describing love the lover has in view a goal for the beloved which his dealings with him will seek to promote. A variety of different phrases and clauses express the one purpose which benevolent love pursues: "He must care for his neighbour that he may love God" (*ad diligendum Deum*); "he must care for them, that they may obtain his Kingdom" (*ad eius regnum obtinendum*); "doing them good for the sake of their eternal welfare" (*propter salutem ipsorum aeternam*); and, with an *ut finale* clause, "so to deal with him that he too may love God," "to work for him, that he too may love God with you."[78] These expressions of purpose are generally introduced by a verb such as *consulere,* "to act in someone's interest," but it is only a short step from this to attaching final clauses directly to the verbs *amare* and *diligere.* This too Augustine does, instructing us to love someone "that he may be righteous" (*ut iustus sit*) and to love evil men "that they may grasp righteousness" (*ut apprehendant iustitiam*).[79]

Two comments may be made about this purposing in benevolent love. In the first place, the subject's purpose is not posited by himself and imposed upon the object of love but is received from without. The subject has discovered that his neighbor has this destiny already given him in his human nature, and in willing its fulfillment he conforms his will to the order of reality. That is why Augustine seems

so often to represent benevolent love-of-neighbor as consisting exclusively in the attempt to bring him to God. It is not that he rejects
other goals which may be adopted from time to time but that this
one is fundamental, for it is the only purpose that the subject can
conceive for the object which he can be absolutely sure is not a will-
ful imposition.

In the second place, the purpose expressed in benevolent love is
not an ulterior purpose. Although the subject does conceive his fellow's salvation as the goal of his action, he does not love him in order
to achieve this goal, subordinating love as means to this end; rather,
it is in pursuing this goal for his neighbor that he loves him. The purpose is "internal" to the action of the verb. "To what end does Christ
love us," he asks, "but that we should reign with him?" But our reign-
ing does not lie the far side of his loving, as an end which it subserves;
it is a goal that has arisen within his love for us, and his pursuit of
that goal is the clearest expression of his love for us.[80] The distinction has to be made clearly because while the internal purpose is quite
proper to true *benevolentia* any external or ulterior purpose is the
denial of it. "To look after one's brother for personal temporal advantage is not to look after him with love; it is really to look after oneself, not him whom one ought to love as himself."[81] In such a context, where we catch an echo of Cicero's repudiation of utility as a
motive for friendship, we can understand those occasional expressions which seem to restrict the notion of true love entirely to love
which regards the object "for his own sake." In the context of benevolent love such a restriction makes sense as a way of ruling out ulterior purposes; the opposite of "for his own sake" at this point is
not "for God's sake" but "for personal advantage."

This then is the last complexity which we must mark in the use of
the phrase *propter Deum* in Augustine's mature conception of the
order of love. We have said that love "for God's sake" is the reason's
acknowledgment that the object has a certain position in the order of
things beneath God; but there is also this note of purpose which is
the will's assent to the neighbor's natural teleology. The fact that Au-

gustine believed firmly in a teleological order allowed him to pass
easily between the proposition and the purpose, between the expression of rational love and that of benevolence: "He therefore who
loves men, ought to love them either *because* they are righteous men,
or *that* they may be so." "He truly loves his friend who loves God in
his friend, either *because* God is in his friend, or *that* he may be so."
"What did our Lord love in us? He loved God in us! Not that we *had*
God, but that we *might* have him."[82] The transition from a *quia-* to an
ut- clause which surprises the reader in each of these examples, marks
the fact that for Augustine a purpose, because it is a *telos* given by
God and not merely a purpose conceived by the subject, is as good a
"reason" to love a man as some feature that is extant.

The preposition *propter* and the verb *referre* continue to be useful
to Augustine as expressions of the simple means-end subordination of
worldly goods to heavenly, even while, in the context of neighbor-
love, they have taken on the more subtle nuances of his mature
thought about ordered love. Thus they form a flexible and imprecise
language which enables Augustine to appeal to more than one aspect
of love at once. The theological point served by this looseness is the
unity of every volitional impulse in the service of the love of God.
The choice of means to ends, the admiration of the neighbor's goodness, the pursuit of the neighbor's true welfare, all these are the subjective aspects of a single movement of the soul which reflects the
one dominant cosmic movement, the return of the created being to
its source and supreme good.

CHAPTER TWO

SELF-LOVE AND THE LOVE OF GOD

The subordination of the second great command to the first leaves the love of God in complete possession of the moral and ethical field. "Love of God" will include any act, thought, or impulse which is in accord with man's created teleology, no matter whether it is a "religious" act, thought, or impulse or, in a narrower sense, a "moral" one. But Augustine also recognized as entirely coincident and coextensive with the love of God the principle of right self-love. The perfection of the one was the perfection of the other. There was no kind of right self-love which did not imply the love of God; there was no way in which God could be loved without the lover loving himself as well. The final state of affairs to which all pursuits were subordinated was "life with God and from God . . . for this indeed is how we love ourselves, by loving God!"[1] On the basis of this association of the two principles we may formally characterize Augustine's ethics as "egoist" or "self-referential."

In maintaining that these two loves are entirely coextensive, Augustine is bound to reject two alternative ways of relating them. On the one hand, self-love might be represented as an area of self-referring duty independent of and complementary to the love of God. For example, the love of God requires that we say our prayers; love of self requires that we do not pray so late into the night that our health suffers. On the other hand, love of God might be represented as a spirit of devotion from which, at the highest moments, all thought of self is strained out, a position maintained by the mediaeval champions of "pure" love. But Augustine has no place either for a virtue of self-love independent of the love of God or for the love of God without self-love.

37

It is easy to see what his objection must be to the first of these possibilities. The totalitarian claim of the love of God would be challenged by any independent source of obligation or value. The pyramidal *ordo amoris* supposes that every subordinate good derives its value from its final orientation to God. To allow a claim for self-love which did not flow from this apex would be to destroy the metaphysical premise on which all of Augustine's ethics were constructed. And so we find frequently repeated the assertion that self-love without the love of God is not self-love at all. "You do not even love yourself rightly if your love for God can be diminished by turning away, even to yourself."[2]

But what of the second possibility? Why does Augustine continue to maintain that self-love must exist alongside the love of God at every level? Why must it always be true that "in loving God one loves himself"? The question is the more puzzling precisely because of the identification of the two. Constantly he stresses that neither can exist without the other and will even go so far as to say that "there is no other love that one has for oneself apart from the fact that one loves God."[3] It is central to his doctrine of the believer's reward that the only prize God can offer to those who love him is "Himself."[4] In Plato's terms, to praise the love of God with reference to love-of-self is to praise it "for itself" not "for its consequences." And since it is plainly self-love, not the love of God, which is persuasively redefined in order to effect the assimilation of the two, we may well ask why Augustine continues to speak of two loves at all. Why not speak simply of "love of God," leaving the term "self-love" free for some other attitude that was plainly different from it? And on occasions we see Augustine tempted by this simplification, more especially when he speaks of "self-forgetfulness": "If the soul loves itself and ignores its Creator, it must become a lesser thing, diminished by love of that which is less, for itself is less than God. . . . And so we must love God . . . to the point where, if it is possible, we are oblivious of ourselves as we love him the more." Self-forgetfulness expresses the total and uncompromising claim made upon our love by the Creator, and

it might be taken to suggest that true love of God will extinguish
love-of-self altogether. "What is there left of your heart for you to
love yourself?" he asks in *Sermon* 34. "What is there left of your
soul? What is there left of your mind? God says, 'With *all* . . .'. He
who made you demands all of you."[5]

But close as he comes to dissolving right self-love into the love of
God, Augustine will not go that far. He continues to speak of the two
loves even while he asserts that they are coextensive. He continues in
Sermon 34: "Do not be depressed, as though there were nothing left
within you to cause you joy. . . . 'But,' you say, 'if there is nothing
left to me for love-of-self, because I am commanded to love him
"with all my heart and all my soul and all my mind," how am I to
keep the second command and love my neighbour as myself?'. . .
Shall I tell you how you are to love yourself? This is your self-love:
to love God with the whole of yourself!" The distinction between
self-love and the love of God is still important. The love which man
has for God is cosmic love, the attraction of the creature toward the
supreme good; the love which he has for himself is benevolent love.
In terms of his destiny within the cosmos, man must love God alone,
cleave to God alone, aspire to God alone, so that God is sole object of
his love. But God can never be served by this love. It does God no
good to be loved; rather, he is himself man's good. It is self, and not
God, that must be the object of benevolence. It is self, and not God,
that is served when one loves God with all his heart and soul and
mind and strength. "Do you think it helps God," he asks, "when you
love him?" "No one would say he had done a service to a fountain
by drinking or to the light by seeing."[6] Augustine's text of Psalm 15
(16):2 reminded him of God's ontological self-sufficiency: "Thou
hast no need of my goods." "It is not only a matter of sacrificial
beasts or any other corruptible and corporeal thing; we are not to
imagine even that God needs man's righteousness. When God is rightly
worshipped, it is wholly to man's benefit, not to God's." Every petition in the Lord's Prayer, "Thy kingdom come, thy will be done,"   *
is really a petition for man's advantage and not for God's. And every

word of praise that man can utter, God desires it, "that you may be helped, not that he may be exalted. There is simply nothing that we can give him in return, and what he demands he demands not for himself but for you." In coupling self-love (benevolence) with the cosmic love of God, Augustine defended the latter against misinterpretation and asserted God's ontological position as the source of all good and of all beatitude—in case anybody should be so foolish as to suppose he could be altruistic toward God.[7]

Furthermore, the coincidence of the two loves was by no means a self-evident matter. The content of self-love, Augustine insisted, had to be taught and learned. "Man must be instructed in a way of loving: that is, he must be taught how to love himself to advantage." "Learn!" he counsels his congregation. "Love God, and so learn to love yourselves!" "Learn to love yourself by not loving yourself!" For the real content of self-love is something which it is possible, even natural, not to know. "If we prefer any other object of love to God, or regard any other object of love as God's equal, that shows that we do not know how to love ourselves."[8] But the Scripture has taken care that man should be instructed: It has set before him for his happiness an *end* to which he is to refer everything that he does. So it is that he learns to love himself. And only when that lesson is learned can a man be entrusted with the responsibility of neighbor-love. "First see whether you have learned to love yourself. . . . If you have not learned how to love yourself, I am afraid you will cheat your neighbour as yourself!"[9]

In the identity of benevolent self-love, properly taught, and metaphysical love of God, we see reflected in Christian terms a cherished dictum of classical ethics, the identity of "the useful" and "the right." Two streams of thought in the classical world defended the claim that "nothing was useful that was not right." There was the Stoic tradition, which had support in Academic circles, notably from Cicero, and was mediated through him to Ambrose. This interpreted the issue as one between the individual and society and defended the identity of the two principles on the ground that otherwise "human society, the most natural thing in the world, would have to be torn asunder." The other tradition, the Platonic, saw the thesis as arbitrating between the external and the internal goods of the individual. The appearance of conflict lay in man's failure to locate utility where it belonged, in his soul.[10] The Stoic version was an apology for social responsibility, the Platonic version an apology for spirituality. Augustine's form of the claim was basically Platonic, though the capacious all-inclusiveness of the first command in Augustine's thought ensured that the social implications were not excluded.

Apologetic, however, exists to defend and not to supplant its object. One may justify a course of action in terms of some feature it possesses without implying that the value of the action is derivative from and secondary to the value of the feature. There is no suggestion either in the classical formulations or in Augustine that virtue can be reduced to an enlightened pursuit of personal utility. The justifying role played by self-love is a modest one. It provides what is sometimes called a "background of intelligibility" for the command to love God and never appears to be the whole point of the exercise. Augustine establishes this point firmly by qualifying "self-love" with the phrase *propter Deum*. As we have argued, the logic of this expression is flexible, and its function is to guard against a suggestion that the movement *from* love-of-God *to* self-love, implied in the idea of "learning" to love oneself by loving God, is anything more than an epistemological movement. The teleological thrust reaches its term in God alone.[11]

AUTHORITY AND REASON

A question which exercised Augustine's mind on several occasions was why, of the three proper objects of love—God, self, and neighbor— the dominical command should mention only two directly. The answers he gave to this question fall into two groups. According to one set, the more common, the answer is simply to be found in the identity of self-love and the love of God. The command has been given us to love God, and "he who loves God will make no mistakes in the matter of loving himself." "True, although the love which God's law requires must be shown to God, self and neighbour, yet there are not three commands but two on which 'hang all the law and the prophets,' that is, love of God and love of neighbour. That is to show that there is no other love that one has for oneself apart from the fact that one loves God. Indeed, any self-love which differed would better be called self-hate."[12] But there is another pattern of answer in which this identification is somewhat qualified. To instruct a man to love himself, he says, would be like instructing him to eat or breathe. All men do it anyway by an unshaken law of nature which applies even to the beasts. All we need is instruction in how to love ourselves to the greatest advantage; and "when love of God is given prominence and set forth as the prescribed way of love so that everything else flows into it, then although nothing is said directly about self-love, nevertheless the words 'Love your neighbour as yourself' show that it has not been forgotten."[13] This does not constitute a withdrawal from the view that the first part of the Great Command is the solution to the question of self-love. Rather, "right" self-love is allowed to have a kind of foreshadowing in a "natural" self-love, common to all, which it is the part of the Great Command to school into right ways. Self-love is not totally given in the love of God. The love of God comes as the answer to a question which has already been posed.

Here is an ambiguity fundamental to Augustine's treatment of the subject. On the one hand self-love is nothing else than loving God; on the other it is a natural phenomenon in need of direction. On the one hand the natural man does not love himself; on the other he does love himself, but misguidedly. But this ambiguity is no more than a reflection of a much more general one, characteristic of all Augustine's epistemology, the ambiguous relationship of authority and reason.

The classical philosophical schools, if we may venture a generalization, regarded the field of human knowledge and experience as a single territory, while Christian doctrines of God and man divided it down the middle. A Stoic or Platonist could cheerfully propose an

intellectual expedition which would start from anthropology or phys-
ics and hope to reach conclusions in theology or ethics; but the
Christian would see in such an itinerary the vain pretensions of human pride in face of an unbridgeable epistemological chasm. It required the merciful self-communication of God to intervene from
yonder side and carry the thinker across. In Augustine's thought we
find this epistemological caution most clearly expressed in the role
of *auctoritas*, standing guard as the censor and guarantor of *ratio*.[14]
There is an overarching continuity on the map of human knowledge
which makes it possible for the perfected mind to understand, but
also a stubborn discontinuity which makes it necessary for the yet
imperfect mind to believe. Substitute "be fulfilled" and "obey" for
"understand" and "believe" and the generalization will apply equally
well to the epistemology of morals. Augustine can treat "self-love"
in either way, as a continuous phenomenon, linking natural and the
perfected humanity, or as a discontinuous one, flowing only from
an achieved virtue which is the gift of grace. But we are more frequently conscious of the latter approach, the approach of authority,
supported by the identification of self-love with the love of God
and making no concessions to natural states of affairs or a priori
perceptions.

The approach by way of authority is well illustrated by a characteristic preaching paradox which tells us that what we call "love" of
self may in reality be hatred. This assertion is intended to be startling:
"Certainly, if I were to ask you whether you loved yourself, you
would reply, 'Yes! Who is there that hates himself?' 'Who is there
that hates himself?' you would ask." Again: "'And who is there',
asks one, 'who does not love himself?' Look! I will show you who!
'Who loveth iniquity, hateth his own soul.'" Self-love, so far from
being the universal predicate that Augustine's flock naturally expect,
is a matter on which it is possible to be self-deceived. Augustine can
shake the conventional "egoist" by taking from him what might
seem to be the most immediate delivery of his self-consciousness.
"Indeed you did *not* love yourself. . . . You *thought* you loved your-

self!" "Do you think you love yourself? You are mistaken!"[15]

While the text, Psalm 10(11):6, "Who loveth iniquity, hateth his own soul," is usually associated with the appearance of "self-hate" in Augustine's mind, we may guess that if Scripture had provided no direct warrant for the expression, rhetorical flourish and philosophical tradition might have conspired to invent it just the same. We are within the magnetic field of the extremely potent Platonic commonplace (the obverse of the identification of the useful and the right) that one who wrongs another really wrongs himself. This dictum, in one form or another, was a part of the philosophical landscape in which Augustine grew up. Plotinus had it and so did Ambrose. In using it Augustine was simply a traditionalist, but in clothing it with the original description "self-hate" he was exercising his own rhetorical genius.[16]

The wicked man's boast that he loves himself is shown to be empty by the terrible consequences he brings upon his own head. What sort of a "love" is it that "ties a noose for the beloved's neck"?[17] Love is love only by virtue of its good effects. In chapter one we showed how benevolent love, as the will for a fellow human being to fulfill his existence, necessarily seeks to bring him to the union with God for which he was made. We did not ask the question: What if this will is misdirected, not perceiving where the other's true well-being lies? In the context of self-love, at least, Augustine cannot avoid this question, and his answer to it is severe: "Such self-love is better called hatred."[18] The criteria for benevolent self-love are objective: one's purposes must correspond to one's given destiny. Self-harm is self-hate, even though unintentional. "Certainly [the mind] does not know that it wills itself evil, for it does not think that what it wills is harmful. But it *does* will evil all the same, since it *does* will what is harmful."

On the face of it, then, Augustine has opted for exclusively objective criteria for benevolent love-of-self. Yet this is not all of his thinking. If we read the last-quoted sentences from *De Trinitate* in their context, we will be left in some doubt as to whether the matter is as clear as it seemed:

The human mind is so constituted that it is never forgetful of itself, never fails to understand itself, never fails to love itself. But because one who hates another is anxious to hurt him, it is not unreasonable to describe the human mind as "hating" itself when it hurts itself. Certainly it does not know that it wills itself evil, for it does not think that what it wills is harmful. But it *does* will evil all the same, since it *does* will what is harmful. Hence the Scripture: "Who loveth iniquity, hateth his own soul." So that if a man knows how to love himself, he loves God; but if he does not love God, even granting that self-love which is naturally instinct within him, yet he may be described not inappropriately as hating himself, since he does what is inimical to himself and persecutes himself like an enemy.[19]

There emerge from this passage two important conclusions: first, that Augustine does not intend entirely to deny himself the idea of a neutrally valued universal self-love simply in order to limit the notion to objective criteria; second, that he sees the oddity of taking nothing but objective criteria to establish a claim for hatred. The real enemy, after all, is intent on doing harm, while the uninstructed lover-of-self does harm unwittingly. In this passage, then, Augustine will go only so far as to say that such a one may "not inappropriately" be described as hating himself. Alongside the objective criteria, according to which self-love depends on the correct identification of the final good, he retains a place for subjective criteria, by which he can say, "The mind never fails to love itself," and, in another place, "Nobody hates himself."[20]

Augustine occasionally refers to benevolent self-love, "the will to serve one's own advantage " (*prodesse sibi velle*),[21] as a duty which we owe to ourselves on precisely the same basis as we owe love to others. The value of this paradoxical way of speaking, once again, is that it strengthens the suggestion of *auctoritas*: self-love is not something which may be assumed to come naturally but is a necessary matter of exhortation and encouragement. "It is improper for a man not to do to himself what he does to his neighbour, when he hears God say, 'You shall love your neighbour as yourself', and again, 'Have mercy on your soul, pleasing God.'" There is a rich vein of remonstrance here, tirelessly quarried for ammunition against theological opponents who risk the fires of hell by refusing to submit to Catholic teaching. Pelagian or Donatist, the adversary is feelingly implored to "spare himself," "show mercy to himself," to recognize that he is his own persecutor and his own enemy. The Scripture instructs him to "Have mercy on your soul, pleasing God" (Ecclus. 30:24). This duty can be imaginatively interpreted as a special case of the "works of mercy" and almsgiving which the Christian is obliged to perform toward the poor. It makes no difference whether we perform these works to ourselves or to our neighbor; in either case their sole purpose is "to deliver us from wretchedness and restore us to blessedness." But we must begin with ourselves, "for almsgiving is a work of mercy, and there is supreme truth in the saying 'Have mercy on your soul, pleasing God.'"[22]

The incongruity of regarding self-love in this way is somewhat reduced when the recipient of the alms is seen specifically as the *soul*. The fate of the damaged or neglected soul Augustine treats in classically Platonic terms of internal division and strife, civil war within the breast. The wicked man will "crucify himself with himself," he will "make for himself a divided heart which will detain him from the vision of God." With a little rhetorical license, Augustine can depict a touching scene. A man confronts his own soul and finds it a beggar: "Whoever you may be that live wickedly, whoever you may be that live in infidelity, return to your conscience! There you will find your soul, beggared, needy, pauperized, care-laden. Not only needy, perhaps, but reduced by very want to silence! Is it beggared? It is hungry for justice! When you find your soul in such a state (it is within you, within your heart, that these things are found!), first give it alms! Give it bread!" When God gave man a soul, he gave him a task: he must care for his soul and make sure that it flourishes. "Who loves the secret chamber of his heart, let him do some good there."[23]

This care may include severe discipline. Just as one who loves his soul "according to the world" hates it "according to God," so, "if it were his wish to give it alms so that all things should be clean for him, he would hate it according to the world and love it according to God."[24] Because in Augustinian anthropology *anima* includes the principle of physical life, the instinct to preserve life at all costs is an error of the soul, not merely of the body. "Perhaps your soul says, 'Tell him not to strike or else I shall have to leave you! If he strikes, I cannot stay with you! Tell him not to strike if you don't want me to go!'" The solution of this mock-pathetic drama comes when the man so addressed by his soul realizes that it is he himself and not some other who is speaking and that what becomes of the body is of no concern to him![25] The one who cares for his soul must free it from this passionate and misconceived desire to remain attached to the body. Augustine wanders with perfect inconsistency between calling this disciplinary attitude "love" and calling it "hate." "It is no self-hate, this ruthlessness with yourself!" he tells us; but then on another occasion: "Utterly amazing that man should love his soul to destroy it and hate it to preserve it! To love wrongly is to hate; to hate rightly is to love!"[26]

The same severely constructive benevolence can as well be expressed toward the flesh as toward the soul. So seriously, in fact, does Augustine take the ontological hierarchy of goods—the good of the soul is God, the good of the body the soul—that it is quite impossible to discern any substantial difference between love of the soul and love of the body. "When God is loved more than the soul . . . then true and complete care is taken of the soul, and consequently of the body too." Asceticism, fortitude in the face of death, self-discipline are equally characteristic of either. Since the good of the body is "not pleasure, not freedom from pain, not strength, not beauty, not speed, not any other quality that might be included in a list of bodily goods, but wholly and completely the soul," true love of the flesh commits us to that subordination of matter to spirit which will enable the soul to resist the faults of the flesh. Then it is that the flesh is properly cared for.[27] The text Ephesians 5:29, "No one hates his own flesh," forbids Augustine to admit a Manichaean unconcern for the body's welfare. It also allows him to develop a mischievous and only half-serious comparison between the proper treatment of a body and a wife. "Its desire is against you, like you wife's! Love it and beat it! Until there is one harmony in one reformation!" Both flesh and wife need healing as part of ourselves, not rejection as something alien. When Julian of Eclanum accused Augustine of contempt for the flesh, he failed to appreciate the warmth of positive regard which wielded the stick.[28]

Such is the benevolent love-of-self that is taught by *auctoritas*.

TRANSCENDING NATURAL SELF-LOVE

The opposite approach, which we have associated with the role of *ratio* in Augustine's epistemology, is marked by the universal claim that all men love themselves naturally. The passages in which this claim is made (rather less frequent, though perhaps also less rhetorical, than those in which it is denied) divide themselves into two groups.[29] Those from the *De Trinitate* have their own distinctive pattern: the universal self-love which they assert is a love of the human mind, an activity of man's self-consciousness belonging with self-understanding and self-awareness. The texts from the *Sermons*, on the other hand, and (with some qualifications) from the *De doctrina Christiana* take as the subject of self-love man as a psychosomatic unity and conceive self-love not as the distinctive feature of human self-consciousness but as something that man shares with the beasts. We can speak, then, of a psychological model for universal self-love (which we reserve for consideration in chapter three) and of an animal model.

There is in every living creature a deep-seated desire to continue existing, to avoid death and to maintain life, a desire "to be at one with oneself" (*conciliari sibi*). "It is the first and greatest word of Nature that man should be at one with himself, and therefore should flee death naturally, so much a friend to himself that he wishes him-

self to be a living creature, vehemently desiring and seeking to live in
this conjunction of soul and body."[30]

Augustine's treatment of this desire is in a clearly marked tradition: *conciliari* is the Latin translation of the Greek οἰκειοῦσθαι, and
both words appear in philosophy primarily as a technical term of
Stoicism. For the Stoics *oikeiosis* was a feature of each individual's
existence from the beginning, a self-relationship which was the presupposition of all growth in that it explained the impulse to obtain food
and ward off danger, as well as of all external relationships and perceptions:

> Immediately upon birth a living creature feels an attachment
> for itself and an impulse to preserve itself and to feel affection
> for its own constitution. . . . In proof of this opinion they [the
> Stoics] urge that infants desire things conducive to their health
> and reject things that are the opposite. . . . But it would be im-
> possible that they should feel desire at all unless they possessed
> self-consciousness, and consequently felt affection for them-
> selves. This leads to the conclusion that it is the love of self
> which supplies the primary impulse to action.[31]

In the first book of *De doctrina Christiana*, where Augustine was at
his most confident about universal self-love, allowing himself a char-
acteristically extravagant assertion of its self-evidence—"only a mad-
man would doubt . . . "—he was also at his closest to the Stoic tradition. Self-love he expounded primarily as "love of one's body." It is
a feature of behavior which man has in common with the beasts.
Thus the grounds on which its self-evident universality is assumed are
empirical; it is an observable feature in all human behavior patterns.[32]

But in his selection of anthropological evidence Augustine imposes
some characteristic personal interests upon the tradition. What Cicero's Stoic sources regarded as an account of the earliest instincts of
the newborn child and only secondarily as an account of the instincts
surviving into adulthood, Augustine turned into a theory to account

for the fear of death. Fear of death is an instinctive feature common to all, even the Old Testament saints, overcome in the Christian church not by any weakening of the love of life (he pours scorn on the Stoics for their *inconsistent* contempt of death!) but by faith in the resurrection. "It is natural," he says, "not only for men, but for all creatures which have any kind of life, to reject death and fear it."[33] Together with the fear of death we may mention related features of instinctive behavior which show love for one's own existence: the shielding of the eyes when an object is about to hit them; care for one's own health and safety; and the most absurd and yet most natural of man's bodily concerns, an anxiety over the fate of his mortal remains. Augustine's Stoicized anthropology, interpreted in the light of Ephesians 5:29, allows him to be generous to this foible so deeply ingrained in the ecclesiastical tradition. "Whatever attaches to the burial of a body is not a precaution for salvation, but a humane duty which corresponds to the impulse whereby 'No one ever hates his own flesh.' It is right to show what care he can for the neighbour's flesh when he who once wore it has left it behind."[34]

But not all of Augustine's interests are with death and its avoidance. The passage of the *Confessions* in which he discusses his childhood instincts also owes something to the Stoic tradition: "Even when I was a child, I existed, I had life and sense, I had care for my safety—a trace of the hidden unity from which I sprang—by interior sense I guarded the integrity of my senses and in small things and thoughts about small things I took pleasure in the truth. I did not wish to be deceived, I had a good memory, I became ordered in my speech, gentle in my friendship, I fled grief, rejection and ignorance."[35] We can see, however, in the mention of "hidden unity," the corrosion of the Stoic pattern through its suspension in a concentrated solution of Neoplatonic Christianity. Not only has it been defined as a "unity of body and soul," which was not quite what *oikeiosis* meant, but it has been taken as a lost aboriginal unity of the unfallen creature, never empirically experienced in this world. What Stoics had seen as a sign of integration, the Christian saw as the ruins of a once integrated, but now disintegrating, human nature.[36]

Animal self-love, the unity of body and soul, can again be analyzed as love-of-the-body on the one hand and as love-of-the-soul on the other. We see natural love of the *soul* expressed in the desire for life (for life is a function of the soul), common to all, even those who in despite of it reach out for martyrdom. Those who fear martyrdom love their souls overmuch. Those who live dissipated and sensual lives, though constantly subjecting their souls to the humiliation of serving bodily desire, yet show their preference for the soul by their readiness to lose any kind of pleasure if need be in order to stay alive. The use of "soul" to represent the principle of physical life, though strange, has a double justification in Scripture and philosophy. The Latin Bible used the word *anima* to translate the Greek ψυχή in all of the Gospel verses which speak of losing "life" in order to save it. This suggested to Augustine that it was the *animal soul* which had to be lost, though only temporarily, for the sake of the *rational soul*. While beasts could not be blamed for fearing death, men, though born with the same instinct, could be blamed for continuing to allow fear to dominate them, since as rational beings they were able to reach toward a higher life than that which they shared with the animals. When man sacrifices his "soul" in martyrdom, he shows his preference for the rational good to the animal and so saves not his rational soul only but ultimately his animal soul and his body with it.[37]

More commonly the self-protecting instinct in man is described as love of the *body*. Here a strong influence is exercised by the text Ephesians 5:29, "No one ever hated his own flesh." Within the scope of this much-used principle Augustine was ready to include a large amount. Here he could locate the fear of death, delight in pleasurable sensation, aversion to unpleasant sensation, rejection of suicide, as well as the other features of self-protective behavior already mentioned. The text is one of the most important in Augustinian anthropology and of particular significance for his anti-Manichaean polemics. His opponents, leaning heavily upon Galatians 5:17, "The flesh

lusts against the spirit, and the spirit against the flesh," supposed that
there was an absolute opposition between the corporeal and spiritual
natures of man. This "carnal error"—the play on words is relished!—
not only misunderstood the text in Galatians, but showed the Manichees to be poor observers of themselves. Did they not evade blows,
avoid falls, take care not to subject their bodies to extremes of tem-
perature just like everybody else? Did they not protect themselves
and think about their health? It is in this context of anti-Manichaean
apologetic that we can best understand the view that natural self-love
is a trace of unfallen goodness still left in fallen humanity. It is a sign
that the body really is the workmanship of a good Creator that,
while the creature does despite to order and unity in his relationships
with God and man, he cannot completely lose his concern for order
and unity within himself. Thus the Neoplatonist understanding of
evil as deficiency is maintained against the Manichaean dualism of
good and evil. Wrong sensuality is good insofar as it is love-of-self and
love-of-body, but evil in that it is despite-of-God and despite-of-soul.[38]

When we contrast these expressions of love for the body and the
soul with those we recorded earlier, we are made aware of the striking
difference that separates the two interpretations of self-love. Everything that is reckoned as "love" from the natural point of view, especially the instinct to preserve life, was seen as "hatred" from the
point of view of divine revelation. Where from the one point of view
Augustine can recognize distinct physical and psychological areas of
interest, values of the body and values of the soul, from the other
point of view he ruthlessly assimilates all the interests of body and
animal soul to the ultimate concern of the rational soul. To such a degree does the authority of the divine command reverse man's natural
assumptions and values.

And yet Augustine is not content simply to set natural and revealed self-love in paradoxical antithesis. He has in mind an apologetic argument: to plead for the love of God by way of reason rather
than authority, starting from the fact that all men love themselves. If
self-love is natural and universal, how can men not be concerned to

love themselves rightly? And if right self-love is nothing other than
love-of-God, what else can we think but that this love is the logical implication of all that men find in themselves by nature? We can
see the argument in a somewhat unpolished form in a paragraph from
De libero arbitrio:

> If you wish to escape wretchedness, love this very thing in your-
> self, that you wish to continue existing. For if you wish to ex-
> ist more and more, you will come near to that which is supremely
> existent. Be grateful, now, that you exist! . . . For the more
> fully you will desire eternal life, and you will hope so to be fash-
> ioned that your sensibilities are not bounded by time, branded
> and imprinted by love of time-bound things. . . . But he who
> loves existence, accepts other things inasmuch as they really ex-
> ist, and loves that which exists for ever.[39]

But there is a difficulty. If, as we have seen, the discovery of perfect self-love "from above" by the teaching of authority suggests a re-
definition of self-love in terms of the love of God, this approach to
it "from below" runs the risk of redefining in the opposite direction
and reducing the love of God to enlightened natural self-concern.
The treasure in heaven to which the argument is supposed to lead us
may turn out to be nothing much more than the small change of human ambition on earth. And so we find that when he employs this
apologetic approach, Augustine is much more guarded about asserting
the virtual identity of self-love and love-of-God, and has much more
to say about the need to transcend natural self-love.

In a passage from the contemporary *De vera religione* we can see
this caution emerging. The argument begins with a universal premise, "We want to be invincible," and proceeds to pursue the claim that
only the Christian achieves what all men want. "He who loves that
which alone cannot be taken from its lover, he it is who is unques-
tionably invincible. . . . For he loves God . . . and his neighbour as
himself." But can his neighbor not be taken from him? Not if he

loves him "as himself," "because in loving himself, what he loves is not that which is apparent to the sight or to any other of the corporeal senses. It follows that to love someone *as* himself is to have him *in* himself." There are two kinds of neighbor-love, then, and only that which is modeled on self-love will lead us to the invincibility which all men desire. But this self-love is itself not an undifferentiated, natural self-love, but the self-love of one who, by loving God, "has" or "possesses" himself entire. He loves himself, as he loves his neighbor, not for "what he is to himself" but for "what he is to God." "That which he loves in them, he has perfect and entire *in himself*." *Apud se,* translating the Greek ἐφ'ἑαυτῷ, gives away the Stoic-Platonic background: We are speaking of the philosopher.[40]

The caution emerges even more clearly in the comparable passage of *De doctrina Christiana* I. There, as we have seen, Augustine identifies four proper objects of love, that which is above us, that which we ourselves are, that which is beside us, and that which is beneath us— our bodies, for only the human will count as a proper object of love, even of "use-love." With respect to the second and fourth of these there was no need of a command, "for however far a man may depart from the truth, he retains his love for himself and his love for his own body." This explanation shows us that Augustine will approach self-love from the point of view of *ratio* rather than from *auctoritas,* basing himself upon a universal love-of-self which is rooted in the original goodness of man's created nature. "For the soul, though it flees from the unchangeable light that rules all things, acts to govern itself and its own body, and so cannot help but love itself and its body."[41]

Here, however, there is a check. The self-love of the soul is corrupted into a desire to rule not only itself and its body but its fellow man too. "Man's perverted soul is inclined to seek and claim as its due that which properly belongs to God alone. Such self-love is better called hatred," a description which is supported, as so often, by an appeal to Psalm 10 (11):6. Yet normally when Augustine attributes self-hatred to the wicked man, he means what he says, but in this case, where he is concerned to build upon an idea of universal self-love, he does not treat the description literally. His last word on the matter is that nobody hates himself. To which he adds: "There has been no argument about this in any philosophical school." Perhaps because none of them had heard the sermons of Augustine of Hippo![42]

The experimental distinction between the self-love of the soul (here *animus*, the rational soul) and the love of the soul for the body has not, in the event, proved very fruitful, as Augustine has had rather little to say about the positive content of the soul's self-love. Turning now to the love-of-the-body to demonstrate that for this love too there is no need of a command, he is on more familiar territory. Ephesians 5:29 is to the fore in response to the Manichaean use of Galatians 5:17. Love for the body includes discipline, "because the more the spirit loves the flesh the more it wishes it subject to that which is better than the flesh." Ascetic discipline is no exception to love-of-the-body except when it is practiced by Manichees, "who wage war against the body as though it were their natural enemy." Nor is it incompatible with such love that one will suffer damage to his body in order to pursue higher goods, for "one should not be thought to have no love for the safety and integrity of the body simply because one loves something else more."[43]

The universal claim having thus been established on both fronts (for self-love and love-of-the-body belong to us by an unshakable law of nature which applies also to the beasts), it remains to forge the link between natural self-love and the command that we should love God. In the first place, Augustine has said that man needs a "prescribed way of self-love, that is, how he is to love himself to best effect . . . and how he is to love his body ordinately and prudently."[44] In the second place, "when love of God is given prominence and set forth as the prescribed way of love so that everything else flows into it, then although nothing is said directly about self-love, nevertheless the words 'Love your neighbour as yourself' show that it has not been forgotten."[45] Thus there is a clear continuity between natural and taught self-love; the difference between them is the "way" which will give a successful issue to the self-concern which all men share. But in reaching this conclusion Augustine has tried not to reduce the gap too much. He has shown that there is indeed a wrong kind of self-love which is arrogant self-assertion; he has shown that love-of-the-body does not mean acquiescence in its disordered impulses. We do not need a command to tell us to do what comes naturally, but we do need instruction to tell us how to do it properly. Even if Augustine does imply that there is a direct road from Nature to Perfection, he knows that there are many beguiling sidetracks and doubts whether anyone will complete the journey without a map.

The journey of the first book of *De doctrina Christiana* is Stoic in its inspiration. Led from the beginning by self-oriented instincts common to all living creatures, the Stoic philosopher experienced a conversion which altered the direction of their leading but did not displace them.[46] So for Augustine self-love is a continuous but artic-ulated personal dynamism. It cannot be removed, but it can be trans-formed. But Augustine will not stand by this position. Although it allows him to call some self-love good, it does not allow him to call it good enough; although it allows him to call some self-love evil, it does not allow him to call it the very root of all human and angelic sin. His next attempt to approach right self-love by the route of hu-man reason will involve him in a more Platonic route. To this we shall return when, in the context of rational-love-of-self, we discuss the later books of *De Trinitate*.

SELF-LOVE AND THE DESIRE FOR HAPPINESS

Benevolent self-love has a number of features in common with the de-sire for happiness which makes a comparison of the two irresistible. We have already commented on the importance which the eudaemon-ist principle "We all wish to be happy" has for Augustine. Most read-ers of Augustine are familiar with the way this principle, which is accorded the status of a priori certainty, is made the premise for an apologetic argument which leads to God as the source of, sometimes

as the reality of, the happy life: the happy life must be a higher good
than ourselves, it must be unchanging and impossible to forfeit, and
it must be universally available. With only small modifications Augustine stood by this argument solidly from his earliest writings to
his latest.[47] Thus the desire for happiness, like self-love, is equivalent
to the love-of-God when it is "taught," but has a natural, nonmoral
area of reference in which it is common to all men. In either case
this articulation is made the basis for a rational approach to man's
goal, more systematically developed with the eudaemonist principle
than with self-love, in which there is a certain amount of continuity
between the natural and the perfected but also a necessary opacity.

But can we go further than the comparison of the two and identify self-love with the desire for happiness? It is an easy identification
for students of Augustine to make, and most of them have made
it.[48] The principal dissenting voice has been that of Ragnar Holte,
and his reasons do not entirely commend themselves. In the first
place, having rejected altogether the presence of what we have called
positive love in Augustine's thought, he cannot take Augustine's as-
surances about the self-evidence of the eudaemonist principle at
their face value. In his view "desire for happiness" cannot be the pursuit of an unspecified, subjectively conceived good; it has to be already, in its fullest sense, love for God.[49] In the second place, Holte's
understanding of self-love is based entirely upon the treatment of
that idea in *De doctrina Christiana* I, from which he conceives it as a
self-standing teleological thrust within the active life alone, thus
missing the point of Augustine's assertions about perfect self-love
being one with the love of God.[50]

Nevertheless, Holte was right to dissent. In support of the differentiation of self-love and the desire for happiness I would make three
points:

   a. In two texts only are self-love and the desire for happiness
      mentioned together in a way that suggests their synonymity.
      As there are some 150 references to self-love in Augustine's
      work, this small number should rather damp our enthusiasm
      for an identification of the two ideas.[51]

b. Augustine regards the desire for happiness as the fundamental
   reality underlying all other desires, a position which arises naturally out of the tradition of discussing the *finis bonorum*.
   Thus one man's desire to be a soldier and another man's desire
   not to be one are equally forms of the desire for happiness.[52]
   But the desire to be a soldier would never be an example of
   universal self-love. It is not the case with universal self-love, as
   it is with the universal desire for happiness, that everything
   everyone does expresses it one way or another. Only some
   things that everyone does, shielding one's eyes, for example, or
   avoiding death, are instances of natural self-love.

c. Although there is continuity and discontinuity between the
   natural and the perfect in both self-love and the desire for
   happiness, the settlement is somewhat different in either case.
   Augustine will say, quite normally, that not all men love themselves and that what pretends to be self-love is often mere self-
   hatred. With the conflict between this and the universal self-
   love he is apparently prepared to live. Universal self-love is never
   presented as an *unsuccessful* groping toward God. But Augustine will never admit that not all men wish to be happy, and so
   he is constantly having to come to terms with unsuccessful desire for happiness. The problem of the continuity between what
   all desire and what only some achieve is always vexing him in
   the eudaemonist context.[53] But with self-love he forgets the
   continuity whenever it is no longer useful for apologetic purposes.

What are we to make of the similarities between the two notions
and especially of the two texts which unambiguously treat them as
equivalent? Augustine's thought about self-love was much less sys-
tematized than his thought about the desire for happiness, which was,
anyway, part of a tradition of thought which he inherited. It is not
surprising if at times his treatment of self-love became attracted by
the stronger magnetic field of the eudaemonist principle. Indeed, we
may reasonably suppose that Augustine's eudaemonism was responsi-

ble for the whole attempt to erect an apologetic movement of thought on the foundation of natural self-love. However, the divergences on closer inspection are more striking than the convergences—and we have made no mention as yet of the fact that there is a radically evil sense of self-love to which no equivalent can be found in the eudaemonist context, simply because the relation between this and the other senses is itself so problematic. Certainly nothing can be gained by the assumption that in talking about self-love Augustine always had in mind one or another form of the search for happiness and vice versa. The study of each, so long obscured by their identification, must proceed in independence.

CHAPTER THREE

SELF-KNOWLEDGE AND SELF-LOVE

Students of Augustine's psychological theory have properly insisted that for our author love always follows knowledge. It is as good or as bad as the information it works on. A false conception of the universe leads to false love of God, self, and neighbor. A true knowledge of the universe brings with it love that is perfect in every respect. The eschatological "wisdom" toward which, according to the *De Trinitate,* redeemed humanity moves is no less a matter of ordered emotions than of rational perceptions.[1]

This gives rise to an idea of self-love which differs from the benevolent love which we have so far been considering. Always corresponding to a degree of self-knowledge, it takes as its watchword the Delphic proverb *Cognosce te ipsum,* "Know yourself." Belonging specifically to the rational, contemplative faculties of the soul which distinguish man from the beasts, it is entirely a human and psychological phenomenon. Of the aspects of love which we outlined in our first chapter, the one which most obviously relates knowledge and emotion in this way is that which we called "rational," and to the characteristic patterns of this aspect Augustine frequently returns when discussing the right and wrong forms which self-love can take.

It affords him more than one way of distinguishing them. In the first place, he can ask what exactly it is about himself that the lover-of-self singles out for approval, for in his own nature he will find some things that deserve his love and others that do not. In the second place, he can ask how the lover assesses himself in relation to other items in the universe, to God in the higher ontological order and to material things in the lower. By measuring this relative self-assessment against the metaphysical realities, he can declare that the love is as good or bad as the assessment is true or false.

Turning first to the former of these questions, we encounter a pair of distinctions that we have noted before: on the one hand, a distinction between the created self and the distortions which have marred it; on the other, a distinction between the self as it now is and that which it is to become.[2] In homiletic contexts Augustine makes constant use of the first of these distinctions, taking the individual's creation and fall as the test for approval and disapproval. Proper self-love is based on the common datum of created humanity, the work of God, in contrast to which the self's own work deserves to be viewed with hatred and fear: "Fear the evil in yourself, that is, your cupidity; not what God made within you, but what you made for yourself. God made you a good servant, you made for yourself a bad master in your heart." "You should hate your own workmanship within yourself, and love the work of God within you." There is apparently no place for self-love based on the actual experience of sanctification: the believer is confronted by an antithesis within himself not of vice and virtue but of vice and Nature. He starts from the premise, "You are an unrighteous man!" and then proceeds to make a distinction along these lines: "I said two things then, 'unrighteous' and 'man'. . . . Love that which God made, hate that which you made!"[3] The wicked man, of course, "hates that in himself which is of Nature, and loves that which is of vice." He is a "friend of his own lust," and "loves his own evil deeds." The virtuous man, on the other hand, in the course of discovering and welcoming his own created Nature, has discovered and welcomed the *imago Dei.* How could he understand his own soul without understanding that it bore God's image? How understand his body without understanding that it was the temple of God? Thus Augustine arrives at the point of saying what might out of its proper context be misunderstood, that "this is the lesson of true justice, to love nothing in oneself but what is of God, and to hate what is one's own."[4]

The second distinction uses eschatology very much as the first uses creation. The present self of our corrupted nature is distinguished from the future self of God's purposing. "Love what you will be!" Augustine urges his congregation. "Let us love the new, so that we need not fear the old!" And this involves adopting an attitude which Augustine does not shrink from calling "self-hatred" toward the empirical reality of what one is. "For anyone who loves himself *as a fool* will not progress to wisdom; nor will one become what he desires to be, unless he hates himself *as he is*." This is no more than the sick man does when he hates himself "such as he is." It is no more than God does when he "hates us evil."[5] We must notice that Augustine is not pleading for a total discontinuity between the self that is and the self that will be. The negative stress in this distinction is balanced by the positive assertions of created goodness in the other. This self-hatred, too, is a selective hatred. The sick man who hates himself sick, hates his sickness; so does the just man, who "hates in himself that which God hates," hate those features of his empirical self which he hopes to see eradicated.[6]

The idea of selective self-approval, then, distinguishes right and wrong expressions of self-love by distinguishing their objects. But Augustine is not limited to the view that certain objects may warrant approval absolutely. Far more fruitfully, though at some considerable risk of confusion, he suggests that there may be *relatively* appropriate and inappropriate evaluations of the self. For rational love takes cognizance of the whole order of things and is capable of discerning not merely that this object is a good but that it is a higher good than that object. The errors to which self-love is liable can thus be charted with considerable precision.

In the first place self-love can go wrong by being deficient. The lover can rate himself too low. We do not often find Augustine saying this but on occasion he does so, especially when he is exploring a Platonic vein of thought about the value of the soul.[7] One instance occurs within a few lines of the beginning of his writing career, when he urges the trouble-laden Romanianus "not to despise yourself, however many things happen to you which are unworthy of your soul." Elsewhere it is worldly pleasures rather than worldly sorrows which are likely to make men underrate themselves: "What is your soul? Think hard! I do not want you to underrate your soul and imagine it is something cheap and worthless! I do not want you to

look for something cheaper than your soul in order to make it happy!"
A third example of the theme shows Augustine directing attention
not to the soul specifically, not to the ontological dignity which it
naturally possesses over and above the material creation, but to the
value vested in man by God's saving acts. "Do not despise yourselves,
for it has not yet been revealed what you shall be! . . . Do not
think yourselves cheap, for the Creator of all and your Creator reckons
you so dear that daily he pours out for you the most precious blood
of his only-begotten Son!"[8]

The second error that may be charted in rational self-love is that the
lover may give too little or no recognition to what is of equal or greater
worth than himself. Occasionally other high values in general are in
danger of being ignored. It would be an "exceptionally perverse self-
love," says Augustine as he contemplates writing the *Retractations*, if
one preferred to lead others astray than to admit one's own mistake.[9]
Such a face-saving author would be blind to the value of truth,
both for himself and for others. More commonly, though, it is our
acknowledgment of the worth of God that is threatened by the
high evaluation, in itself not inappropriate, that we have of ourselves:

> There is nothing in creation attaining to the dignity of
> divinely-instituted natures of greater excellence than the
> rational mind. It follows that a good mind is more satisfied
> with itself, more delighted with itself, than any other
> creature could be. Yet how dangerous—no, how utterly disas-
> trous is that self-satisfaction, when it is the occasion of
> bloated swelling and diseased inflation! When it does not see,
> as it shall see in the end, that ultimate and unchangeable
> good, by comparison with which it despises itself, in love for
> which it becomes cheap in its own sight, and is so filled with
> its mighty breath as to prefer it to itself, not by the exercise of
> reason alone but in undying love as well!"[10]

From this we can see why Augustine describes this evil self-love as *amor sui usque ad contemptum Dei* and its opposite as *amor Dei usque ad contemptum sui.*[11] The force of the qualifications, missed by commentators who simply refer to *amor sui* and *amor Dei*, is to emphasize that the attitudes contrasted are *comparative* evaluation. The city of this world loves itself so much that it despises God by comparison, the eternal city loves God so much that it despises itself by comparison.[12] Augustine regularly qualifies the phrase *amor sui* when it appears in a bad sense with such expressions as, "If he did not love himself, but put God before himself, . . ." "Whoever has dismissed God and loved himself, . . ." and "If the soul loves itself and ignores its Creator. . . ."[13] In all of these expressions the critical idea is that the love has lost its proper grasp on the order of things: it has put second things first and first things second. The obedient believer, by contrast, has a love that is perfectly ordered to the proportions of reality. He has the "perfect justice," which is "to love the greater objects more and the lesser less."[14] He "knows himself" not in an individualistic sense but generically, by understanding that he is a man, which is the whole of humility. But even this does not mean that he is to undervalue himself: "You are required to be humble, not to turn yourself into an animal!"[15]

In the third place a whole series of possible mistakes is opened up when the fault of comparative misevaluation is brought into conjunction with Augustine's dichotomous anthropology:

If the mind's self-love is less than the being of its object merits, as, for example, if the mind of man were to accord itself that amount of love that is appropriate to the human body when in fact it is worth more than the body, this is a sin, and such love is not perfect. Again, if the mind accords itself love greater than its being merits, let us say to an extent that would be appropriate to God though in fact it is incomparably inferior to God, this too is a gross sin, and this self-love is not perfect. But even greater the perversity and iniquity when the *body* is accorded that amount of love which is appropriate to God![16]

   The three possibilities which Augustine here so carefully distinguishes present us with something of a puzzle. The meaning of the
second is clear enough; it is the same as that comparative misevaluation
which we have just been discussing. But what about the first, confusing
the order of soul and body? Are we to take it that this mistake is
compatible with giving God his proper primacy or is it a general confusion of the spiritual and material realms? If the latter, how does
it differ from the third? And what is the difference between the two
ways of slighting God's majesty that are here distinguished, excessive
love of body and excessive love of soul?

   At one point Augustine is prepared to assert as an a priori truth,
"universally agreed," that men love their souls more than they love
their bodies. The evidence for it is that which anyone can confirm by
introspection: however immorally one lives, however devoted one's
soul may be to the pleasures of the body, when death threatens the
soul will fight for itself (that is, for life).[17] Elsewhere, however we
are told of the real possibility that our preference for soul over
body might be reversed. "Who is there who does not love himself?
Look! I will show you who! 'Whoso loveth iniquity hateth his own
soul.' You are not going to say that someone loves himself when
it is his flesh he loves and he hates his soul, to his own destruction,
the destruction of his soul and his body? Who is it, then, who loves
his soul? The man who loves God, of course, with all his heart
and mind!" In this clash of testimonies we see the strains which
Augustine's monist adaptation of the Neoplatonic value system has
imposed. Pulling in one direction is the claim that the soul is the
good of the body and directly responsible for the body's physical
life. Pulling in the other is the claim that the good of the soul is
God.[18]

   The confusion generated by these relative evaluations of soul and
body cannot easily be resolved. However, Augustine does explain
at some length what he means when he speaks of the soul's loving
itself "as a body," and his explanation suggests a partial resolution of
our difficulty:

What then can be the purport of the injunction, Know thyself? I suppose it is that the mind should reflect upon itself, and live in accordance with its nature; that is to say, strive to be ordered according to its nature, under him whom it should be set under, and over all that it should stand over—under him by whom it ought to be ruled, over all that it ought to rule. For perverse desire makes it act often as though it had forgotten itself. . . .

Its love has been devoted to the material things with which the bodily senses have involved it in a persistent familiarity; and because it cannot take with it into the inward realm of immaterial being the material objects themselves, it collects and carries along images of them, formed in itself and of itself. . . .

Now the mind goes astray through uniting itself to these images by a love so intense as to make it suppose its own nature to be like theirs. It becomes as it were conformed to them, not in reality but by supposition: supposing itself to be, not an image, but the actual thing of which it carries the image in itself. . . . Thus the mind, supposing itself to resemble its own images, supposes itself to be a bodily thing. It is well aware of its own domination over the body; and this has caused men to ask what part of the body has most power in the body, and to consider this to be the mind or even the whole soul. . . . This theory identifies the soul with an actual part of the bodily viscera which can be exposed by anatomy.[19]

In this passage Augustine directs our attention behind the quantitative notion of the proportions in which a man may love body and soul, to the qualitative issues about the nature of the soul, and particularly to erroneous materialist theories. To love the soul as a body is to conceive of it in materialist terms. This should alert us to the true significance of the expressions in which false love is described as quantitative deficiency or excess. By Augustine's own admission the materialists are well aware of the superiority of the soul to the body—

to the rest of the body, as they see it—and so, if right love of the
soul is to be simply a quantitative matter (neither as much as God
nor as little as the body) they might stand as good a chance as any
of us of getting the proportion right. But for Augustine the Neoplatonist, the given ordering of all possible objects of knowledge and love
in ontological dignity demands of the soul more than a purely quantitative ordering; the knowledge and love must themselves reproduce,
as it were in imitation, the qualitative distinctions which it finds in
reality. These quantitative terms are intended to convey a quasi-
qualitative distinction between the knowledge and love of one kind
of thing and the knowledge and love of another. Only so could he
have claimed to detect a kind of "consubstantiality" in the perfected
mind's love and knowledge of itself, which he would even dare to
believe was an image of the divine Trinity.[20] The materialist, whose
mind "knows" itself as a material thing and loves itself as such, is
said to have a "lesser" self-knowledge and self-love than his mind
merits, and so to miss the image of the consubstantial Three-in-One.
But what is called for is not a mere subjective intensification of
self-knowledge and self-love, but a qualitative equivalence to the object. The mind must grasp itself as it really is.

THE CONVERSION OF SELF-LOVE

The mind's love of the material world, of itself, and of God are not
seen by Augustine as simply *coexistent* attitudes, whether in proper or improper proportion. Such an account of their relations (essentially that presented by Ragnar Holte)[21] misses the constant interest
which our author takes in the transition from one love to the other,
that is, in the mind's conversion from over-involvement in the material universe, *via* an integration with itself, to contemplation of God.
There is, in other words, a concern to trace a vertical movement,
which takes self-love as its midpoint, as well as the horizontal relation
in which the self is both subject and object of cognition and delight.
But this requires the use of a third aspect of the love-of-self besides

the benevolent and rational aspects that we have so far observed. We have to think of self-love as part of the cosmic movement of the universe to its final cause, a movement in which the gathering of each entity around its own center of being is an important but only pre-liminary stage.

At first it is difficult to imagine how the picture of cosmic motion and rest can be applied to a rational being's relationship with itself. In the tenth book of *De Trinitate* Augustine develops extensive ob-jections to the idea of the mind's "seeking itself." [22] Is he likely to be any happier with the thought of its being attracted to itself or clinging to itself? But this conceptual problem has been posed for him by the Neoplatonic tradition of spirituality, a tradition in which he has been steeped far too deeply to allow himself to be scared off. He pictures the movement-to-self not as falling and rest, like the movement of a stone pulled by gravity, but as a contraction, some-thing like the closing of a flower or the retreat of a snail into its shell. But as this movement then has to be integrated into the upward movement toward God, perhaps we may be permitted to venture another simile: it is rather like the smoke from a fire which has bil-lowed out into the room, but which, once the flue has been opened, is sucked back into the grate by the draught and then thrust up the chimney. But let this incongruous illustration give way to a survey of how contemporary Neoplatonism thought of it, a survey which is not intended to suggest direct dependence of or on Augustine, but merely to sketch the content of ideas with which he was, and ex-pected his readers to be, familiar.

To be in matter is to be in space. The intelligible realm, which is neither in matter nor in space, may be said to be "in itself." This phrase expresses three ideas. First, it suggests that the intelligible is *self-sufficient*. The material realm is the image, dependent upon the archetype, but the archetype, the intelligible realm, is not dependent upon anything except itself. It has its good wholly within itself and from itself. [23] Secondly it conveys the notion that the intelligible is *be-yond spatial dimension*. Porphyry writes: "If to be in space is to be outside self, having proceeded into mass, and if the one is reflection, the other archetype, then that which is in space has existence relative to the intelligible while the intelligible has existence in itself."[24] Thirdly it expresses the idea that the intelligible is *unified*, and even though it is not without the suspicion of subdivision in its parts, nevertheless it forms a cohering, self-according unity.[25] It was natural for the Christian Platonist to draw upon this language to express what he knew of the being of God, who "remains always within himself."[26]

The mind and soul of man may exist in one of two states: separate, detached from the world of matter, "in itself"; or in association with the material, having proceeded from itself to what is alien to it. The former condition is often described as "self-presence," its opposite as "distance-from-self."[27] Plotinus in particular was fond of metaphors of "contraction," "gathering," and folding to express the withdrawn state of the soul separated from the material universe. In this state alone could it be self-sufficient and enjoy a stable satiety.[28] And because it was fundamental to the Neoplatonic outlook that the mind of man was truly the man himself, this withdrawal of soul from body was the main purpose of Neoplatonic spirituality. Augustine summarized the message of Porphyry's lost *De regressu animae*: "We must shun every material thing, that our soul may be happy with God for eternity."[29]

The spiritual task of withdrawal could be presented in more than one way. Where Plotinus liked metaphors of contraction, representing a gathering of the scattered force of the soul from the periphery to the center, where the true self belonged, Proclus in a later century used the verb ἐπιστρέφειν, not strictly "to be converted" or "to turn," as of a sudden, decisive event, but "to be oriented toward" or "to turn upon," an attitude rather than an act.[30] And yet for Plotinus as much as for Proclus it is characteristic of the intelligible realm that it turns upon itself; for whatever turns upon something external to itself is metaphysically inferior to that which it turns upon. And for Proclus as for Plotinus the content of true wisdom is self-direction, a retreat into one's own nature to discover the true dignity and beauty of the soul. The contemplative sage is transported with a passionate delight and longing to collect himself from his body, to be with himself. He is helped by the "instinctive sense of belonging, with which his soul greets every kind of beauty." [31]

In Ambrose's Christian Platonism so frank a repudiation of the material world could find no place. And yet the call to the individual to direct his attention inward upon himself is no less clear, attributed, however, not to Plotinus but to more authoritative sages. " 'Give you attention,' says Moses, 'to yourself alone,' " and with this call Moses is seen also to repromulgate the Delphic motto, the heart of ancient mysticism, "Know yourself." [32] But in Ambrose we notice idiosyncratic variations on the Platonic tradition, both of them owing as much to the influence of Latin Stoicism as to Christianity. One is the strong emphasis on personal unity or integration, an emphasis not entirely absent from Plotinian thought but less characteristic of it. It was bound to appeal to the monotheist, anti-Arian Christian bishop. "God is one! . . . You, in the similitude of God, are to be one likewise. . . . Moral inconsistency makes a man change his identity." [33] The second, of great significance for the student of Augustine, is the identification of the inner self with the *conscientia*, a term which, by fluctuating between simple psychology—as "self-awareness"—and moral psychology—as "conscience"—opened the door to a moralizing interpretation of Platonic spirituality. The delight in one's own conscience which Ambrose encourages among his flock is less a matter of contemplation and mystic withdrawal than of moral earnestness and self-examination. [34]

We need only turn to Augustine's accounts of his own conversion to see how thoroughly he had assimilated the Neoplatonic spirituality. [35] The "books of the Platonists" released within him a motion of the soul exactly similar to that which they described.

> And counselled from this source to return to myself, I entered into my inner being with thee as my guide. I could do so,

because thou wast my helper. I entered in, and saw, with the eye of my soul such as it was, something above the eye of my soul, above mind, an unwavering light, not the common light which all flesh sees, nor something of the same kind but greater as though the daylight was much clearer and extended to fill the whole. That light was not of this kind at all.

Lo! when certain books "packed full" (in Celsinus' phrase) had wafted Arabian delicacies upon us, when they had let fall a very few drops of most precious ointment upon that little flame, it was incredible, Romanianus! incredible! and beyond what even you will believe of me perhaps (what more need I say?), and incredible to me too, what a fire they stirred up. . . . Straightway I began swiftly to return wholly to myself.[36]

What Augustine had experienced became the model on which he understood all Christian experience. The soul must be encouraged "not to pour itself out into the senses more than it is strictly compelled to, but rather to collect itself from them back into itself and become a child again for God." Augustine is free with exhortation to "return to yourself," or "not to go outside."[37] "Outside" is shorthand for the whole material realm, which is not the proper environment of the soul. Augustine could say about it what he says about the image of it held in the mind's eye: "to love it is to estrange oneself."[38] With his usual flair for lighting upon a text of scripture which incapsulates a doctrine in a word or two, Augustine linked this view of conversion with Luke 15:17, where the Prodigal Son is said to "return to himself." The whole parable is expounded as an allegory of Platonic conversion at *Quaestiones Evangeliorum* II.33, while shorter treatments and brief references are not rare.[39]

Like Ambrose, Augustine identifies the inner self with the conscience. Not only does this add a moral dimension to the spiritual quest, it shifts the attention from the once-for-all self-discovery of conversion to the constant spiritual discipline of self-scrutiny. "Pay

attention to such a treasury," he urges, "that you may be rich within!" In Galatians 6:4 he finds a text which carries this emphasis:
"Let every man examine his own work, and so he will have his boast
in himself alone and not in another." His comment: "That is, in
his own conscience." "You have your boast within yourself, because your boast is God, and he is in your conscience." The constant
care of the conscience is the Christian's greatest concern. "Hammer your conscience, if you want to be free from fear! Don't be content to stir around on the surface! Get deep inside yourself, into
the inner recesses of your heart!" When we read that the "return into a good conscience" has come to involve the active service of the
Gospel for the salvation of others, we know that the metamorphosis
of pagan spirituality into Christian is complete.[40]

Yet for all the transformation that the Platonic theme undergoes,
it retains its mystical overtones. Detachment is prominent in the
earliest works: Augustine twice propounds the view that the soul of
the wise man is not actually present in his body because he is "with
himself," and then has to wrestle with the problem of how the
wise man can still converse with us.[41] In his notes on Job he takes the
words, *non enim sum mecum*, "I am not with myself," to mean that
"he clings to what is outside," and, reversing the picture, he uses
the text Psalm 37 (38):11 in the description of his own conversion
to say that the light of his eyes was "within" while he was still
"outside." The most elegant adaptation of Scripture to Platonic
mysticism must surely be the treatment of the sleep of Adam while
God made Eve from his rib, which is seen to point to the inner
contemplation-of-self in which one discerns the difference between
the ruling and the ruled parts of the soul.[42]

At the heart of this mystical spirituality lies a premise in the doctrine of God: God "remains in himself," still and self-possessed.[43]
So does the Word, "remaining constantly within himself without grow-
ing old, and yet making all things new." It is a striking feature of
Augustine's Christology, and one that marks an affinity with the

Alexandrian tradition of his day, that the Incarnation does not involve
the Word in leaving his place in the Universe. He "orders all ages from
his Father's bosom while he consecrates this day from his mother's
womb. In the one place he remains, from the other he comes forth."[44]
From beginning to end God's being has been at rest in himself, a
fact signified to us by the institution of the Sabbath day: "not the
day on which God began to work, nor the day on which he finished,
lest it should seem that God's joy was in any way enhanced by the
making or completion of his creatures, but the day on which God rested from making them, in himself. Never has he been without that
rest." Man is invited to purify himself, becoming still and self-collect-
ed, that he may share God's rest. The institution of the Sabbath is
by way of being a veiled proclamation of the eschatological Gospel:
"For he who is always still conferred stillness upon us, when he
showed us that he rested from his labours."[45]

Nevertheless, whenever the mature Augustine leads us up the mystical ladder of Plotinus, through the collection of the self to the stillness of the divine, he is careful to insist that self-knowledge and the
knowledge of God are distinct, that over and beyond the recovery
of self-identity there is a further step to take. "Return to yourself, for
the truth dwells in the inner man. But when you find your own nature
to be susceptible of change, go beyond yourself! Remember: in
going beyond yourself, you go beyond the thinking mind." In this
phrase, *transcende et te ipsum*, we see what the unambiguous theism
of Christianity has made of the Plotinian ecstasis. Any suggestion
that the soul is itself an extension of the divinity has to be undercut.[46]
In the account of his own first ecstatic experience in the seventh
book of the *Confessions* Augustine insists that what he saw was not
the light of his soul, but "something above the eye of my soul, above
my mind, an unwavering light." Comment on this passage which
points to its dependence on *Ennead* I.6 should always be qualified by
some note of the seriousness with which Augustine maintains the
gulf between man and God in face of the tendency of his model to

obscure it. Lest there be any room for doubt about this "above," he goes on: "Nor did it rise above my mind as oil above water or as the sky above the earth: it was above me because it made me, and I was below it because I was its creature."[47] Such an emphasis on the two stages of the approach to God is entirely characteristic, too, of his popular presentation: "Return to yourself!" he will say; and then, adjusting the cliché to the point of destroying it, "But don't stay there!"[48]

There is an obvious affinity between the ascent of cosmic love to its goal in God and the "apologetic argument" which we discussed in chapter two. They are in reality two sides of the same ascent, now seen from an epistemological, now from a metaphysical point of view. Nevertheless, there are some striking differences which require us to approach the two, as we have done, separately, and those differences are especially obvious in the matter of self-love. In the epistemological ascent, this is taken as the universal starting point: every man has, and knows that he has, a benevolent love for himself, and the task is to explore the implications of this until they lead him to pursue his own true welfare in the love of God. In the cosmic ascent the movement-to-self is already the first step in the direction of redemption. The starting point is self-estrangement. This, we may guess, is why Augustine generally avoids the term *self-love* when he is thinking along the lines of the Neoplatonic spirituality, easily as he might have used it.[49] It would have introduced a good self-love that was not coextensive with the love of God, a natural self-love that went beyond the neutrally valued benevolence-to-self that was expressed in instinctive animal self-preservation. Nevertheless there was one massive philosophical undertaking in which Augustine attempted to draw together all these elements, the Plotinian ascent from self-estrangement, the epistemological ascent from universal self-benevolence, and the proportioned rational self-love by which we know ourselves aright. The remainder of this chapter will be given to an all-too-scanty review of this great synthesis, the last eight books of *De Trinitate*, still one of the landmarks of Western thought.

SELF-LOVE IN THE *DE TRINITATE*

The first interest in the later books of *De Trinitate* is to establish a
model for the relationships within the Holy Trinity by analogy from
human psychology. A secondary interest, yet so strong that it almost
comes to dominate the first, is the epistemological transition from
the model to the original. The successive psychological trinities which
Augustine expounds in these books are more than a series of approx-
imating models; they are a description of the route to the knowledge
of God. In this way his trinitarian "analogies" serve a purpose which
the analogies of the earlier Fathers did not. Man's knowledge and
love of himself is much more than a helpful illustration of three-in-
oneness, like source-stream-sea or root-branch-fruit. Because man
is made in the image of God there is an ontological rationale for attempting to understand the Godhead through the structure of the
human soul. Anthropology and theology (in the strict sense) are thus
inseparably interwoven and taken with equal seriousness. But precisely because it is taken with great seriousness, the anthropology
must not be abstracted from reality, but must start from the existing
condition of mankind as fallen and blind, in need of redemptive
grace even for the very task of understanding anthropology and theology. Thus the whole enterprise takes on the lineaments of the
doctrine of redemption, which, for Augustine, means the Plotinian
ascent refashioned in the light of faith in Christ.

In the following summary we are concerned mainly with the
interaction of the "horizontal" and "vertical" interests as it affects
Augustine's treatment of self-love. How far has the upward thrust of
the Plotinian program influenced his treatment of the purely natural
self-love which is coordinated at each stage with self-knowledge?
Has the convergence of the vertical and the horizontal resulted in a
new settlement in favor of *ratio* over *auctoritas* or is it still the
case that he who would learn to love himself must submit to the discipline of love-of-God?

Book VIII: The function of the eighth book in the structure of
the work is explained in a retrospective note in Book XV:

> We may recall that it was in the eighth Book that the manifes-
> tation of the Trinity to our understanding began. There we
> essayed to lift up, so far as might be, the effort of our mind to
> the understanding of that most excellent and changeless being
> which is other than our mind. In contemplation we were aware
> of it as not far from us and yet above us—not spatially but by
> its own most reverend and wonderful excellence, so that we
> found it present in us in virtue of its own pervading light. But so
> far we had no glimpse of the Trinity, because we could not in
> that dazzling brightness direct our mind's eye steadily to look
> for it. All that we could with some clearness distinguish was
> that it was no measurable mass in which the quantity of two or
> three must be believed greater than that of one. Only when
> we came to consider charity, which in Holy Scripture is called
> God, the light began to break upon a Trinity, consisting in
> lover, the beloved, and love. But from that ineffable light our
> gaze flinched away: we had to confess that our mind in its
> weakness was not yet strong enough to be conformed to it.
> And therefore, in order to recruit our labouring efforts, we
> paused in the pursuit of our undertaking and turned back to
> the more familiar consideration of that same mind of ours, in
> which man has been made after the image of God; and from the
> ninth to the fourteenth Book we occupied ourselves with our
> own creaturely nature in order that we might be able to appre-
> hend and perceive the invisible things of God through the things
> that are made.[50]

We are instructed by this note to treat Book VIII separately from the
books that follow it. The decisive road to the knowledge of God will
be begun in the ninth book. The eighth is something of an intro-
ductory essay to the method of the later books. Its subject is explicitly

the knowledge of God, whereas in the following books, from IX to XIV, the attention is temporarily diverted to the knowledge of the *imago Dei* in the human mind. It is important to register Augustine's clear suggestion that the attempt of Book VIII was a failure. He has described the enterprise in language not unlike that used for the "ecstasies" of *Confessions* VII–IX: he rises to a point at which the light of truth "shines out" for a moment, only to fall back as the material world clouds his vision and the perception of truth is lost. We could suggest that the speculation of Book VIII in the *De Trinitate* stands to the following laborious intellectual ascent rather as those ecstasies stand to the careful dialectic ascent of *Confessions* X.[51]

The "interior route" which he announces is an approach by which "the essence of truth may be mentally perceived without mass and without motion."[52] It is an avowedly rationalist route, contrasting with the deliveries of *auctoritas* in the preceding books. By frequent reference to the truths of faith proclaimed in the first seven books we may become very familiar with them. But there is a problem: as soon as we try to give them some imaginative content, our minds become confused. The route of reason is intended to help the believing mind over this difficulty. According to the retrospective note, again, the attempt of Book VIII is in two stages, the first having the limited philosophical aim of enabling us to see that there is no question of mass in God's being, the second with a more theological content, affording a momentary glimpse of a Trinity. The first stage begins with an apologetic argument of the characteristic Augustinian form, working from a universally accessible a priori: "You love nothing that is not good."[53]

Starting from this a priori (and it is an a priori, despite the appearance of empirical substantiation), Augustine shows us that there are continuities between a natural psychological response to a multitude of good things and the contemplation of God. All good things are good by participation in the One Good. Therefore we all love by implication the One Good which is God. And so we *ought* to love God (*sic amandus est Deus*). But some explanation has to be given of why there is any question of "ought," why the love of God does not automatically follow from the love of good things. This is necessary not only to preserve Christian theology from a complete surrender to philosophical continualism but to defend the philosophical enterprise itself from reduction to triviality. And so Augustine distinguishes an *act of will*, whereby the soul is converted to loving God, from the *natural love* which draws it to the multiplicity of good things. Love of the many is common to man: love of the One requires voluntary conversion.[54]

Now a further element of discontinuity is introduced, this time by distinguishing different senses of the predicate "good." All "good" things except the Good itself can from another point of view be described as "not good." It could never be guaranteed that the soul's love of things "good" in *that* sense would commit it without further ado to the love of "the Good in its own right." Nevertheless, despite these qualifications, love of the highest is indeed implied in the love of good things: a human mind, for example, attracts us because of its origin in the realm of truth.[55] Thus, when the mind does turn toward the Good, which is Truth, the will is acting in conformity with its nature. Furthermore, even without such conversion there is an irreducible goodness about the soul *as creature*, in that it continues to be superior to the body. Though such a soul cannot enjoy the good which would be accessible to it did it so will, yet that good is "not far from every one of us. For in him we live and move and have our being."[56] So the program is spelled out: there is a fundamental continuity between the natural loves of the soul, created in truth, and the Good which it is called to love supremely. Yet such love is not easy or obvious, but requires an act of the will. We should not underestimate the significance of this distinction between *voluntas* and *amor*, two terms which Augustine usually keeps in harness.

The first stage was limited to establishing the philosophical point that God stands to material goods as the One to the many and that he is without mass and motion. The second builds on the first, making further use of the idea of conversion of the will. But it starts by positing a new, decisively Christian discontinuity: "'We walk by faith, not by sight,' we do not yet see God, as the same apostle says, 'face to face.'" Christian eschatology poses a serious threat to the prospect of a reason-based epistemology (4.6). It is characteristic of the mature Augustine that he will not, as once he might have done evade the implications of eschatology. Instead, he attempts to develop a theory of knowledge-by-faith which has room for it, showing a continuity between what may be known and loved now and what may only be known and loved then. "Sure faith is the beginning of knowledge." Only the beginning: he will not, like pagan Neoplatonism, absorb both anthropology and theology into an undifferentiated theory of the cosmos.[57] Yet it is no less than the beginning. For without some kind of sight, the deliveries of *auctoritas* could have no content. When we hear the stories of Paul we imagine a face (4.7); and so it is with faith in God, that we must have some kind of model drawn from experience, even though we have no genus or species under which to subsume the Holy Trinity (5.8). What we hear and receive cannot be absolutely unknown, though it cannot absolutely be known either.

And so Augustine makes use of "the idea of the good imprinted in us," which he has just demonstrated to be implied in all of men's loves, the knowledge of which, however, is not identical with the vision of God. Here every man has the necessary epistemological aid to understand what "righteousness" is when it is predicated of a man like Paul. To have this innate idea is not to be righteous. The will must turn upon it in love (the distinction between *voluntas* and *amor* now forgotten) if it is to be a righteous will. There is, in fact, a threefold division: there are those who cannot gaze upon this form, those who gaze upon it and yet are not righteous, and those who not only gaze upon it but willingly cleave to it, and by so doing become righteous. (Thus the ground is prepared for a later model of the Trinity: *mens, notitia,* and *amor*).

Although this form is clearly *within* (it is called the *veritas interior praesens*), such a conversion of the will is not called self-love.

Augustine holds to the position that the form is "ours" (*apud nos*) but not "ourselves" (*nos ipsi*). Self-love, in fact, makes an appearance by quite another door. When we love ourselves, we do so in just the same way as we love other people, by comparing ourselves to the *forma*; and indeed Augustine finds it convenient, though ill-suited to the order of the dominical love-command, to mention love of neighbor before he mentions self-love. We love ourselves, as we love our neighbors, "either because they *are* just, or that they may be so." Self-love, at this appearance, is not part of the movement of cosmic love, but is love in its "rational" aspect only. It plays no part at all in escorting the soul on its upward journey to the knowledge of God. Consequently Augustine can afford to treat it at this point entirely in an *auctoritas*-oriented way: the criteria for self-love are objective, and Psalm 10 (11):6 is taken at its face value (6.9).[58]

At this stage in the argument there is a slight but discernible change of gear, as Augustine substitutes for the "idea of the good," by reference to which we love our brother, the "love itself" with which we love him. Augustine does not clearly justify his equation of the two: It is probably simply that both "the idea of the Good" and "love itself" denote God, insofar as God may be known by faith.[59] The question of knowing God can now be reduced entirely to the question, "What is love?"; but still the door is prevented from swinging open too wide by the stipulation that only *real* love will count. To attempt to discern the nature of God in a carnal love would be to "seek God through those powers which preside over the world or its parts," and to "go outside, deserting one's inner being, than which God is yet more inward" (7.11). But one who loves his brother with "spiritual charity" sees God who is charity itself (8.12). This charity is essentially trinitarian by virtue of its subject-object-copula form (10.14). It is something of an embarrassment that this form is characteristic of all, including carnal, loves, while Augustine has insisted that only true love will allow a glimpse of the Trinity which is God. But only in real love does one mind love another mind, and so (to guess at what Augustine's answer would be) only in the trinity of true love is there an approach to consubstantiality, the three members being the loving mind, the mind of the loved brother, and either the "form within" (in the earlier part of the argument) or "love itself" (in the latter).

The program of Book VIII was to prove that the Supreme Good was "not far from any one of us." But in drawing the lines of continuity between the Supreme Good and the mind of man, Augustine has defended himself with remarkable thoroughness against a possible charge of glib continualism. It is *only* real love which reveals the trinitarian nature of God. It reveals it *only* to faith and not to sight. Furthermore the voluntary cleaving to the inner form, the foundation of true love, is not accounted for in terms of a "natural" love of the good, but is left unexplained. In this cautiously guarded assertion of continuity, self-love plays no role. Like love-of-neighbor, self-love arises from a love for the "form," which is both logically and metaphysically prior to it. It has no foothold in Nature, but belongs within the setting of divine *auctoritas.*

Books IX–XIV: Whereupon Augustine ceremoniously makes a fresh start and, abandoning the trinity of external love (*amans, amatus, amor*), which could not entirely establish unity of substance, concentrates on the reflexive relationships of the mind to itself. The subject-object-copula structure, which afforded a trinity in the one case, will now yield a pair only; but when there is predicated of the mind not only self-love but also self-knowledge, the one subject-object and the two copulas form a trinity, *mens, notitia, amor,* equal in ontological dignity, one in substance, three in relationship (IX.2.2ff.). It remains only to demonstrate (a) that in the human mind this self-approving self-knowledge has a permanent existence, unshaken by variations in the knowledge of and emotional response to empirical objects; (b) that *notitia* can properly be called a "Word" and described as "begotten" in a way that *amor* cannot. Then the model of the Holy Trinity will be complete (IX.6.9–11, 9.14, 10.15; 7.12, 11.16–12.18). If Augustine's concern had merely been to perfect a "model" of the Trinity which would improve on those models commonly used by his predecessors, he could have concluded the *De Trinitate* at the end of the ninth book.[60] The fact that he goes further, first to expand upon the psychological theory which the model presupposes (Book X) and then (Books XIff.) to trace a series of ascending trinities as the mind engages itself with a succession of objects of perception and contemplation, demonstrates how seriously he takes the secondary interest of his work, the perfection of a theory of the *imago Dei* and of the route by which man comes to know God.

In the course of the freestanding enterprise of Book VIII Augustine demonstrated the trinitarian structure of human love only in relation to "real love," the love which the Christian has toward his brother. It was even an embarrassment that the same structure could be discerned in a measure within "carnal" love, which is not that love which Scripture identifies with God. The tenth book, however, is entirely devoted to denying this exclusiveness and to demonstrating that the trinitarian model of *mens, notitia, amor* can be discerned in the reflexive relationships of any human mind whatsoever. This reversal is plainly dictated by consideration of what is to follow: the *similitudo Dei*, as tradition had taught, was discernible in all men; the *imago Dei* only in perfected manhood. Thus the way is prepared for a frankly continualist program of ascent from the universal self-love of the natural human mind to the perfected self-love of the mind engaged in contemplation of the Divine.

In confirmation of the universal claim Augustine demonstrates that the mind's search for knowledge of itself in response to the Delphic "Know yourself" is of quite a different order from its search for knowledge of any other kind. Augustine does not like the expression "self-questing" in connection with the mind, though he continues to use it (X.4.6., cf. 10:16). Other quests for knowledge are motivated by an *appetitus*, which does not presuppose knowledge of the object of the search (though it does presuppose knowledge of *some* kind, IX.12.18; X.11.17). Quest for knowledge-of-self, however, presupposes knowledge-of-self and so does not belong in the category of *appetitus* but of *amor* proper. Of course, if such a seeming

quest can be conducted at all, there must be some differentiation between kinds of self-knowledge, and this differentiation Augustine
marks by the words *notitia* and *cogitatio* (X.5.7). (There is no comparable terminological differentiation in the sphere of love.) When
a mind undergoes philosophical conversion and returns to itself, there
is no new knowledge of self and no new love of self. What happens
is best described as a "sorting out" of confusions: erroneous materialist concepts which had obscured the mind's self-knowledge and had
attracted its self-love are now removed (X.9.12). The self-knowledge
and self-love which were always present are now enabled to function
without error and ambiguity.

Here is a most sweeping assertion of universal self-love, which we
can understand only if we remember that here alone in his work
he is concerned exclusively with self-love of the mind. The Plotinian
influences in his treatment of the mind's self-consciousness have
often been charted. Augustine stood in a tradition which regarded such
self-consciousness as the decisive characteristic of the mind and of
the whole immaterial realm. While we may find reflexive relational
predicates peculiarly difficult to apply intelligibly, Augustine's
difficulty was the opposite one: how were they not perpetually predicable of the mind?—for it was impossible to conceive of a mind's
knowing other minds if it did not know itself, since "there is nothing
that could be more immediate to it than itself."[61] Identity appeared
to be the supreme case of relational proximity, and yet the Delphic
proverb and the mystical aspects of Neoplatonism all insisted that
there must be some change in the mind's relation to itself. This was a
conflict posed by the classical tradition itself, not by its meeting
with Christianity. The universality of the mind's self-love and also its
differentiation arise from the need to combine a philosophy of
mind with a program for mystical enlightenment.

Augustine's final maneuver in the tenth book is to replace the
trinity *mens, notitia, amor* with a new one, *memoria, intelligentia,
voluntas*. There can be no doubt that the two are meant to be broadly
equivalent: The earlier trinity is later recalled and reaffirmed

(XIV.14.18), while at this point Augustine is careful to insist that this new trinity is "included" within the things that everyone knows about himself a priori (10.16) and to demonstrate that as a model it works as well as the other did (11.18). The change has perplexed commentators. Some have seen in it an improvement on a model which allowed priority to the first person of the Trinity and so carried a hint of subordinationism. Others have accounted for it as a mere recapitulation to persuade the unconvinced.[62] However it may be, one immediate gain which Augustine reaps from the change is that the new trinity can have "external operations." The memory, imagination, and will enjoy not only mutual relations but relations of perception with other objects, both material and spiritual. St. Augustine is ready to begin the exercise which has never been far from his mind, the recapitulation of the Plotinian ascent from perception of sense-objects to the contemplation of God.[63]

Book XI inaugurates this exercise at the same time as it continues the search for models of the Trinity. It is concerned with the two trinities "in the external man," i.e., in the activities of perception and imagination. This starting point is justified by reference to the "weakness" of our mental habits, which are always seeking material images (XI.1.1), a somewhat disingenuous excuse after what has gone before. It only serves to emphasize the independence of this new beginning. At two points Augustine underlines the vertical, Plotinian interest. One is when he makes (otherwise gratuitous) moral criticisms of those who "live by the trinity of the external man" and links them with the doctrine of the *imago Dei* (XI.5.8). The *imago* is not simply the most perfect of trinitarian models; it is the perfection of man himself, and it is to this that Augustine's method is leading us. The other point is the discussion of proximate and ultimate terms of the will (XI.6.10). The *voluntas* in the exterior trinity of sight is directed to the vision; "But this is not the will of man as such, which is directed entirely to beatitude, but only this immediate will, directed to this one thing, can be said to have 'vision' as its end, whether or not it then refers it to something else." The will in the lowest trinity,

directed to the perception, is connected through it to the ultimate
goal of man, as by an intermediate to an ultimate end. "When wills
are rightly directed, there is a connexion between them which
forms a route of ascent to beatitude. . . . Blessed are those who by
deed and life sing the song of ascents!" (XI.6.10).

The twelfth book prepares the way for the two trinities of the inner man (i.e., reason) by introducing us to some key concepts. Human
reason has a higher and a lower function, "wisdom" and "knowledge,"
sapientia and *scientia*, corresponding to the distinction of male and
female within humanity. When the higher and lower are considered
separately, only the higher bears the image of God; but considered
together as the one mind that they are essentially and will be
entirely when they pass beyond the realm of time and change, they
bear the *imago* together. (Thus, in one stroke, Augustine reconciles
Genesis 1:27 with 1 Corinthians 11:7, promises the eschatological ab-
olition of sexuality, and warns us that the *imago* belongs in the contemplative activity of the mind!) Just as the senses and the memory in
the trinities of the external man had as their proper object "material
things," so the upper mind (the "wisdom"-reason) has as its proper object "eternal and unchangeable, spiritual things" (XII.12.17). But
there is no exact equivalent for the lower mind (the "knowledge"-
reason), for its function is not only to discern but to direct (XIII.1.1).
It is concerned with the "science of action"; it instructs the body
in the use of material things and is thus the rational force which controls *appetitus* (XII.12.17). The upward thrust from *scientia* to
sapientia is even more unambiguous at this point than at the lower
stages. *Scientia* is teleologically oriented to *sapientia* as *usus* to *fruitio*
(XII.14.22). However, within the sphere of *scientia* a major disjunc-
tion is apparent; for the lower activity of the reason is capable of
thrusting in a quite different direction, downward to the "private
sphere" which is the body and outward to become entrammelled in
material things. It may move to the image of God or to the image of
the beasts.

What will determine the difference? What decides whether the

"knowledge"-reason will move in one direction or the other? There is
no difference in the will because "all men wish to be happy"
(XIII.4.7). There is no difference in what the agent knows since everyone who thinks about happiness will agree that it consists in rightly
directed will in secure possession of its object and that it requires immortality (XIII.5.8). The difference lies entirely in the presence or
absence of faith. Not all believe that immortality is possible. Those
who lack faith compromise with inferior goods. Those who possess
faith, grounded "not in human argument but in divine authority,"
pursue true beatitude (XIII.7.10–9.12).[64] The latter half of Book XIII
is devoted to a resume of the saving acts of the incarnation and
crucifixion which forms the authoritative message which faith accepts.
The incarnate Word stands to the eternal Trinity as lower reason to
higher, so that *scientia*, directing the body's acts within her own economy in conformity with the temporal acts of the divine economy, is
led upward by the one Christ into *sapientia*, eternal blessedness in contemplation of eternal truth.

　　An admirer of Augustine has much to satisfy him in the thirteenth
book of the *De Trinitate*, which brings together the psychological
and eudaemonist motifs of the Cassiciacan dialogues with the theology
of grace from the anti-Pelagian period, as well as including the author's best thoughts on the incarnation and atonement. But there is
much to puzzle and confuse in an argument which one commentator
has dubbed "tout d'abord déconcertante." The upward thrust has
now completely replaced the trinitarian analogies at the center of attention. The trinity of the lower reason is mentioned only as an
afterthought at the end of the book (20.26), and when it does appear
it is not a trinity of *scientia* at all but a trinity of "faith." The de-
tails of this trinity are never explained to us; we are left to surmise
from hints earlier in the book (1.4) that the object of *scientia* is the
significance of the saving story and to construct our own triad on
that basis. We might have supposed that a trinity of *scientia* could as
well be traced in those who did not believe the saving story as in
those who did, for such a universally agreed a priori truth as the

eudaemonist premise is also an object of *scientia*; but we are told that
only those who live in faith live "according to the trinity of the inner man," the others presumably having gone entirely to the dogs.
Yet, if the success of Book XIII is due more to its richness than to its
perspicuity, the fundamental point is quite unmistakable. The universal will to happiness must accept in faith and on authority the
message of the Christian Gospel or else be frustrated. The book is thus
the most important "retractation" Augustine ever wrote. He has re-
built the Platonic stairway of reason to the epistemological specifications of authority: *credo ut intelligam*.

At the final stage of the ascent the object of the mind's contemplation becomes "eternal things," not (as might be supposed) God, but
the mind itself. And so in the fourteenth book we are referred back
to the reflexive trinity temporarily abandoned in Book X, now cast into a new form: self-memory, self-understanding, self-love (XIV.4.6f.).
In a long section of recapitulation we are reminded that this trinity
is always present in every human mind in an implicit form as *notitia*
(or *cognitio*) rather than as *cogitatio* (6.9). Thus the steps by which
the mind has ascended from the memory-understanding-will of sensory
perception to that of faith correspond to the *cognitory* self-memory,
self-understanding, and self-love; while the last step, from faith in saving
history to contemplation of things eternal, corresponds to that transition from *cognitio* to *cogitatio* which has already been explained to us.

Corresponding again to this distinction is that between the *imago
deformis* and the *imago reformata*. Hitherto we have observed a series
of ascending *similitudines* in the perceptive operations of the mind.
But this is not the only relationship of fallen man to his perfection. Parallel with the series of *similitudines* and distinct from it was the deformed
image, the noncogitative self-directed relationships. Two points deserve comment here. First, in this way Augustine insists on the continuity of the *imago* in Nature and Grace. The deformed image was an
image nevertheless because of its "potential" (4.6, 12.15). The perfection of the image in *cogitatio* is the explication of something already
implicit in all humanity. Secondly, whereas the *similitudines* could be

traced in an ascending series, the deformed image can be seen only retrospectively from the vantage point gained in the fourteenth book. Thus the narrow door of faith through which *scientia* had to pass in order to become *sapientia* remains the only access to perception of the image in any form whatever and so the only access to the knowledge of God.

The *imago Dei* is found perfected in the conscious self-relationships of perfected man, and yet those perfected self-relationships can only exist in conjunction with the contemplation of and the worship of God. Here is something Platonic and at the same time Christian. The Platonic habit of identifying knowledge of the ultimate realities with self-knowledge is maintained. (There remains, of course, the distinction between "self" and "above self," but at this point it is not stressed.) Yet by a dramatic Christianization of all this Platonism, the true self-knowledge of *cogitatio* is attainable only eschatologically. "The likeness of God is perfected only when the vision of God is perfected" (XIV.17.23). Thus the Platonic program is fulfilled only at the climax of the walk of faith. Those wicked men who do think about eternity even while they are on this earth do not do so by virtue of the achieved image. The self which they contemplate when they contemplate their own nature is not an eternal self (15.21). Immortality can be predicated of the unperfected human mind only "in a sort of way" (4.6). Thus any knowledge the wicked may have of the spiritual realm is only by a reminiscence of God which dwells in them.

This account of the self-relationships of the *imago*, perfect and imperfect, yields a treatment of self-love (XIV.14.18) sharply contrasting with that which we met in the eighth book. Augustine begins from the assertion of universal self-love in the mind, which is "so constituted that it never fails to remember itself, understand itself, love itself. But because to hate someone is to try to harm him, the human mind too may be said, not incongruously, to 'hate itself' when it does itself harm. True, its ill will toward itself is unwitting, since it never thinks of itself as obstructing its own wishes; nevertheless, it does wish ill for itself, it does wish for what is obstructive, and that is why

Scripture says, 'Whoso loveth iniquity, hateth his own soul.'" As we have already observed, this is a much weaker defense of Psalm 10(11):6 than we expect from Augustine outside the context of *ratio*; it jars noticeably with VIII.6.9, where that text was allowed to have the last word. But in the context of this psychologically conceived self-love literal self-hatred would be an impossibility. What follows is slightly evasive: "So then, whoever knows how to love himself, loves God"— that would pass muster in an *auctoritas* context—"but anyone who does not love God. . . ." Here he is in difficulty. He cannot say that such a one does not know how to love himself because within the terms of the present work he still does love himself. So he must proceed differently: "Even though he retains that self-love with which he is naturally endowed, he may yet not unsuitably be said to hate himself, since what he does is against his own interests and he is persecuting himself like an enemy."

Here we must recall what this universal self-love was supposed to consist of. It was the will holding before the mind its implicit knowledge of itself, a very reduced notion indeed but essentially human and rational. Now, without explanation or defense, Augustine associates with it the universal animal self-love of the *De doctrina Christiana*, afraid perhaps that unless he gives it some substantial behavioral content it will vanish altogether! "It is a horrific mistake," he tells us, "that when all wish to serve their own advantage, many do only that which is most harmful to themselves." Hardly less horrific is the mistake he himself then makes. He adduces, as an example of self-love operating destructively, Vergil's account of how the farm animals destroyed themselves and backs this up with a comment reeking of Stoicism: "Every animal is naturally (*natura*) at one with itself (*conciliatum*) so that it protects itself (*se custodire*) as much as possible."[65] And as if this were not bad enough he continues with the argument that every mind "so loves itself, that if it had to choose one or the other, it would prefer to lose all that lies below it than perish," an argument with which Augustine's readers are familiar enough to know that it requires *anima*, not *mens*, as its subject.

Self-love, for the purposes of the *De Trinitate*, was a universal phenomenon which might be articulated into two forms corresponding to the deformed and the renewed image, an unconscious or self-conscious will for metaphysical self-presence. We may well discern in the fourteenth chapter of the fourteenth book a distinct unease in Augustine's mind about this universal psychological datum, an unease which has led him to cast around for support in the wrong places. It is indeed vital for him to establish this notion of self-love if he is to argue a fortiori to self-knowledge and self-memory and so establish the claim that not similitudes merely but the very image of God, though deformed, is characteristic of all humanity. But in doing so he barely escapes the total disaster of proving that it is characteristic also of the farm animals in Vergil's *Georgics*!

It does not serve our purpose at this point to follow Augustine into the fifteenth book and examine his comparison of the image with the original. We have established all that we need in order to draw some conclusions about the role of self-love in the continualist program of the *De Trinitate*.

First, we observe that while "faith" is the dominant discontinualist, *auctoritas*-oriented motif of the ascent the chief force for continuity is the desire for happiness. *Amor sui* does not carry the responsibility for the upward thrust which will bring the mind to its goal, any more than it is responsible for putting obstacles in the mind's way. The distinction between self-love and the desire to be happy is as clear in the *De Trinitate* as it could possibly be. True, both of them are predicable of all human minds, but they perform quite different functions. Psychological self-love is the operation of the will in holding the concept of self before the self-perceiving mind. It is not the occupation of the will with its *ultimate* term; it therefore has nothing to do with the teleological thrust of the will toward beatitude.

Secondly, self-love is articulated into two kinds, the self-love of the *imago deformata* and the self-love of the trinity of contemplation. The role of faith in marking and bridging the chasm between the natural and the perfect has its implications for every activity of the mind, and so the mind's self-love too must be seen as natural on the one hand, perfected on the other, and the two aspects not confused. This is the authentic Augustinian pattern. The later mystics who associated with the mind's ascent a final discarding of self-love at some exalted stage of piety were modifying Augustine's conception in order to make of it a unitary, rather than an articulated, phenomenon. Even in this continualist context Augustine did not speak of outgrowing self-love, simply because he had no need to. He expressed what the mystics wished to express by speaking of the "instructed" self-knowledge and self-love of the perfected image.

Thirdly, the lower self-knowledge and self-love is comparable with the higher only formally; in its content it is sharply distinguished. The self-love of contemplation is part of the conscious activity of cogitative reflection upon self. Until the stage of perfection is achieved, the mind is incapable of such cogitative reflection since, even when it does think about itself, it is confused by material images. It is hard to find much substantial matter for comparison between the two. Indeed, as we have observed, Augustine finds it hard to find much substantial matter in universal psychological self-love at all and is driven to use irrelevant ideas to support his case.

Fourthly, the perfected self-love of the self-cogitative mind is coterminous with but not identified with the love of God. We are told that the trinity of memory, imagination, and will is perfectly the *imago Dei* when the mind is itself the object of its own contemplation, but that this can happen only when it remembers, know, and loves God. The perfected image is never present other than with the vision of God, and yet the two activities, love of self and love of God, are not the same. Thus Augustine appears to have reached the same conclusion about the relationship of the two by the route of *ratio* as he did by the route of *auctoritas*. In fact, however, the convergence of the two routes is not entirely accurate. The perfected self-love of *auctoritas* was a benevolence toward self, the supreme pursuit of one's highest and best interests which follow from the discovery that God himself is the supreme good. The perfected self-love of *ratio*, ı the other hand, is something more rational in content, a contemplative reflection upon self which, by a Platonic magic never quite explained, is not only compatible with but indissolubly linked with the loving contemplation of God.

There remain, then, moments of incoherence in the Augustinian account of positively valued self-love and its relations to the love of God. The discoveries of *ratio* do not perfectly coincide with the deliveries of *auctoritas*. However, the major features are clearly marked and constant, from whatever point of view Augustine approaches the subject. Perfect self-love is achieved only when God is loved to the fullest extent. Such a state is reached not by drawing out the implications of a natural self-interest but by a faith in the incarnation. If we have given disproportionate attention to the places in which natural, neutrally valued self-love plays a significant part, it is only to show that in the end, by articulating the concept of self-love sharply into two stages, Augustine still maintains the role of *auctoritas* in leading the believer to a perfected love of God and self. The Stoic program of the *De doctrina Christiana* and the Platonic program of the *De Trinitate* impose modifications upon the usual pattern, to be sure; but it remains the case that the man who would learn to love himself aright must sit down in the school of Christ and learn to love God.

THE PRIMAL DESTRUCTION

"Two loves made two cities," wrote Augustine in a famous and much-quoted passage of the *City of God*. "Self-love to despite of God made the earthly city, love of God to despite of self the heavenly."[1] Remarkably, this idea of a self-love diametrically opposed to the love and worship of God is a late arrival in Augustine's pages. It is impossible to identify its first appearance with complete certainty, for not all the relevant passages can be dated; we can safely say, however, that it is after A.D. 400 and that the earliest example is either in the exposition of the forty-fourth Psalm or in the eleventh book of *De Genesi ad litteram*.[2]

We have remarked that Augustine's use of the phrase "self-love" cannot be explained adequately by reference to merely literary influence; this applies particularly to the special case of perverse self-love. His Christian Latin predecessors do not have it. Cicero's use, when it does not conform to the Stoic model, is too weak to account for Augustine's. There is no parallel expression in contemporary Neoplatonism. In Greek moral theology, certainly, there is the vice *philautia*, which appeared at least once in Latin before Augustine as *seipsum diligere* in Rufinus's translation of Basil.[3] There is the scriptural text, 2 Timothy 3:2, "Men will be lovers of themselves," which Augustine quotes eight times in the course of his writings, beginning with the exposition of Psalm 44 (45) in which evil self-love makes its first appearance; and to reinforce the direct influence of this verse, there is the Gospel paradox about loving one's soul: "Whoever loves his life will lose it" (John 12:25). Yet neither Rufinus nor the scriptural text is sufficient to explain why Augustine rather late in the day should have adopted a manner of speaking which had marked incon-

veniences for him. We must look for pressures internal to his thought.
The pressures can be traced back to Plotinus's doctrine of a fall
of souls. The soul's fall, for Plotinus, is the exact opposite of the soul's
redemption. If redemption proceeds by turning inward upon itself,
the fall occurs when it "goes forth from itself," "stands out from itself," "is scattered abroad." With all its faculties extended toward
the material universe, it is stretched and pulled away from its spiritual
center of gravity in the intelligible world. In this extended condition
it is vulnerable to bewitchment and deception; it can be caught up in
the material world and satisfied with material images of spiritual reality. "In rebelling from itself, it rebelled from reality at the same
time."[4] From time to time, however, we find this rebellion described
not only in terms of separation from the self, but as a form of mistaken attraction to the self: "But it leaves that conjunction; it cannot
suffer that unity; it *falls in love with its own powers and possessions*
and desires to stand apart; it leans outward, so to speak." "The evil
that has overtaken them [the souls] has its source in self-will, in the
entry into the sphere of process, and in the primal differentiation
with the desire for self-ownership. They conceived a pleasure in this
freedom and largely indulged their own motion; thus they were
hurried down the wrong path, and in the end, drifting further and
further, they came to lose even the thought of their origin in the
Divine."[5] So insistent is Plotinus as a rule that dispersion in matter
is alien to the soul's nature, that the path of true selfhood is the
path of spiritual withdrawal, that these expressions come as a shock.
Yet we can see that his system has need of some such notion. Plotinus had to account for disruption and disunity in a way that would
impute no fault to the totality of things. By speaking of the self-
assertion and self-differentiation of the part from the whole he could
admit the fact of division without seeming to fragment the ultimate
cosmic unity.

It is in the context of the doctrine of the Fall that Augustine's perverse self-love first makes its appearance. The passage in the Genesis
commentary which introduces us to the "two loves" theme is con-

cerned with the Fall of the Angels. Two groups of angels are each
characterized by its own love: "the one holy the other defiled, the
one sociable the other private, the one concerned for common utility in supernal fellowship, the other reducing even common affairs
to private power in order to arrogate dominion." This evil, restricted
love is the result of *superbia*. "The beginning of all sin is pride,"
says the book of Ecclesiasticus (10:15), a saying which can be harmonized with St. Paul's dictum that "the root of all evil is avarice"
(1 Tim. 6:10) if "avarice" is understood not specifically but generally to mean "that by which one seeks something more than one
ought for one's own promotion and for love of one's own concerns."
Augustine proceeds: The connection in Paul's mind between the
general and the specific can be seen in his progresssion of thought at
2 Timothy 3:2: "There will be lovers of self, lovers of money. . . ."
The juxtaposition of this text with the others makes it clear that
"self-love" and "pride" are to be regarded as equivalent. Pride "turns
from the communal to the personal good in perilous self-love." Its
contrary, charity, "does not seek her own" (1 Cor. 13:5), which is to
say, it takes no delight in promoting private interest.[6]

The identification of self-love with the *superbia* of Ecclesiasticus
10:15 is found once again in the "two loves" passages of *City of
God*, to which the Genesis commentary looked forward. Here too the
Fall, of Adam this time, is under discussion. Pride is the beginning
of Adam's sin, both sin and fall alike amounting to an ontological deprivation, a "turning to self, so that he is less than he was when he
clung to the supreme Being. To abandon God and to be in oneself,
that is, to take pleasure in oneself, is not quite annihilation but ap-
proximates to it." In Augustine's account of the Fall, self-love is to
reject the good common to all, God himself, in favor of some limited
personal good; and its result is the disruption of a human nature
deprived of its only true good. "For man can relate only destructively
to himself when he holds God's will in contempt, and so it is that
he learns to tell the difference between clinging to the Good common
to all and taking pleasure in his own good. For in loving himself man

is given over to himself." According to the final summary of the section, it was the two loves that *created* the two cities: self-love is aboriginal to the earthly community.[7]

In the first commentary on Genesis to which Augustine set his hand there is no clear reference to perverse self-love. There are, however, anticipations of it in the context of Adam's Fall which must interest us. "If the soul," he writes, "deserting God and turning to itself, desires to enjoy its own power as though there were no God, it puffs up with that pride which is the beginning of all sin." And later: "This is what the serpent persuaded them to do, to love their own power to excess and to desire equality with God, so making evil use of that middle position they enjoyed, as of the fruit of the tree set in the middle of Paradise."[8] Adam's sin was still engaging Augustine's mind when he was writing the concluding pages of *De libero arbitrio* a few years later: "Pride it was that turned him from wisdom. Stupidity was the consequence of his turning. . . . How did this turning happen? He to whom God was the good, wished to be his own good, as God is to himself." "If the soul turns the wrong way and takes pleasure in itself, perversely imitating God, and desires to enjoy its own power, it is diminished proportionally to its desire for aggrandisement. This is what the text means, 'The beginning of all sin is pride' and 'The beginning of man's pride is apostasy from God.'"[9] In these early passages we observe that the place of self-love is taken by the phrase "loving one's own power," an expression which Augustine continued to use after he had introduced *amor sui* alongside it. There is an interesting parallel between an assertion in a letter of 410/11, "The primal sin is delight in one's own power," and that of Sermon 96, probably from 416/17, "The primal destruction of man was self-love."[10]

The opposite of "love of self" (*amor sui*) is always "love of God" (*amor Dei*), and yet the opposite of "love of God" is usually "love of the world" (*amor mundi* with plain allusion to 1 John 2:15, and often also *amor saecli*).[11] It is, however, just when Augustine is speaking of the root of human sin in the Fall that "love of the world" will not serve, for Adam did not yet have a corrupt and fallen world to fall in love with. It was in this context, then, that Augustine began feeling his way toward an alternative expression. Besides "love of one's own power" and "delight in one's own private matter" there were other possibilities. Of the fallen angels he could speak, in *De vera religione*, of "loving self more than God" and of its opposite, "loving God more than self." "This is perfect justice, to love the greater objects more and the lesser less."[12] We have commented elsewhere on the difficulties inherent in such proportional conceptions. They were not well suited to express the sharp contrast of alternative attitudes which gave rise to the two cities. Lovers of self and lovers of God were not disagreeing merely on a matter of priority and proportion. They were traveling in opposite directions. Thus, when Augustine expresses the same contrast in a later work, he modifies it to allow a revealing imbalance: "They [the humble] have loved God *above* themselves. They [the proud] have loved themselves *instead of* God."[13]

It is not enough for Augustine to say that Adam had a high evaluation of himself. It is not enough for him even to say that Adam's self-esteem was too high, his esteem of God too low. He needs to stipulate that Adam had a profound misunderstanding of the relationship between God and man. Each occurrence of *amor sui* in this sense carries with it, as an identification tag, a phrase to mark the radical atheism which characterized the wrong self-assessment: it is self-love "dismissing God," "neglecting God," "to the point of despising God."[14] The same goes for the phrase *sibi placere*," to be self-satisfied." With the assertion that men are satisfied with themselves goes the corollary that they are dissatisfied with God and believe they can do without him. "If your works have not been God's praise, then you are beginning to love yourself; and you will belong to those of whom the Apostle says, 'There will be men who love themselves.' Be dissatisfied with yourself! Be satisfied instead with him who made you!"[15]

In the first book of the *De doctrina Christiana* it appeared briefly that the phrase *sui fruitio* would be available to connote this rebellious self-love which refused to accept subordination to God. "Nor ought one to 'enjoy' himself . . . because he ought not to love himself for his own sake, but for his sake who is the proper object of 'enjoyment'. . . . But if he loves himself for his own sake, not referring himself to God but turning to himself, then he is no longer turned towards something which is unchanging. So one who 'enjoys' himself is diminished because he would be better if he cleaved and clung wholly to the unchanging good than he is by slipping back from it, even into himself." However, by the third book he has adopted the easier and "loose" expression, whereby he can speak of "enjoying self for God's sake," and that or its variant, "in God," becomes his normal way of speaking.[16] The task of making the distinction, where necessary, between right and wrong self-love is thus assumed not by the pair of verbs *uti-frui* but by prepositional phrases with *propter* and *in*. The two prepositions carry very much the same sense: they point to the *self-evaluation* implied by self-love and to the *movement* away from God which it effects. If they are to be distinguished at all (and there may be the hint of a distinction at one point where he says, "ourselves in him, *yet* for his sake"), the difference will be that *propter* points more to the subjective, less to the ontological; but to force such a distinction on all the texts would be difficult.[17] Augustine likes to use the phrase *se in se ipso diligere* to contrast with love of self "in God" (its opposite is *se in Deo*, not *Deum in se*): "If you love yourself-in-yourself, and satisfy yourself by yourself, you ought to be seriously alarmed if you are not alarmed! . . . To love oneself-in-oneself and to be satisfied with oneself is not the love of justice but the emptiness of pride. . . . What is cheaper than man without God? Look at what a man who loves himself-in-himself and not himself-in-God is really loving!" The same phrases will qualify the love that he seeks from others: "He [the enemy] would like us to be loved and feared, not for Your sake but in Your stead. . . . May we be loved for Your sake! May Your word be what men fear in us!" "We would be loved by you," the pastor tells his flock; "But not in ourselves! Love us in Christ!"[18]

SELF AND THE FALL

The radically evil sense of self-love demanded by Augustine's reflections on the primal sin formed a kind of mirror-image of the ideas we examined in chapter three. Like them, it applied both the "rational" and the "cosmic" aspects of love to the subject's love of himself. It understood his sin both as a misevaluation based on false understanding and as a movement within the universe which carried him away from God.

The former line of thought was important to Augustine's anti-Pelagian polemic. The doctrines of Pelagius arose, Augustine believed, from a false account of human nature. He attributed possibilities to natural man which could not possibly be realized without the direct (rather than merely indirect) intervention of grace. In particular this came from underestimating the damage done to human nature at the fall, but there is more than an occasional suggestion that Pelagius's account of man claimed excessive autonomy for mankind as such and would be mistaken even as a description of Adam before the fall. The good in man was treated as though it were now independent of the one who gave it. As a result of the grace of creation man had de facto become the immediate source of his own good; and "he necessarily loves God too little who imagines that good is effected not by God but by himself." "Self-love" in this context is an admiration of oneself for being what in fact one is not, the source of one's own value and potency. Suppose someone believes that it is love that keeps him from sinning but thinks of that love as "his own," i.e., understands it primarily in terms of his own immediate agency as subject: "You will love yourself, because you will love the source of your love."[19] Augustine grasped at a text of Saint Paul which seemed to confront this mistake decisively. He had used it in various contexts in his early writing, but it was only later in his career that it became a firm favorite in his weaponry, a hammer to break the Pelagian rock in pieces: "What have you that you did not receive?" Paul had asked the Corinthians, "and if you received it, why do you boast as if it were not a gift?" Cyprian's comment was most apt: "We must boast of nothing, since nothing is ours to boast of."[20] The piety of the Pelagian was the piety of the Pharisee in the parable who confronted God with a certain confidence in his moral achievement instead of abasing himself in utter dependence. "Whatever good you think you have from yourself you have detracted from the praise of God." True worship takes place only when man ceases to boast in himself and boasts in the Lord. The suggestion that false love-of-self could represent *relatively* false assessments of human nature in relation to divine is banished by this sharp alternative. The two boasts are mutually exclusive, and there is no third way.[21]

The cosmic movement toward self away from God can be understood as a direct reversal, presupposing the same cosmic topography, of the conversion of the soul from external things, via itself, to God. Indeed, the very phrase "conversion to self" is used for the movement of rebellion as well as for the movement of ascent. By converting to self, "that proud angel" expressed his pride; and for man to "turn to" or "lean to" himself means that he leans away from God; it is the opposite of "cleaving to" God. "In leaning to himself he became less than he had been when cleaving to the One who is supreme existent." "In turning to himself he is no longer turned toward something which is unchanging."[22] Augustine is fond of quoting Psalm 41 (42):7, which read in his Latin version *Ad me ipsum conturbata est anima mea*, "Toward myself is my soul disturbed." His general use of the text can be observed from the comments he makes when expounding it in its context: "Could the soul be disturbed *toward God*? No, it is disturbed *toward myself*. Toward the unchanging, it was restored; toward the changeable, it was disturbed. . . . Do you wish it to be undisturbed? Then let it not remain within yourself. Say, 'To thee, o Lord, have I lifted up my soul.' Hear this more plainly: do not hope in yourself, but in your God; for if you hope in yourself your soul is disturbed toward you, for it finds no source of security in you."[23]

√   Behind this, of course, lies the Platonic cosmology whereby the

soul of man occupied the middle place in the universe, beneath the
divine and above the realm of matter. Its turning to itself was the
first step down as well as the first step up. Augustine understood "the
tree in the middle of the garden" in Eden to be an allegory of man's
turning away from God: "That is why they are said to hide at the
tree in the middle of the garden; it means, *in themselves*, for they are
in the middle of the order of the universe, below God and above
matter. So they hid in themselves and were tormented by wretched
errors, having abandoned the light of truth which was other than
themselves."[24] But in order to conceive the possibility of the soul's
movement in relation to itself (for it does not transcend its human
nature as an absolute subject) we must imagine it as capable of expan-
sion and contraction. Man stands, as it were, with his feet in the
center of the universe, able to stretch upward toward God or to con-
tract back upon himself and fold himself away from God. Several
times Augustine calls upon this physical picture of the soul's activity,
distinguishing between man erect and man bent. "God made you
to be something good. He made something less good than himself,
and something less good than you. You are placed beneath something
and above something. Do not abandon the higher good and bend
down to the lower good. Stand upright, that you may receive praise,
because 'all who are upright in heart shall receive praise.'" "'Renew
an upright spirit within my inward parts.' He means, 'By my deed
the uprightness of my spirit became aged and bent.' In another Psalm
he says 'They have bent my soul.' When man makes himself prone,
looking downward to earthly desires, he is, as it were, bent double;
but when he is lifted upright toward the heavens, his heart becomes
erect, so that God becomes his good." In such passages Augustine
will usually speak of man's bending downward to the earth beneath
him rather than simply to himself; but the two physical metaphors—
recoiling upon himself and stooping down to the earth—are part of
the same pictorial scheme.[25] With a metaphysical gloss on Philip-
pians 3:13 Augustine speaks of the soul's failure to strain forward to
what lies ahead (that is, God) and to forget what lies behind (that

is, material pleasures) and describes that failure as "deserting God and turning to self." Elsewhere, with a liturgical allusion, he can describe "leaning to self" as a failure to heed the Sursum Corda: "It is good to lift one's heart on high—but not to self, which is pride, but to the Lord, which is obedience, only possible for the humble."[26]

However, when Augustine comes to characterize this "middle place" in the universe more closely, it appears to be a very different place on the downward journey from what it was on the way up. The significance of the return-to-self in the conversion of the soul to God was that the soul became "gathered," participating in the self-sufficiency and unity of the spiritual order which transcends spatial limitation. The turning away from God to self, on the other hand, has nothing to do with the spiritual characteristics of God in which the soul participates. It is a matter of turning to the partial away from the whole. The soul abandons its access to the totality of being in favor of the partial being which is itself. It is attracted, of course, by the idea of making itself ruler, of positing a universe in which it is itself the chief power; from that point of view its move can be described as "coveting something greater." But what appears subjectively as aggrandizement is, in objective reality, diminution. A creature can never really be God. When self-as-subject posits self-as-object as ruler of the universe, far from actually promoting self-as-object, self-as-subject is abased by being cut off from its proper object, the supreme being, and confined to participation in a derived and inferior being. "In loving its own power, the soul slipped away from the shared whole to its own restricted part; and, although by following God in the created whole it could have been governed by his laws in the best possible way, by desiring (in that rebellious pride, called the beginning of sin) something more than the whole of things, and in struggling to govern it by its own law, it was thrust back, since there is nothing greater than the whole, into a purely partial concern. So that by coveting something greater it became something less."[27]

Worse is yet to follow. The sphere of the private is not only a diminished sphere, it is also unstable. The only stability in the universe is God, so that delight in the private sphere inevitably leads to descent yet further down the ontological scale toward the transient and material. The rebellious soul finds itself on a greasy pole where the only safe place is the place it has just left, the top. Augustine laid great stress on the sequence of thought in 2 Timothy 3:2, "Men will be lovers of themselves, lovers of money. . . ." "He begins with self-love and the desertion of God; then, by loving external things, he is driven out of himself, so that after the words . . . 'Men will be lovers of themselves' the same Apostle continues immediately, 'lovers of money.' You see, now, that you are outside yourself! You began by loving yourself. Stay put within yourself if you can!" Again: "Did I not tell you that you would not stay put within yourself? Money! Is that what you are? Look! First you left God, and now you have left yourself too, and come to a bad end!" This rhetorical trope enables Augustine to harmonize the two uses of self-love which Platonism gave him by showing that evil turning-to-self cannot in the last event be a clinging-to-self at all. The unfortunate soul is carried past her stop and ends up not exactly at nothingness but uncomfortably close to it.[28]

Adam and Eve were pursuing "their own interest," *commoda privata*. For Augustine the idea that one person's individual interests could clash with another's was simply a mistake: The only true interests had to be communal because the only true goodness was God, who gives himself freely and totally to all. "Private interests," then, are always defectively conceived and, if achieved, defectively enjoyed.[29] Neglect of the "common good" is not simply neglect of other agents and their needs but neglect of the transcendent good common to all agents. Yet the deprivation which results has a horizontal as well as a vertical aspect. Commenting on a text in Psalm 103 (104), "The waters will flow through the midst of the mountains," Augustine insists that the waters of life are "in the midst," that is, publicly available. "If they are not 'in the midst,' they are like private property, and do not flow for the public benefit: I have mine, he has his, and there is nothing 'in the midst' which I and he both have. But that

is not the way with the glad tidings of peace!" The social deprivation
which man experiences when he pursues a purely imaginary "private good" is a necessary consequence of his vertical, ontological
deprivation because the good which comes to him through others is
precisely the same good which he has proudly refused. "Man is his
own worst enemy when he seeks what is his own and not what is God's.
In God's inheritance, which is himself condescending to offer himself
for our enjoyment, we shall suffer no such limitations in our fellowship with the saints as are imposed here by the love of our own limited interests."[30]

In this context we must notice the remarkable use Augustine
makes of a text from St. John's Gospel. Jesus' words about the devil,
"When he lies, he speaks according to his own nature" (8:44), appeared in Augustine's Latin version as a generalization, *Qui loquitur
mendacium, de suo loquitur*, "Who speaketh a lie speaketh of his
own"; and this generalization he deploys to point the contrast between the "private" sphere of activity and that in which God is
acknowledged. He who speaks *de suo* is not speaking what is God's.
Even in the faulty Latin version this text cannot sustain the weight
Augustine lays on it, especially on the word *suum*. We have to recognize one of those cases in which a scriptural text is significant to
him because it fits something already present in his thought. This text
fits the fall of Adam and Eve very well: "There came an angel fallen
from heaven, turned serpent now because his purpose was the subtle
spreading of poison. He spewed out his poison, he spoke of his private realm, of his own realm, for 'who speaketh a lie speaketh of his
own.' Unhappy were they to hear him! They abandoned that which
was common, and betaking themselves to their own private realm
in perverse ambition to be like God—for this is what he had said: You
shall be like Gods—, by striving for what they were not, they lost
what they had received." *Suum* has become an objective, ontological
category, more than the mere reflexive relative, since Satan by speaking *suum* could make Adam and Eve grasp *suum* too. It has become
the category opposed to God, as lying is the category opposed to

truth. "Whoever speaks truth, speaks from God, 'for whoso speaketh
a lie, speaketh of his own.'" Again: "All sin is lying. Whatever is
counter to Law and Truth is called lying. So, what is it the Gospel
says? 'Who speaketh a lie speaketh of his own.' That means, whoever sins, sins of his own. Note the converse of this: if whoever lies
speaks of his own, it follows that whoever speaks truth speaks from
God."[31]

THE PERVERSE AND THE NATURAL

Certain texts, comments, and epigrams in Augustine's writing co-
here in distinctive patterns, so that when the reader reaches a familiar
landmark he feels that he could write the next paragraph himself.
Perverse self-love belongs in such a group of ideas and associations, its
own well-defined thought-context, and does not simply develop out
of, merge into, or even share common conceptual territory with the
other notions of self-love which Augustine can deploy. It carries with
it its characteristic reference to the radical opposition of self and
God which underlay the Fall of angels and men. When Augustine
speaks of evil self-love this reference enters the discussion, so that
the various attitudes of men in their relative and historical situations
are interpreted in terms of a fundamental refusal of the *summum
bonum*. It speaks not of *any* sin and selfishness but of *the* sin and *the*
selfishness. It has been observed as a general contrast between the
moral theology of the West and the East that the latter moves from
sensuality to pride, from the temptation of the flesh to the temptation of the spirit, and the former moves in the opposite direction.
In Augustine's work *amor sui* stands for the Western starting point.[32]

It is therefore a misconception of Augustinian self-love to interpret it as "original sin," the abiding taint of Adam's sin in all men, a
natural feature of the fallen universe.[33] Augustine did, of course,
reject all forms of perfectionism in the interests of a strong doctrine
of grace and a strong eschatology, so making himself the grandfather
of modern "neoorthodox" realism. But he did not predicate radical

evil-intent of all baptized Christians. Proud self may be the starting point, but humble Christ has come "to pull men down from themselves and bring them over to himself, healing their swelling and nurturing their love." The possessions of "private concern" may be constantly with us, but "if we cannot abstain from possessing them, let us at least abstain from loving them, and make room for the Lord." Evil motives and daily sin may persist to harrass the Christian in his pilgrimage, but self-love, *this* self-love, is an attitude of opposition to Christ which he must, and can, have done with: "Do not love yourself! Love him! If you love yourself, you close the door against him; if you love him you open to him."[34] A neoorthodox interpretation of Augustine can be so concerned with the self-love of the *civitas terrena* that it forgets that there is also a city of God to contrast with it, albeit a city on pilgrimage and far from its final peace.

This point is well illustrated by Augustine's treatment of two verses which might very well have contributed to the concept of perverse *amor sui* but did not do so. Both are from St. Paul: one is the critical judgment he passed on his fellow church leaders, "They all seek their own interests, not those of Jesus Christ" (Phil. 2:21), and the other is a phrase from his hymn to love, "Charity seeketh not her own" (1 Cor. 13:5). We are no longer in the Garden of Eden when Augustine deploys these texts (often in harness). We are, as St. Paul was, in the church of Christ and surrounded by the ministers of Christ, who are making not the ultimate decision of Adam and Eve but the small ethical decisions arising in the course of their ministry, which may or may not express their total commitment to God and God's people. Augustine will remind his friend and fellow ecclesiastic Alypius that "if there is any spark within us of that love which seeketh not her own" they, as ministers of God, must be concerned not to offend their congregation. In this same spirit of unselfish love, nuns should be prepared to have their clothing in common. Conversely, a churchman may be motivated by self-seeking in the most religious activities: in preaching, in exercise of the pastoral ministry, in desiring the gifts of the Holy Spirit, even in remaining a Catholic instead of becoming a Donatist.[35] To "seek one's own" in this context is not to choose the radical alternative to the worship, praise, and love of God but to carry over into Christian discipleship some traces of the old Adamic spirit, some reservation about total and unconditioned self-giving. Religious deeds so performed are performed "impurely, that is, not from a spirit of pure and sincere love." It is to love Christ "unchastely"; it is to seek a return in the temporal sphere rather than loving God for God's own sake, *propter Deum*.[36]

There are, of course, points of connection between the *sua quaerere* of these texts and *amor sui* as the radical rejection of God. Augustine does from time to time quote the Pauline verses in the metaphysical context as well as in the ethical. But with the exception of one passage in the Tractates on John we do not find *amor sui* used in the context of ministerial ethics to which these two texts, taken on their own, seem to belong; and in that one exception, the introduction of *amor sui* into the new context does not deprive it of its distinctive *timbre* but has the effect of interpreting the issues of ministerial ethics as a matter of ultimate choice. It is in the course of a fine exposition of Jesus' commission to Peter, "Do you love me? . . . Feed my sheep!" that Augustine moves from that text to speak of self-love and the warnings of 2 Timothy 3:2; and as he does so the great pastoral charge begins to echo with distant but distinct resonances of ultimate refusal and perdition. "Let us not love ourselves, but him. In the care of his sheep let us seek his interests and not our own. For, paradoxically, he who loves himself and not God, does not love himself at all; while the true lover-of-self is he who loves God and not himself. For one whose source of life is outside himself, self-love is death; and that is no true self-love which is really self-destruction."[37]

Another scriptural point of departure which develops a line of thought in similar independence is the text John 12:25, "He who loves his soul will lose it, and he who hates his soul in this world will keep it for eternal life." As we have observed, Augustine takes *anima* in this context to mean the animal soul of man; he points out that "losing one's soul" means "losing one's life" and not "sacrificing one's eternal destiny."[38] Had he gone on to refer to the improper love of one's animal soul as "self-love," we would, of course, have classed it with the neutrally valued animal self-love which we discussed in chapter two. Interestingly he never does so. Wrong love-of-soul operates without reference to the language of self-love. This strange independence may be due in part to a complicating factor in the exegesis: Augustine is in genuine doubt as to whether he should interpret the two limbs of the verse as antithetical or, treating *perdet* as a concealed imperative, complementary: "He who loves his life *should* lose it." His better judgment takes him to the antithetical understanding whenever he acknowledges and discusses the doubt, but on more than one occasion, even when his argument really demands the correct exegesis, he expounds *perdet* as *perde* or *perdat* without considering the alternative.[39] This idiosyncrasy of exegesis enabled Augustine to evade for some time the biblical witness to a wrong love of one's soul, but even when this route of evasion was closed, the love-of-soul which is fear of death continued to be treated without reference to *amor sui*, whether "natural" or "perverse."

For all the independence of evil "self-love" from other uses of the phrase, Augustine was well aware that he was using the one term in more than one way. He delighted to exploit the paradox which this ambiguity created; it brought out the orator in him, a character never far below the surface especially when he occupied the preacher's chair. Yet recognizing the paradox, he attempts no reconciliation, offers no dénouement of the linguistic puzzle, sounds no deeper harmony over which the discord is resolved. As we look over the passages in which he places the good and the evil senses of *amor sui* alongside one another, we are confirmed rather than disturbed in our opinion that each operates in its own way without reference to the other. Sometimes he aims no more than to stun his congregation with contradiction. "Learn to love yourself by not loving yourself!" "Do not love your lives in this world! Do not love them, if you love them, so that by not-loving them you may save them, since not-loving is the better form of love!" "Let him deny himself if he loves himself, for by loving himself he loses himself!" They were listening to an accomplished performer, a *prestidigitateur* in words, who, like any good showman, was capable of unbounded amazement at the various surprises that came tumbling out of his hat. "In some quite inexplicable way," he muses (*Nescio quo inexplicabili modo*), "he who loves himself, not God, does not love himself," and the expression of wonderment tells us that the preacher's tongue is in his cheek.[40]

In other passages, no less characteristic, Augustine arbitrates between the two self-loves, yet without resolving the paradox, and declares that only positive self-love, which is to love God with heart, mind, and soul, is true self-love. Psalm 10:6 is allowed to win over 2 Timothy 3:2. "Who loves himself otherwise than he should, loves himself unrighteously . . . and so does not love himself. For 'whoso loveth iniquity, hateth his own soul.'" In chapter two we suggested that these passages reflect a preference for objective criteria for benevolent love. Had Augustine chosen to regard intention rather than effect as the criterion of true love, he would have agreed with the assumption that everyone loves himself, and so could have differentiated perverse and righteous self-love as foolish and enlightened manifestations of the one universal impulse. But generally this is not his way. His congregation are surprised to be told that their assumption is wrong, that there are indeed those who do not love themselves. Perverse self-love is really self-hate; it can be called self-love only by qualifying it as "false" as opposed to "true."[41]

But what of those contexts in which Augustine propounds a universal, neutrally valued self-love? Does this not commit him to establishing a connection between false and true which elsewhere he avoids? On one occasion he manages to escape this conclusion. In *Sermon* 330, although he begins by articulating universal self-love into a "right kind" and a "wrong kind," he immediately goes on to say that only right self-love is successful in making self the object of love

at all. From there he has easy access to his usual treatment of 2 Timothy 3:2, showing that self-love is unstable, leading either upward
to God or down and out into the material world. The result of
"wrong" self-love is loss of self, and so this passage fits neatly alongside the others which deal with the paradox by disqualifying evil
self-love altogether.[42] In two other passages, however, Augustine accepts the consequences which follow from his use of a neutral self-
love and so diverges considerably from his normal position. Both
passages treat true and false self-love as modifications of an underlying neutral attitude; correspondingly, both are reserved about the
text Psalm 10 (11):6 and incline to treat it as a rhetorical exaggeration. Not surprisingly, perhaps, they are passages already familiar to
us for their somewhat problematic arguments.

In the first book of *De doctrina Christiana*, where he writes of
a self-love which "claims as a right for self what is properly due to
God alone" (we are allowed to assume that this is the *fruitio sui*
which has been criticized a little before), Augustine declares: "Such
love is better called hate. It is unjust; it strives to subjugate what
is below it, and refuses to be subject to what is above. It is most aptly
said 'Who loveth iniquity hateth his own soul.' That is how the mind
becomes weak and is tormented by the mortal body."[43] Although the
language of self-hate, prompted by the scriptural text, is apparently
endorsed, the careful reader will notice that Augustine stops short of
his characteristic assertion that evil self-love is "really" self-hate.
And indeed he begins the next paragraph unexpectedly, oblivious of
the text, "Nobody, then, hates himself." The "most apt" description was obviously not intended literally in this case, and, indeed, if
it had been, it could not have been accommodated to the theory
of love propounded in this rather uncharacteristic book. For the
purposes of *De doctrina Christiana* I all men love themselves, and they
love their bodies with a natural love akin to that of the animals;
right self-love differs from wrong as "use" from "enjoyment." It is
right as it regards self as a means to the proper end of love, wrong
as it regards self as itself the end.

In a passage from the fourteenth book of *De Trinitate* Augustine is even more doubtful about Psalm 10 (11):6, for which he offers the weak defense that "even granting that self-love which is naturally in him, yet he may not unsuitably be described as hating himself."[44] Here too the departure from the normal emphasis is occasioned by a concern to develop a theory of natural self-love. A nature-based apologetic which wants to predicate self-love of all men has difficulty with the assertion that wicked men do not love themselves at all. In neither case, we observe, is it any part of Augustine's concern to demonstrate a *homogeneity* of perverse and natural. Had he wished to do so he could have forgotten Psalm 10 (11):6 as easily as he forgot 2 Timothy 3:2. Rather we see him struggling to preserve some distinction between the perverse and the natural while being yet unwilling to declare that *amor sui* is used in two utterly different senses; and so, when the natural form has to be asserted universally, it is not as completely disentangled from the perverse as he would like. The evil self-love of the *De Genesi ad litteram*, the *City of God*, and the homiletic works is essentially discontinuous from the other forms. But Augustine is hard put to maintain its independence within the continualist programs of the first book of *De doctrina Christiana* and the later books of *De Trinitate*.

CHAPTER FIVE

YOUR NEIGHBOR AS YOURSELF

The "second great command," "You shall love your neighbor as your-self," dominated Augustine's moral thinking. In one or another of its biblical contexts, or indifferently, it is quoted or referred to on more than a hundred and twenty occasions. Unlike his predecessors, Augustine does not pass over the final words of the saying without comment; but neither, unlike some of his successors, does he treat them impressionistically, as a loose way of suggesting the totality of the demand, "a pick," as Kierkegaard's expressive metaphor has it, which "wrenches open the lock of self-love and thereby wrests it away from a man." "As yourself" is taken with some degree of lit-eralness and is called "the measure of love," *regula amoris.* [1]

But which of the various kinds of self-love is it that Augustine takes to be the measure of our love for the neighbor? Evidently he does not suppose that we should love our neighbor in the way that Adam loved himself in his moment of rebellion, even if some con-tent could be given to that analogy. Nor is it plausible to think that the psychological self-love of the *De Trinitate* is in question, as that is essentially a function of self-identity; and in any case the text was a favorite with Augustine long before his psychological specu-lation reached maturity.

When he elaborates the content of neighbor-love, Augustine does not give much prominence to the natural needs of body or soul which we may suppose the neighbor to have. In practical terms, love of the neighbor is evangelism. He is a man, and men find their blessedness in God. The only service of lasting significance that we can render him is to lead him to that blessedness. Time and again this principle is repeated in different ways. "If souls please you," he writes, apostrophizing his own soul, "love them in him: snatch them, as many as you can, to him with you." The Christian is to be "on fire to lead them to that for which he was on fire with love." An enthusiastic supporter of a charioteer or of an actor sets out to persuade others to become enthusiasts as well. The more committed his own support, the more extravagant the praises with which he furthers his favorite's reputation, the more his determination to melt the most frosty indifference.[2] All this suggests quite clearly that the love we owe our neighbor is modeled on that perfect self-love which is expressed in love for God. And yet when the text speaks of loving the neighbor *as* we love ourselves, it seems to suppose a concept of self-love as a *specific* activity or attitude, such that our responsibilities to others are analogous to it; whereas the love of God (and therefore *that* love of self) is, as we have seen, an all-inclusive moral category from which every other moral obligation, including all forms of neighbor-love, is held to be derived.

So long as the verb *to love* is used with its "rational" aspect to the fore, the comparison implied by the phrase "as yourself" is a purely qualitative one and the problem does not arise. In that case love-of-neighbor-as-self is no more than the recognition that his dignity and his supreme good are the same as mine. "This is the lesson taught in the house of learning: love for God and love for neighbour, God as God, neighbour as self. You will find no equal to God of which it might be said, 'Love God as you love that.' For your neighbor, though, there is a standard, because you have found an equal to him in yourself."[3] Love in this instance is a matter of recognition: of God, as one without an equal, and of the neighbor as being equal in dignity to ourselves. In a passage from *De vera religione*, which we have discussed in another connection, Augustine argues that even in ourselves that which we love is not what lies on the surface, evident to the eye or other bodily sense, but bare humanity; and so it is with our neighbor, that it is his humanity we must love. Only then can love remain undisturbed by changing outward circumstances, for "he has *in himself* him whom he loves *as himself*." If a man does

not love "as himself," then he will love "as pack animal, bath or
painted talking-bird, to gain some temporal pleasure or advantage
from him." But the case is not better if he loves "as [literal] brother
or son or spouse or cousin, as relative or fellow-citizen." All these
loves are "temporal." "No one is his own father, son, relative or anything like. To himself each man is simply man."[4] The sense which
the comparison "as yourself" bears in this passage is again qualitative
rather than quantitative and the force of the verb is evaluative: we
are required to *estimate* our neighbor *as equal humanity*. And it is
just the same pattern of thought in the controversial passage from the
first book of *De doctrina Christiana*, where neighbor-love is clas-
sified as "use" because we love him *propter Deum*. Inappropriate as
the use–enjoyment contrast may be to express it, the point is simply
that our neighbor is an ontologically dependent being, "a 'thing'
of a very high order, made in the image and similitude of God" with
his own created teleology. To "use" him, as to "use" ourselves, is
to recognize this fact and to respect his rank and destiny.[5]

Far more frequently, however, the comparison is presented quan-
titatively, and the verb carries its "benevolent" sense. "How much
good, you ask, should I wish my enemies? As much as you wish yourself!" Here we reach the classical form of the golden rule: "The
good one wishes to happen to oneself, one must wish for the other
man as well; the evil one does not wish to happen to oneself one
should not wish to happen to him; this is the attitude one should
adopt towards all men." While formally the comparison turns on
the quantity of love awarded to self and neighbor, in effect it turns
on its content, since the good wished in either case is nothing less
than the supreme good. Augustine is encouraged in this understanding of the *regula* by the thought that the supreme good may be
shared without limit and without loss; it is therefore entirely the opposite of worldly dominion, the object of carnal ambition, which
cannot brook a rival. There is no place for rivalry in the supreme good,
for "the good they receive in becoming good is not taken from your
store. It will not be charged to your account!" On the contrary, the

more the merrier: the presence of companions actually contributes something to this "most agreeable association in the enjoyment of God and of one another in God."[6]

But this simply focusses the problem more sharply, so that we can see in it the lineaments of the issue which dominated our discussion in chapter one: how Augustine is to reconcile the monism of classical eudaemonism adapted to the purposes of Christian theism with the importance accorded to the neighbor by the two-fold love-command. If the supreme good is the only true end of all human action, anything that it is right for man to pursue must, at least by implication, be included in its content. But is the neighbor's enjoyment of the supreme good itself part of the content of the supreme good? As we see, Augustine would sometimes like to think so, but how can he defend the coherence of his eudaemonism on these conditions? The very fact that the supreme good for Augustine was both transcendent and eschatological prevented him from accepting the classical resolution of the difficulty. Reasons could be adduced to show that a historical supreme good would have to include a social life. Classical moralists argued that life without friends was insupportable.[7] But this argument could not apply to a transcendent supreme good which, established as it was on a priori argument, was incapable of being defective. To identify the end-of-action as "eternal life in God" Augustine had to show that this alone completely satisfied the specifications of human need. He could not then turn round and say that "eternal life in God" would be intolerable without other people there to keep us company. That is why, in the section of *City of* XIX.1.3 *God* where the comparison with classical eudaemonism is most thoroughly elaborated, Augustine so carefully distinguishes the question "about having friends or not" from the question "about the supreme good itself." While he was playing the strict eudaemonist he could not allow society to be any part of his theory of the good. And yet, although the pursuit of the neighbor's good cannot be justified on the rational grounds which support the rest of his eudaemonist theory, it is always present, appended as an afterthought on the basis of the love-command.[8]

Since, then, the duty of love-to-neighbor is derived from the duty of love-to-God—as a specific duty from the most general and all-inclusive one—simply by way of a command, it cannot be on an equal footing with love-of-self, which is not a specific duty at all but is coextensive with the love of God. It is logically impossible to take the requirement that one love one's neighbor *as* oneself literally since love-of-neighbor as an expression of love-of-God is simultaneously an expression of self-love. The awkwardness to which this formal incompatibility gives rise may be illustrated by three sentences from the tenth book of *City of God*: "That man should learn how to love himself, there was set before him an end, to which he might refer all that he did that he might be happy; for one who loves himself wants only to be happy. The end is this: to cleave to God. So therefore the man who knows how to love himself, when instructed to love his neighbour as himself, must take his instruction to mean that he should commend to him as best he can the love of God."[9] Despite the *regula*, the love which this man bears his neighbor is not the same love that he bears himself, for the end of action is cleaving to the supreme good, and that is something one can do only on one's own behalf. There is an imbalance between the "cleaving" which he does for himself and the "commending" which he does for the neighbor. Loving his neighbor "as himself" can mean only that he seeks to instill in the neighbor a self-love similar to his own.

Someone might wish to defend Augustine against this objection by arguing that the identity of self-love and cleaving to God is, in philosophical terms, "synthetic" and not "analytic." The obvious fact that an agent cannot cleave to God on another's behalf and that his neighbor-love too will be an expression of the cleaving which he does on his own behalf still does not mean that the term *love* is used in a different sense in the two phrases "love of self" and "love of neighbor." Let *love* mean simply "to seek the welfare of X," an exact translation of Augustine's verb *consulere*; and then it has the same sense whether X is the self and love is expressed by cleaving to God or whether X is the neighbor and love is expressed by commending the love of God to him. But this defense will not help Augustine's position;

for the whole point of saying that evangelism must be the content of
neighbor-love was precisely that one must show love to the neighbor in exactly the same way that one shows it to oneself. It hardly
matters whether we choose to defend the univocality of the word
love while allowing that it has different expressions or whether
we deny its univocality altogether; for in either case we concede that
Augustine has failed to transfer the whole content of eudaemonist
self-love without modification to the neighbor.

But this quibble, overnice as it may seem, is of some significance
for an appreciation of Augustine's fundamental concerns. An accusation often brought by modern critics in the tradition of Karl Holl is
that Augustine's literal understanding of the *regula amoris* led him
to "reduce the demand" of Christian ethics. Always set under the intrusive rubric of self-interest, "the most inward essence of neighbour-
love, its meaning as the will for self-denying community, remained
hidden from him."[10] Quite the opposite is the case. According to the
strictly formal demands of eudaemonism, self-love (insofar as it is
equivalent to the pursuit of the *summum bonum*)[11] should have been
determinative of neighbor-love and neighbor-love justified only in
terms of self-love; and there might have been no very great harm in
that, provided it was clearly enough understood that self-love was only
a formal and not a material category. But as though to avoid the
very appearance of evil, Augustine has sacrificed the coherence of
his eudaemonism in order to speak of neighbor-love as the equal
of self-love. Consistency has been of less importance to him than
a maximal view of the requirement of neighbor-love. And the tool
with which he has cracked the eudaemonist framework open is
precisely that with which he is accused of securing it, the words
as yourself.

We seriously misunderstand our author unless we appreciate that
the *regula* confers the highest possible status upon the obligation
to love the neighbor. Love-of-neighbor-as-self is never, for Augustine,
a second best to love-of-neighbor-more-than-self. This view he
might conceivably have sustained on the model of Kierkegaard's "pick
to wrench open the lock," so that love-of-neighbor-as-self was seen

as the first step to something higher;[12] or else he might have held it in
the way Holl imagined he did, in conjunction with a double-standard
theory, so that love-of-neighbor-as-self was the acceptable minimal
level above which it was saintly but unnecessary to aspire. Had either
of these understandings of the *regula* been his, Augustine would at
some point have alluded to love-of-neighbor-above-self as a higher possibility. This he never does, and for the simple reason that in his language loving one's neighbor as oneself is loving him to the uttermost.

This interpretation is supported by a few passages in which Augustine does actually allude to the possibility of loving the neighbor
more than self, only to declare that it would simply be wrong. From
every point of view, of course, this is paradoxical: it offends the
plain sense of the text, makes the existing confusion over the comparison of the two loves worse, and obscures Augustine's general concern
to maximize the neighbor's claim. But it does confirm that love-of-
neighbor-as-self is a maximal, not a minimal, standard.

The origin of the view that one should not love another more than
oneself, quoted in the *Soliloquia* as "that most just rule of friendship," appears to be Cicero's *Laelius*.[13] Within the Aristotelian tradition of writing on friendship it is perfectly comprehensible; for on
the one hand that tradition founds friendship on mutual respect for
the other's reason, so that one may quite sensibly speak of the
friend's reason as something that must be equivalent and not superior
to one's own, while on the other, even where mutual benefits are
in question, it is plausible to argue that the stability of friendship requires a certain reciprocity and equilibrium and that heroic self-
sacrifice unreciprocated could actually destroy the relationship. But
friendship and Christian love may be two very different things, and
Augustine's use of the thesis is very awkward when he transfers
the "most just rule of friendship" without apology into an exegesis
of the love-command.

The fullest example comes from *De mendacio*:

Once it is settled [that "God hates all who work iniquity, and

destroys all who speak falsehood"], who that affirms these
truths will be shaken by those hard cases: What if a man takes
refuge with you and you could save him by telling a lie? and
so on? The death of which they are so foolishly afraid (while
they are yet not afraid to sin!) is that which kills the body
but cannot kill the soul, which our Lord warns us in the Gospel
not to fear. But "the mouth that lieth slayeth the soul" (Sap.
1:11) and not the body. . . . Is it not, then, sheer perversity to
maintain that for one to live physically another should die
spiritually? For even love of the neighbour has been set a limit
by the love that a man should bear for himself. Scripture says,
"You shall love your neighbour as yourself." Is it loving him
"as yourself" to give him his temporal life at the cost of your
own eternal life? Indeed, if someone sacrifices his own temporal life for another's temporal life, even that is not loving him
as himself but *more than* himself, and going beyond the rule of
sound teaching. How much less, then, is he intended to lose
his own eternal life for another's temporal life by telling lies![14]

It is clear what the supposed father of Situation Ethics is telling us:
Lying is always a sin, and we must not commit sin even to save
another's life, for the preservation of life is not always the highest
moral value. This is expressed in difficult and misleading terms,
with self-love representing the principle of moral right and neighbor-
love the principle of saving life. The rule that we must not love
our neighbor more than ourselves amounts to no more than the truism
"If in any circumstances the protection of life (neighbor-love) is
not coincident with the morally right (self-love), then we ought not
to pursue it!" The problem which this triviality raises is entirely
due to its expression. Augustine himself acknowledges that "self-
love" and "neighbor-love" in this context are not parallel in sense,
the one being concerned with fostering the life of the soul (i.e.,
the principle of moral right) and the other with preserving the life of
the body (the principle of saving life). Fleetingly he confronts the

question of whether the rule "neighbor no more than self" still obtains when only the physical welfare of the two is at stake and in a moment of weakness toys with the idea of forbidding self-sacrifice in this more obvious sense. This is something like what the classical principle meant and equally something alien to an account of Christian love. The application with which Augustine is really concerned, however, is quite inoffensive and not at all what the classical principle meant. Augustine's use of the "rule of friendship" to express something so different and his consequent flirtation with a view somewhat closer to its true meaning arose from its superficial resemblance to the "rule of love" expressed in the words *as yourself*.

Once again he had failed to register that eudaemonist self-love as a general category inclusive of all moral virtues was not a directly comparable form of love to substantial love of the neighbor. This failure led him on several occasions to say things which offered more than a little opportunity to critics. When he repudiated with some warmth the suggestion that St. Stephen prayed kneeling for his persecutors and standing for himself because he cared more for his persecutors than for himself or when he insisted that self-love must always accompany neighbor-love because almsgiving is worthless unless done for the sake of one's own blessedness, it sounds very bad indeed. But the intrusion of "self" on these occasions turns out on inspection to be purely formal, a confusing distraction arising from the eudaemonist category. What he really wants to say is good moral sense: Even gestures of kindness and goodwill toward other people have to be ordered within the total context of God's demand. They are not ipso facto authentically moral acts simply because they are neighbor-directed. Such alms as are done outside this moral order are not really expressions of love in its fullness at all. They are the alms without charity of which St. Paul spoke; they "profit me nothing."[15]

THE RECIPROCATION OF LOVE

"If you love those who love you, what reward have you?" Prompted

by Christ's question, thinkers and preachers have affirmed throughout
the Christian centuries that love without a risk is of no account in
the moral order. The demand that we should love our enemies and
pray for those who persecute us presents our love with its supreme
test; it is the case which shows up most clearly the generosity of
Christian love at its widest. Love which can bear a hostile response is
agape on the model of Christ's own love. And yet, in apparent tension with this, though with equal scriptural warrant, Christians have
also needed to stress the peculiar riches of that mutual love which
exists only within the church. To theologians whose inclination is to
discount this latter emphasis (and we may class Holl and Nygren
with that group, along with such greater luminaries as Kierkegaard),
the attempts of an Augustine or a Barth to include both universal
and special love are bound to carry the threat of compromise.[16]

Augustine was original, according to Hélène Petré, in his use of the
terms *neighbor* and *brother* to distinguish the universal and the
special love.[17] Hitherto the idea of "brotherhood" had tended to
carry a universal rather than a special reference among the Latin
theologians, while in their attempts to answer the famous question,
Who is my neighbor? they had been plunged into some confusion. They mentioned, only to reject, the idea that the *proximus* was
to be understood literally as a close relative. Tertullian fleetingly
entertains the idea that he is oneself.[18] Most favored among the earlier
Latin fathers was the view that the neighbor was Christ. This at once
allowed them to explain the status given to the second great command
and to understand the strange inversion of Luke 10:36f.: the neighbor was "the one who showed mercy." Not before Jerome do we find
a definite statement of principle that "the neighbor" is every man,
though in fact there had also been an undefined use of the word in
this universal sense which supported his understanding.

For Augustine it became a firm rule of interpretation. He was
aware that the Hebrew text of Leviticus did not carry this sense, but
this, he believed, was one point at which the New Law had achieved
a greater understanding than the Old. The Christian command of

love for the enemy implied a universal neighbor-love a fortiori. "Because a man, therefore a neighbor," he says; and, "Every man is a
neighbour to every man."[19] Petré has distinguished two justifications
of this doctrine: one, largely Stoic, based on the community of
reason, the other, largely Christian, based on the fact of Adamic
descent.[20] Either way it encompasses humanity *qua* humanity and
is thus distinguished from that more restricted love shown to
"brothers" who share with us a hope of the heavenly inheritance.[21]

A characteristic difficulty for any theory of universal love is that
of "proximate relations": friends, family, colleagues, fellow-Chris-
tians, and others.[22] If we are to extend our love to all on the basis
of humanity alone, irrespective of how they are related to us, do
we not declare any preferential attachment illegitimate? At the time
of the *De vera religione* Augustine seems to have thought so, or,
at least, if not illegitimate, to have thought that they were forced upon
us *faute de mieux* by the conditions of human fallenness. This opinion he later withdrew, recalling that even if man had remained in his
Paradisal state, he would still have had wives and children, some of
whom, by being his own and not other men's wives and children,
would have made special claim on his regard.[23] How could such claims
be justified in terms of universal neighbor-love? And how could such
a love tolerate the special requirements of "love for the brethren"? It
was not open to Augustine to find that these restricted claims had
their source in some other moral principle than neighbor-love, for it
was an avowed part of his ethical program that all obligations of
every kind should be traced back to the twin commands of love for
God and neighbor. He replied instead that these special responsibilities were imposed by the limitations of time and opportunity. "In
the first place, a man bears responsibility for his own: for it is to
their care that he has simpler and easier access, whether in the order
of nature or in the order of human society." "It is necessary that
love, like a fire, should cover the nearest terrain before it spreads
further afield."[24] It is doubtful whether this answer is really adequate.
Can it explain, for example, how we may have certain obligations

to members of our family which would be positively offensive if we attempted to extend their scope? Perhaps "the order of nature" must introduce more kinds of differentiation than the merely quantitative one which Augustine recognized. Yet it is plain that if Augustine errs, he errs toward inappropriate universality rather than to inappropriate particularity. The *regula*, in so far as it is used in this context, enhances rather than diminishes the universalist tendency.[25]

It is an interesting illustration of the importance for Augustine's thought of soteriological categories, that he must make life more difficult for himself by establishing universal neighbor-love on a redemptive basis too. It is as though humanity has not been fully specified unless mention has been made not only of its origin but of its destiny. "Every man must be our neighbour, not only on the ground of common humanity . . . but also in hope of that inheritance."[26] The two ways in which this is done are already familiar to us. First, Augustine speaks of a possibility in every man, which is to be acknowledged and respected while we do not know how he will turn out. The non-Christian is to be regarded as *not yet* a member with us of the body of Christ. "Each one of us ought to regard any other as though he already were what he hopes he will be, even though he has not yet become it." Our ignorance of the future leads us to a universal charitable assumption: "Love all men, for you do not know what he will be tomorrow, who today is wicked." It may even be that we are mistaken about the state of a man's heart at present; one reason for loving our enemies is that we "may not hate our friends unawares."[27] Secondly, passing from the rational to the benevolent aspect of love, Augustine instructs us to love the neighbor "that he may be righteous." To love the neighbor is to do him good, both his body and his soul. Augustine's favorite analogy is that of the doctor and his patients. "How is it that doctors love the sick? Surely they cannot love the sick! If they love the sick, they must wish them sick for ever! No, they love the sick to an end, not that they should remain sick, but that they should recover from their sickness and be well."[28]

This raises in a new form the problem of hidden self-interest. Does the lover's ambition to see the enemy within the fold not qualify the freedom with which his love is offered? Does it not constitute an ulterior motive which subordinates the highest of responsibilities to some other end? This question becomes acute when the lover's purpose is defined not simply in terms of reconciling the neighbor to God but as reconciling him to self and so turning him from an enemy into a friend.[29] And we should not underestimate the importance to Augustine of reciprocity in love. We are all anxious to be loved, he tells us, and our natural response to love is to return it. There are a number of examples within his own autobiography: The notorious theft of pears at Thagaste is accounted for by "the pleasure of the offence which derived from the company of fellow-offenders"; his association with the *eversores* at Carthage was due to delight in their friendship; his affection for the bishop of Milan was aroused as he saw him "not at first as a teacher of the truth but as a man who was kind to me."[30] He thought that all the natural relationships of love, husband and wife, parent and child, brother, sister, and all the rest depended on the confidence that love was returned. As for Christians, who owed love to all men, it was nevertheless true that they "gain much delight (and properly so!) from those who in turn regard [them] with a holy and pure affection."[31]

We may detect two influences at work in this doctrine, both of them well evidenced by the following passage from *De catechizandis rudibus*:

> There could be no greater reason for our Lord's coming to earth than for God to demonstrate his love in our midst, urging it strongly upon us; for "while we were yet sinners, Christ died for us." And all because "the end of the commandment" and "the fulfilling of the law" is love; so that even if we were initially reluctant to love God, we might be less reluctant to love him in return for the love which he showed us first. For there is no greater incentive to love than for the other to love first. It

would be an exceptionally stubborn spirit that could refuse, not simply to offer love, but even to return it . . . .

If this rule applies to the more degraded loves, how much more is it true of friendship! There is no impression that we are more anxious to avoid giving than that we do not love our friend, or that we love him less than he loves us. Once let him think that, and he too will cool towards that love in which men enjoy one another's company in shared intimacy. . . .

Another point deserves our notice. Although it is true that superiors wish to be loved by their inferiors, take pleasure in their polite attentions and love them more the more conscious of such attentions they become; nevertheless, there is a peculiar strength in the love of an inferior for a superior who he can see loves him. For love is more welcome when it does not owe its heat to drought and need, but spills out in superfluity of kindness.[32]

One influence is the theological principle stated here in the words of Romans 5:8 but perhaps more commonly justified by reference to 1 John 4:19, "We love because he first loved us." Augustine has taken this principle of the man–God relationship as the supreme example of a rule that is primarily true of human intercourse. The other influence is, once again, the Ciceronian tradition of writing about friendship, betrayed in this passage by the term *amicitia*, which Augustine was not inclined to use very widely, the unusual verb *redamare* "to love in return," and the generally un-Augustinian idea of friendship between social superiors and inferiors.[33]

It may be useful to distinguish two possible theses about reciprocity in love, a strong thesis and a weak one. The strong thesis states that neighbor-love depends on a consciousness of being loved, the weak that it simply includes a desire to be loved in return. Both these theses are maintained by Augustine.

In the strong thesis it is undoubtedly implied that all human love has had an element of self-interest at least in its beginnings. Augustine believed that no man can discover what it is to love unless he first experiences what it is to be loved. And yet it would be quite wrong to regard this view of the genesis of neighbor-love as evidence for what he supposes the obligation to amount to. The Christian life, after all, is a convalescence from the disease of sin; the life of virtue is entered from a position of great disadvantage. Our need of the incentive is more a testimony to our initial weakness than a permanent limitation of our responsibility. The progress of our convalescent love is charted in three stages: "Extend your love to your neighbours (but that is hardly an extension since you are almost loving yourself if you love those who are attached to you.) Extend it to those you do not know, who have done you no harm. Pass even beyond them, and reach the point of loving your enemies."[34]

It could appear that this doctrine institutionalizes, and thereby authorizes, the restricted love of the beginner; and so it might be thought that it takes the first step to establishing the *iustitia minor*, or double-standard morality, characteristic of mediaeval ethical theory (though confined in Augustine's mature thought to his theory of monasticism).[35] Certainly the passing allusion to self-love in the passage just quoted appeals to the Stoic concept of natural self-love rather than to Augustine's more usual idea. From this we can see how the later tradition, as exemplified by St. Bernard, could build a theory of ascending stages which slowly accomplished the supersession of Nature by Grace until, in a moment of mystical excess, pure love was achieved.[36] But this development is still a long way off. The significant feature of the theory of stages in Augustine's version is that the highest stage, so far from being relegated to the eschaton or to rare and favored moments of mystical contemplation, is nothing more than the ordinary Christian duty of loving one's enemies. We are all expected to reach the stage where we can love our enemy without any encouragement or return. The Catholic church must continue to love the Donatists (in its well-known fashion), not seeking the privilege of being loved itself but that of seeing Christ loved. "Let them speak against us what they will, we must love them willy-nilly!"[37]

There remains the more modest thesis, the claim that even when not dependent upon reciprocation, even when the desire for return is hopeless, love must still desire it. In defending this thesis, Augustine is content merely to guard against a possible misunderstanding. A desire which has no place in true love is the desire for material reciprocation. "Often," he writes, "a concern for this life's necessities hurts our inward eye and causes it to film over; in effect it creates a double heart within us, so that all our dealings with men which appear righteous are in fact not conducted with a pure heart as the Lord commands. We do not act out of love for mankind, but because we want to get something out of them to provide for the necessities of life. We ought to do them good for the sake of their eternal salvation, not for some personal and secular advantage."[38]

There is thus an exact correspondence between right and wrong motivation in the case of love for neighbor and in the case of love for God. In both cases love which has in mind some extrinsic material reward is deprecated, while love which desires simply the benefits intrinsic to the relationship is considered "free." The word *gratis*, most frequently applied to love for God, also belongs to the province of human love, to the relationship of friends and the mutual love of man and wife.[39] The rules of the means-end language do not, of course, encourage Augustine to speak favorably of "loving the neighbor for his own sake" as the classical tradition could do; but in other respects he is close to the Ciceronian rule which he quotes: "Friendship is to will good things to another for his own sake, and to have this will reciprocated."[40] Of a love which has no interest at all in establishing friendship Augustine has no knowledge.

GOD AND THE WHOLE

In general Augustine ties his anthropological and cosmological principles so closely to "theology" in the narrow sense that it is no surprise to find him anchoring his doctrine of love to the relations that obtain within the tripersonal, consubstantial Godhead:

The Holy Spirit too belongs in the same unity and equality of substance. For whether he is regarded as the unity of the two, or the holiness, or the love, or whether he is the unity because he is the love, or the love because he is the holiness, it is evident that he by whom the two are joined, he by whom the Begotten loves, and is loved by, the Begetter, not by participation, not by gift of some superior being, but essentially and by their own nature "preserving the unity of the Spirit in the bond of peace," he is not himself one of the two. By grace we are commanded to imitate the life of the Godhead with respect both to God himself and to one another—the two commands on which hang all the law and the prophets. Thus are these three one God, alone mighty, wise, holy and blessed. Our blessedness is from him and through him and in him; for by his gift we are one among ourselves and one spirit with him, our soul drawn closely after him as though attached by glue. For us "it is good to cleave to God," for "he shall destroy all who go whoring from him." The Holy Spirit, we have shown, must be some element common to the Father and the Son, whatever that element may be. In fact he is their community itself, consubstantial and coeternal with them. If it seems convenient to call this community "friendship," very well; but "love" is better. This too is substance, because God is substance, and Scripture says that "God is love."[41]

This paragraph contains everything central to Augustine's doctrine of love. All love originates in the immanent love of the Godhead, which is at once a mutual relation between subject and object (the first and second Persons), the expression of the unity between them (which has its ground in the identity of divine being), and at the same time an independent subsistent (a third Person) alongside them. We will conclude our chapter by exploring this statement in some greater detail.

In the first place, the view that *the love between subject and object is itself a third subsistent* is demanded by Augustine's hostility to

"Macedonianism," the fourth-century heresy which denied the Spirit's ontological equality with the Father and the Son. Augustine believed that he had found in Hilary's account of the Spirit as *usus*, "a kind of ineffable embrace between Father and Son" as he explained it, a valuable defense against this deviation. By allowing him to assign the word *love* as a particular designation of the Spirit, it put at the disposal of his argument the text 1 John 4:16, "God is love."[42]

But the objective subsistence of love as a third beside its subject and object is assumed as well of human as of divine love. In his first unsuccessful attempt to plot a trinity in the soul of man Augustine proposed the triad "lover," "beloved," and "love" (*amans, quod amatur, amor*); and although he abandoned this pattern, it does not seem to have been the status of *amor* that worried him but the difficulty of establishing unity of substance between the lover and the object of his love.[43] We find another illustration of the principle in the strange thesis which has already attracted our notice, that to love something means that we also love the love itself, as a second object of our love. "Is the love itself also the object of our love? Certainly! Without it we could not love the other!"[44]

It follows from this starting point, in the second place, that *love must be a mutual relation*, that is, that every subject is also object and every object subject. If love were conceived, as we tend to conceive it, as an attitude of the subject alone, it would be an irreversible predicate. From the fact that James loves John it could not be concluded that John loved James. But for Augustine, love in its perfection is *mutual*: it must be the case that if the Father loves the Son the Son loves the Father. For this is the logical implication of the belief that their love is a third, not simply something which the Father does or feels toward the Son but someone who stands between them. Once again, the divine love sets the conditions for human love: among men, too, *caritas* must be *mutua*, and this is the significance of the "new commandment" which Christ gave his disciples, that we love "one another" (*diligere invicem*).[45]

Unreciprocated love was always a defect in the universe as Augus-

tine understood it. He could not glory in the fact that the Word "came
to his own, and his own did not receive him," as a triumph of self-
giving love in its own right. The teleological thrust of love was always
toward exact mutuality of subject and object, a state that must obtain when "God shall be all in all." We must bear this in mind when
thinking about the passages, discussed above, in which the desire
for reciprocation of love is given some prominence. This is not a desire with narrowly personal reference: The lover desires to be
loved not for some privately conceived gratification but because this
is the fulfillment of love as such, a fulfillment which is owing to
God and the universe as much as to himself.

This train of thought sheds some light upon Augustine's use of the
text Romans 5:5, a matter on which he is much misrepresented. The
text, a favorite, speaks of "the love of God . . . poured into our hearts
through the Holy Spirit which has been given to us." Even the sym-
pathetic Burnaby joins the chorus of complaint that Augustine dis-
torted St. Paul's meaning by treating the words "of God" as an
objective rather than a subjective genitive, referring the verse to our
love for God instead of to God's love for us. On St. Paul's meaning there may, of course, be more than one opinion but however
that may be it is misleading to say that in Augustine "the genitive is always objective in default of a note to the contrary." It is true
that on one occasion Augustine rules out the interpretation with a
subjective genitive; but in its place he proposes not an objective genitive but a causative: The love of God is "the love by which he makes
us his lovers."[46] For Augustine "love" is not a *nomen actionis* for
which the distinction between subjective and objective genitive is relevant; it is a *nomen personae*, and the "love of God" shed abroad
in our hearts is nothing other than the Holy Spirit who sheds it.[47]

In the third place, love is *the expression of an ontological ground
of unity between subject and object*. The unity of the Father and
the Son, of course, is a unity of being and as such has its source not in
the third but in the first Person of the Trinity, who is the "fount
of deity." But at the level of relational subsistence in the Godhead its

unity is its love, the Holy Spirit who binds the Father and the Son in one.

The connection of love and unity was, of course, by no means an idea original to Augustine. When he wrote of a youthful friendship, "I realized that my soul and his had become one soul in two bodies," the metaphor was already worn smooth from long use.[48] But it achieved a new sharpness in the context of the Augustinian metaphysic. The role of *caritas* was to "bind us together and make us one." By love we "dwelt inside" one another. Love built a "unified structure."[49] It was a fire which welded, a glue which made things stick, a chain which linked together. In the Acts of the Apostles he found confirmation of his view in a description of the early church as "one soul" and "one heart." As we would expect from the identification of God's love with the Holy Spirit, it is in the church that the unity of man with man is revealed to the world.[50]

Corresponding to the two conceptions of love as mutual relation and organic unity were two interchangeable ways of using the verb: one could say either that the subject-objects of love "loved each other" or that the unified whole "loved itself." This interchange was assisted by a linguistic coincidence. All that the Latin language possessed by way of a reciprocal pronoun was the adverbial form *invicem*. To "love each other" had to be written in Latin in one of three ways: *diligere invicem, diligere se invicem*, or simply *diligere se*. This last form plainly invited confusion with the reflexive *self-love*, a confusion which on the whole Augustine carefully avoided but occasionally exploited for his own purposes. In the following passage, for example, we can observe his use of the ambiguity to enable him to jump from a favorite remark about mutual love to another favorite remark about self-love and, perhaps, back again:

> This, then, must be our reason for loving one another [*nos invicem*], so our love will be distinguished from that of the general run of mankind, who do not love each other for this reason because they do not really love each other at all. But

those who love themselves/each other [se] for the sake of possessing God do indeed love themselves [se]. That they may
love themselves [se], therefore, they love God. But not all men
share this love. Few there are who have this reason for loving
themselves/each other [se] that God may be all in all.[51]

But this is not mere confusion of language, whether accidental or intentional. Augustine states it as a principle that "when the members
love each other, the body loves itself." This is not supportable, of
course, on purely logical grounds, for it by no means follows that
whatever the members of a group do to one another the group as a
whole does to itself. It can only be true as a stipulative definition
of love. Love is the force which draws every part to its completeness
in the whole, and the self-love of the whole is that state of achieved
cohesion in which there is no more separateness or division left in the
universe. Mutual love stands to this achieved self-love as the many
"sons of God" stand to the Son. In some moods Augustine was capable of hinting at an extraordinarily collectivist Christology. In a
phrase which has become almost as popular a tag as the notorious
totus Christus, caput et corpus, he speaks of one who loves God's
sons becoming a member of God's Son, joined in love in the structure
of Christ's body: "and then there will be one Christ, loving himself."[52]

Certain obligations confront the individual who discovers himself
to be a part of this larger, self-conscious whole. "The whole is more
important than the part. . . . Any soul purged by piety has to that
extent learned to take less delight in its private welfare and to look to
the law of the whole, devoutly and gladly giving way to it."[53] The
contrast so often drawn between the "common good" and the "private good" has this concept of "the whole" (*universitas*) as its context. Adam's choice of the private was not simply the decision of an
individual agent to pursue this or that good; it was a choice about
what he would be or even about *what* would be, whether there would
be a cohering whole with Adam a part of it or a divided whole with

Adam as a separated individual. The food for man is "common" not only in the sense that it is the same for everyone and capable of infinite extension to satisfy all but also in that it can only be enjoyed by a communal subject. A typically flamboyant comment on the text "The waters will flow through the midst of the mountains" shows us how Augustine can exploit this idea:

> What is said to be "in the midst" is communal. Communal property on which all may live on an equal basis is "in the midst" and does not belong to me, but is neither yours nor mine. Which is why we say of some men, "They have peace 'among themselves,' 'they have faith among themselves,' 'they have love among themselves.'" You know this expression: "among themselves" really means "in their midst." And what does "in their midst" mean? It means that it is their common possession. [54]

If the individual's submission to the common good is the primary obligation to which this collectivist metaphysic gives rise, the second is that he should assist in the genesis of the whole by drawing others into as close a relation as possible with himself. The assumption behind this demand is that identity is the ultimate term of proximity. Those who are very closely related to us are almost ourselves, their "otherness" reduced to nothing by the extreme intimacy of the bond.[55] Love is a fire, spreading out from a central point to engulf all that lies around it, extending the scope of its identity. "It is necessary that love, like a fire, should cover the nearest terrain before it spreads further afield. Your brother is closer to you than mankind in general. Again, he whom you never knew will more easily attach to you (*adhaeret*) than will your enemy who is actually at odds with you." In this passage, the continuation of which we quoted above,[56] the verb *adhaero* expresses the accumulation of new parts to the whole. The neighbors, already attached, are "almost yourself." The attachment of those who stand at one further degree of remove will extend the scope of the self yet further toward universality.

The collectivist trait in Augustine's metaphysic can be traced without much hesitation to Stoic influence mediated through Plotinian Neoplatonism. The holistic community of gods and men, in which the individual is but a fragment of the whole, is a favorite theme of the Stoics; and with the picture of love as an outward extending, all-embracing locus of identity we can hardly fail to compare their doctrine of *oikeiosis* in what Kerferd calls its "outward-looking aspect."[57] Yet there is another strain of Augustinianism not easily harmonized with this. The battle between the collectivist Augustine and the individualist is responsible for a number of the logical puzzles we have noted in his handling of the rule of love. There are moments when he can view Stoic collectivism with withering scorn, especially when it leads, as short of intervention from revelation it must lead, to a defense of suicide: "A happy life indeed that seeks the aid of death in terminating itself!"[58] But in the nineteenth book of *City of God* he is, as we have observed, the strict eudaemonist and so also the strict individualist. There may no doubt be two opinions about which is the better Augustine, even about which is the real Augustine. But there can be no dismissing this deep-rooted tension in his thought and no quick labeling of one side as classical and the other as Christian. The collectivist and the individualist alike are classical by education and Christian by conversion.[59]

In the fourth place and lastly, all these points in common between human and divine love demonstrate that *human love reflects the divine reality as ectype reflects archetype*. If love can make one soul and one heart of a diverse multiplicity of men, we can be certain a fortiori that the Father and the Son are, in the fount of love, One God.[60] In the titles used of the Holy Spirit as the love of the Father and the Son we may discern precisely the same ambiguity between mutuality and unity. When it is convenient to stress the equal and mutual relation of the Father and the Son, the Spirit is called "the love which the Father and the Son have for *each other*," while when it is the unity and coinherence of the Godhead which is to be emphasized, the Spirit is simply "self-love," the third in the triad, *sapientia, notitia sui, dilectio sui.*[61] The self-love or mutual love of the Godhead is the link through which the self-love of the universe, the love of man for man and for God, is derived from the divine being. On one occasion in the fifteenth book of *De Trinitate* man's love for God is explicitly identified with the title "Gift" of the Holy Spirit. But such an identification is implied even where it is not expressed: The long arguments of Book VIII of the same work to demonstrate the trinity of love constantly apply the text "God is love" to the "true love" of a man for his brother;[62] the pouring of love into our hearts of which the text Romans 5:5 speaks is always, for Augustine as well as for Paul, the work of the Holy Spirit. The glue of the universe is simply the love of the Godhead in his *operationes ad extra.*

One Augustinian scholar has recently provided some strong arguments to demonstrate the presence in the early Cassiciacan dialogue of the Stoic–Plotinian theory of the World-Soul. He was not concerned with the later works but had he been so he might have found much to intrigue him in the words we have already quoted from *De Trinitate* VI: "By his gift we are one among ourselves and one spirit with him, our soul drawn closely after him as though attached by glue."[63] In the context we can hardly plead that *anima nostra*, "our soul," is a distributive expression referring to our several individual souls, for is it not precisely Augustine's point that in love we are no longer many but one? And yet it is equally unthinkable that he is referring here to a holistic World-Soul to be understood as an item of cosmology, for he has spoken of the unity of the redeemed as a gift of God's grace. We may fairly claim to see the Stoic idea fossilized in Augustinian rock, a permanent record of the materials from which it came to be. But the unified soul is no longer an immanent fact about the cosmos but an eschatological achievement, the accomplished work of the Holy Spirit in the church of Christ. The one soul of mankind is evangelical proclamation, a truth of the same order as the one spirit of man with God. And it is no nostalgia for lost unity but an imperious summons from above which has effected this attachment, both horizontal and vertical. By this double movement of re-unification, the love-of-neighbor acting as cradle for the love-of-God, the Spirit whose name is *Dilectio* completes his redemptive work.

CHAPTER SIX

CONCLUSIONS:
SELF-LOVE AND EUDAEMONISM

In tracing Augustine's use of the phrase "self-love," we have been forced to make a number of distinctions. We have distinguished different evaluative tones which the phrase may carry: an unfavorable tone, with which it represents the root of all sin and rebellion against God; a neutral tone, to represent the natural condition either of man's animal or of his rational nature; a favorable tone, to represent man's discovery of his true welfare in God. We have tried to show that although a bridge of moral apologetic is sometimes constructed between the neutral and the favorable there is no such commerce between the unfavorable and either of the others; and that evil self-love relates to natural and to right self-love only in paradox. We have distinguished, too, different aspects of love which may be presupposed by the idea of self-love: benevolent, rational, and cosmic. Benevolent self-love, the promotion of one's own true welfare in God, we have seen used in association with the favorable tone, and sometimes, rather ambiguously, with the neutral. Rational love, the evaluative estimation of oneself, false or true, we have seen associated with both favorable and unfavorable tones. Cosmic love, the idea that love is a movement through the universe, encompassing self as the midpoint, we have also seen used in connection both with man's fall and with his redemption. The fourth aspect of love, which we called "positive," we have not found in any intelligible reflexive use.

All this may tempt us to conclude that there is no such thing as a "concept" of self-love in Augustine's thought. There are too many points left unresolved and incoherent. Is it, in the end, possible not to love oneself? In what sense do we love our neighbor "as" ourselves? Although the term is the product of Augustine's most important

psychological and theological speculations, it is not in itself a finished, self-conscious theological artifact.

Nevertheless, it would be wrong to suppose that the idea is without its own wider significance. For, as we have also seen, self-love,
however rough-hewn, forms part of the supporting structure of the Augustinian "eudaemonist ethic," his theory of morality and human
action, related in the classical way to the ideas of happiness and fulfillment.[1] In saying that self-love finds its only true expression in love
of God Augustine is formulating in one of many possible ways a
principle fundamental to his metaphysical and ethical outlook, namely
that all moral obligation derives from an obligation to God which is
at the same time a call to self-fulfillment. This principle has generated
much controversy in the course of this century, and our purpose in
the course of this chapter will be to examine it and the role that "self-
love" plays in its formulation.

THE CRITIQUE OF HOLL AND NYGREN

We approach our task by way of a highly influential critique of Augustine first voiced fifty years ago by Karl Holl in his paper "Augustine's Inner Development."[2] Holl wrote with the primary purpose of
refuting Harnack's contention that Augustine's intellectual conversion to Christianity happened in two stages, the former stage bringing
him no further along the road than to a barely Christianized Platonism,
and that the *Confessions*, written from the latter stage a decade
afterward, reinterpreted the events of his earlier conversion to fit
his mature, Pauline theological persuasion. Holl argued that an account
of Augustine's conversion in essential agreement with that of the
Confessions could be pieced together from the dialogues of Cassicia-
cum, virtually contemporary with the events, and that Augustine's
later development could best be understood as an exploration of themes
implicit from the beginning. And yet Harnack was not mistaken in
detecting contradictions in Augustine's thought: not, as he had maintained, contradictions between the early Augustine and the mature

but between the Catholic Augustine and the disciple of St. Paul, contradictions that were present from the first and never resolved throughout his intellectual career. Augustine never grasped the full implications of the Pauline Gospel (which, Holl made no secret of believing, is *the* Gospel). St. Paul was always tempered by a Platonic and Catholic interpretation, and nowhere was this more evident than in the Augustine ethic.

Augustine approached religion from the point of view of classical eudaemonism, in pursuit of "the happy life." "The conversion," says Holl,

> represents nothing more than a change of taste. The fancy for earthly good is replaced by the sweeter fancy for heavenly good. Enjoyment reaches its peak in self-forgetfulness, and yet it is clear that the self-forgetful man (as he appears) is really busy thinking of himself all the time. Augustine does not shrink from the claim that in the "love of God," as he presents it, self-love at its highest is provided for at the same time.[3]

Nor is the situation very much improved when Augustine includes love-of-neighbor with love-of-God as the supreme obligation. For

> when he expounds the command in greater detail, he constantly intrudes self-love between love-of-God and love-of-neighbour. It is the point of reference from which the two other articles gain their inner relationship and proportion. . . . In connexion with this, we notice that Augustine could only grasp the commands of the Sermon on the Mount in their negative aspect. The most inward essence of neighbour-love, its meaning as the will for self-denying community, remained hidden from him.[4]

This approach has serious implications for the doctrine of grace:

> Under the category of grace he has never been able to comprehend

more than that sudden discovery of a taste for the spiritual and
eternal which eradicates man's craving for things of the senses.
It is still true for Augustine that the will cannot be set in motion
without something to attract it. Augustine now designates this
more exalted longing, consistently with the biblical vocabulary,
preferably as *caritas*, sometimes as *dilectio* or *amor*; but fundamentally it is still the old Platonic *eros* which shines through.
Apart, of course, from Augustine's new insistence that this *caritas*
does not arise from within man himself, but is "poured" or
"breathed out" upon him, unpresumed, from on high. For it is
God's way to allow man what he longs for. So it is with *caritas*,
and that is why it is a gift of grace. Interpreted in this way
Romans 5:5 becomes a basic point of reference for Augustine.
Moreover it squares with this concept of Grace that, for all the
self-accusation with which the *Confessions* proceed, forgive-
ness-of-sin never achieves the same decisive sense that it has in
Paul.[5]

As the concept of grace is weakened, so is the force of the divine command:

Augustine is quite clear that one can only really deserve the
highest good when he loves it "for its own sake." But this means
no more than that he must not use it as a means to an end,
aiming at some other good. He will never say that one should
love it *selflessly*, without reference to his own happiness. Rather
he continues to stress, as before, the true fulfillment of self-
love in the love of God. This principle is repeated again and again:
"right self-love is love of God." [(It is plain that Augustine found
no difficulty here, although he was constantly stumbling over
the inner contradiction. *Amor sui* serves him as the root of sin,
and yet he finds *se ipsum diligere* unexceptionable, just so
long as it is expressed in the form of loving God!) *Holl's note*.]
Here we find substantiation for the claim that Augustine, on

the face of it inebriated with the love of God, is the first to ex-
pound that attenuation of the command as concerns the duty
of loving God on which scholasticism later built. An actual fulfillment of the command to love God with all the heart is
only possible in the life beyond; here we must be content, as
he says explicitly, with a *iustitia minor huic vitae competens*.[6]

We may summarize Holl's critique under two heads: In the first
place, the *eudaemonist structure* of classical ethics is the main object
of attack. There are specific points of content to criticize, but it is
the form which causes him the more profound discontent. Augustine
should not have taken the quest for happiness as the model for
Christian ethical thought. He should not have accepted the classical
legacy of a teleological analysis of human action and will. Eudaemonism elides the distinction between the way of God's requiring and
all other ways which man may devise. Christian ethics requires a different model, a different form, to do it justice. Secondly, it is *the
part of self-love* in Augustine's thought to represent the eudaemonist
structure as a whole. The intrusive presence of this third love alongside the two loves commanded in Christ's summary of the law is an
indication that love of God and love of neighbor are both conceived
eudaemonistically. They are measured and controlled by self-
love because self-love is nothing other than the quest for happiness,
without which no ethics, in Augustine's view, can be conceived.
That self-love plays this role in Augustinian ethics is demonstrated
by its moral ambivalence: Either sin or virtue may be called *amor
sui*, for both are the product of the soul's quest for some beatitude.

Holl's critique was elaborated in the much more widely known
work of Anders Nygren.[7] Nygren, despite his disavowal of value judgments, finds Augustine's mixture of Pauline and Platonic elements,
the "*caritas*-synthesis" as he dubs it, every bit as disagreeable as Holl
did, and the features which unsettle him are precisely those which
alarmed Holl. "*Caritas* is in essence love to God. Yet according to Augustine, all love, even that which is directed to God, is acquisitive

love, and so, in a certain sense, self-love."[8] *Amor sui* is taken by Nygren to be an analysis of what Augustine conceived love-as-such to be. Whenever he spoke of love, whether as *caritas, dilectio,* or *amor,* he had in mind an impulse both acquisitive and self-referential. This impulse is properly described as *self*-love. Nygren too wishes to direct criticism at the form rather than the content of Augustine's ethics. There is no question of a reprehensible egotism or selfishness, no question of Augustine's urging us to pursue our own interests when we ought to be pursuing those of God and neighbor. The problem is simply that even when he does commend the love of God and neighbor he cannot break free of the self-referential framework. In the last analysis everything is justified by its place in the "acquisitive" pursuit of beatitude.

Nygren has his own way of dealing with the strange ambivalence of *amor sui.* It is not enough, he tells us, for a critic merely to distinguish two senses of the phrase, mutually contradictory, and opt for one or the other as "typically" Augustinian.[9] *Amor sui,* he thinks, describes something wrong when it specifies the *object* of love (because God is the only good for mankind) and something right when it specifies the *nature* of love (because all love is acquisitive love).[10] This seems to mean that when *amor sui* carries a negative tone it specifies a moral attitude susceptible to ethical evaluation, while in its positive sense it simply represents love as such, as yet unspecified. In the one case the objective genitive is a direct object, so that "self" stands in the same place as "God" in the phrase *amor Dei.* In the other case the genitive serves as a kind of indirect object and the phrase interprets what love, any love, amounts to. Thus Nygren's complaint is fundamentally the same as Holl's: Augustine is guilty of pouring substantively good ethics into an inadequate formal vessel which will not hold them.

Our analysis of Holl's critique, then, will serve for Nygren's as well: First, there were the objections to eudaemonism as an unsuitable vehicle for Christian ethics; secondly, there was the role of self-love, seen as a representative expression for the eudaemonist approach. Leaving the first and more general objection for discussion later in the

chapter, we will give our immediate attention to the relationship between self-love and the eudaemonist categories, taking up in turn two
pivotal claims in the Holl–Nygren case, the intrusion of self-love upon neighbor-love and the equation of self-love with the desire for
happiness.

THE INTRUSION OF SELF-LOVE UPON NEIGHBOR-LOVE

"The most inward essence of neighbour-love, its meaning as the will
for self-denying community, remained hidden from him." We may now
reasonably suppose that what Holl found lacking in St. Augustine's
treatment of Christian love was not so much "community" as "self-
denial," an element which has come to play a major part in modern
treatments of the theme, especially Protestant ones. It has appeared
(in Gene Outka's words) as "the inevitable historical manifestation of
agape insofar as *agape* was not accommodated to self-interest."[11]
Holl's view is taken rather further in the direction of self-negation by
Nygren, who sees the Cross as the normative expression of *agape* and
characterizes this Christian idea of love as "sacrificial giving," which
"lives the life of God, [and] therefore dares to 'lose it.'"[12] And
if Outka can distinguish two different positions with respect to self-
denial—an extreme position which regards sacrifice as the "quintes-
sence" of love and a more modest one which allows it "only instrumental
warrant . . . in promoting the welfare of others"—that is a difference
of opinion which can be kept within the family of Augustine's critics.[13]
For the position which Augustine is accused of holding is far removed
from either of these. It is a position in which self-sacrifice in the
neighbor's interest can never be recommended on any grounds because
the measure and limit of what we owe to any man is constantly declared to be our own self-love.

   Some apologists for Augustine are content to admit this implication.
Etienne Gilson among them says "Loving another with one's whole
soul does not mean disowning or sacrificing oneself; it means loving

another as oneself, on a basis of perfect equality. The one I love is my
equal and I am the equal of the one I love. . . . All charity for another's
person seeks its own good as well. This is self-evident because the
definition of love implies desire for a good we want to possess, and if
a person sacrificed himself in favour of the object of his love, he
would possess nothing."[14] Such a position might, of course, be pressed
to yield a norm of *physical* self-sacrifice, assuming that after death
there is a Heaven in which the subject may continue to exist and enjoy
the object of his desire. Even without a Heaven, if one believed as
the Stoics did that certain states of consciousness (including, perhaps,
the awareness of not having done everything possible to save the
beloved) were less to be desired than total extinction, one could argue
for a form of suicide which would at least have sacrificial elements.
But a sacrifice so controlled by considerations of the subject's own
welfare is not at all what is meant when *agape* is said either to consist
in or to involve self-sacrifice in the neighbor's interest. What is
required is subordination *in principle* of self to other; and that, according to apologist and critic alike, is what Augustine cannot concede.

A slight unevenness in Gilson's defense draws our attention to an
ambiguity in the accusation. He defends self-love at one moment
on a basis of equality with neighbor-love, at another on the ground that
all love implies desire for some good. In the first case self-love is legiti-
mized as one love *alongside* others, in the second as the *presupposition*
of all loves. In a more technical treatise Gilson might have made the
scholastic distinction between self-love as *amor benevolentiae*, a specific form of love with the self as its conscious object, and self-love
as *amor concupiscentiae*, implied by the quest for good which is an
aspect of any love. It is in the latter that we recognize the characteristic
structure of eudaemonism, self-love sharing with the love of God the
position of highest generality in the hierarchy of values. But the objections to Augustine's use of the *regula* are actually directed at the
former. The critic would like to have it both ways. Objecting, in the
first instance, that Augustine shortchanges the neighbor by measuring
his claim alongside that of the self, he then goes on to object that

Augustine derives the neighbor's claim from that of the self. But really
he must choose between these two incompatible lines of attack. If
the self-love in question is the ultimate value which, together with the
love of God, is taken to be the source of all obligation, it cannot be
measured, for good or ill, alongside the altruistic principle, since altruism
too is an expression of it. If on the other hand this self-love is a sub-
stantive moral claim, a genuine rival to neighbor-love (and this is surely
what the command in its original context suggests), then it has nothing
to do with the central principle of eudaemonist ethics. Holl and
Gilson may perhaps be forgiven for missing this distinction, which, as
we observed in chapter five, often eluded Augustine also.

THE EQUATION: SELF-LOVE, QUEST FOR
HAPPINESS, LOVE

When Augustine says that true self-love is love of God, he is saying
something not unlike what he means by the claim that God is man's
happiness. Both express the principle that duty and self-interest ultimately coincide. Holl appears to have concluded from this that self-love
and the quest for happiness were in all contexts synonymous, something we have shown not to be the case.[15] Nygren took the equation
further with his suggestion that "self-love was what love, in Augustine's
thought, really amounted to." Thus we have the equation of self-
love, the quest for happiness, love. Why did it seem obvious to Nygren
that this equation held true for Augustine? My tentative suggestion
is that he found in contrasting *mediaeval* philosophies of love echoes
of his own disagreement with Augustine and so inclined to credit
Augustine with later, mediaeval views, in particular those of St. Thomas.

Pierre Rousselot's veteran monograph, *Pour l'histoire du Problème de
l'Amour au Moyen Age*, a work known to Nygren, distinguished two
conflicting conceptions of love in the theologians of the twelfth and thirteenth centuries, one which he called the "physical," one which he
called the "ecstatic" conception.[16] The names are a little unfortunate
and may suggest a kind of contrast which Rousselot did not intend.

What he had in mind was this: Thomist and pre-Thomist treatments explain the love of one being for another in terms of a metaphysical framework which embraces both subject and object, while the other tradition presents love as a confrontation of two absolutely individuated beings in which the loving subject suffers a kind of disintegration in face of the object of his love. For the Thomist, love is comprehensible as part of the rational movement of the universe toward integration and unity; for the "ecstatic," love is neither rational nor comprehensible. For the one, the subject is related to the object within a subsisting ontological continuity which enables it to be conceived as an extension of the subject's self. For the other, the object is so completely alien that the relation involves a disruption or dissolution of the subject's self. From the former view, rooted in Platonist cosmology, comes the Thomist tradition; from the latter, equally rooted in Platonist mysticism (though Rousselot does not acknowledge this ancestry), come mysticism, quietism, voluntarism, even Reformation and post-Reformation views of love.

The treatment of self-love in these two traditions reveals their critical divergence. For the physicalist, represented by St. Thomas, "there is a fundamental identity between the love of God and self-love" (p. 3). For the ecstatic, although love may have its beginnings in self-love (p. 8), unless it leaves this starting point behind, it remains imperfect and flawed (p. 58). Self-love is incompatible with perfect love. Gregory the Great, in a sentence much quoted in the Middle Ages, distinguishes two kinds of love and reserves the word *caritas* for a love completely rid of self-concern.[17] Other writers do not even acknowledge the possibility of a lower, self-referential love worthy of the name (p. 58 ff.).

To judge from one or two suggestions, Rousselot is inclined to place Augustine in the physicalist camp, and it is obvious that a strong case can be made for this. Augustine identifies true self-love with the love of God. He declares that no one can hate himself and, like St. Thomas later, he believes that all operations of the will express the quest for beatitude. He does not, it is true, take the step which in Rousselot's

view wins for St. Thomas the metaphysicians' crown; he does not
overtly extend the notion of unity so as to conceive of every agent
simply as a part of the whole, though we have observed tendencies toward this solution.[18] There is left in Augustinian thought a certain
duality between self-love and the love of God which it remains for St.
Thomas to erase. But the essential characteristics are already discernible. Self-love is evil only when the self is imperfectly understood
and conceived of as an independent item apart from the rest of the
universe. A true self-love, a self-love based on true self-knowledge, must
coincide with love-of-God because it involves a love of the whole of
which self is understood to be a part, the love of Being itself instead of
love restricted to the self's artificially individuated being.

And yet such a characterization, though initially plausible, must
leave us uneasy. Our own conclusions suggest three reasons for uneasi-
ness: First, we remember that for Augustine the equivalence of self-
love and love-of-God can be maintained only when both are in their
perfect state. True, he gives a very qualified assent to the view that all
beings love God in some way or other; also, he subscribes from time
to time to the view that all animate beings love themselves.[19] But these
two phenomena are not the same: The universal love of God, insofar
as it can be maintained at all, can be maintained only on the ground of
ultimate metaphysical tendency, while the universal animal self-love
is a matter of empirically observable behavior. Only of *perfect* self-love
and *explicit* love of God can it be said, "Herein you love yourself,
by loving God." And so the whole Thomist construct of a natural tendency which, as much in its inchoate as in its achieved form, is at
the same time love-of-God and love-of-self is left without an essential
supporting pillar. Secondly, the identification as one single tendency
of love-of-God, love-of-self, and love-as-such, an identification central
to the Thomist scheme, fails as well at the second link as at the first.
It is not the case in Augustinianism that all love is reducible to love-of-
self. True, all love, that is, all operations of the will, can be explained
in terms of the quest for beatitude—in that St. Thomas and St. Augustine are at one; but, as we have shown, the identification of the quest

for beatitude with self-love cannot be maintained. Nowhere in Augustine's page do we find the classic "psychological egoist" argument that since the very notion of appetition implies the desire to possess, all appetite is self-referential.[20] Then, thirdly, perverse self-love is never treated by Augustine simply as a special case of the natural tendency. The wrong choice of the Fall, which could be interpreted from the Thomist point of view as an inherent risk in created nature, is for Augustine an absurdity.[21] Although it is true for him, as well as for St. Thomas, that self-love in its corrupt sense belongs to a diminished and ontologically false concept of the self (amor rei privatae), it is not the case that right self-love is simply the same impulse with the misconception corrected. Corrupt self-love is to be classed, according to the rough classifications we proposed, as either "rational" or "cosmic"; true self-love (outside the fourteenth book of De Trinitate) is a matter of love as benevolence.

Augustine and Thomas are both "eudaemonists," but there is a wide difference in the way that their eudaemonism is worked out. The difference may be summed up briefly: Where St. Thomas understands the equation of self-love and the love-of-God in terms of the analogy of being, for Augustine it is a datum of revelation.

Such a characterization of Augustine's eudaemonism as against that of Rousselot's "physicalist" school may lead us to suspect that the gulf between Augustine and the "ecstatics" is not so wide as Rousselot supposed. They too are unwilling to account for true love as something natural, as ordinary as selfishness. There is more than a suggestion that love is a transcendent, even a demonic, force. There would be something of lèse majesté in the attempt to dignify with the title "love" anything that belonged simply to normal human motivation. In this context we can find clear anticipations of the Reformers' concern not to "reduce the demand" of God's law. Abelard, for example, is strongly insistent that the love-command of the Gospel is something far and away more serious than anything in the law and the prophets, and he precludes any reference to the eternal blessedness we may hope to gain from the object of our love. And in quoting Augustine in support

of this "gratuitous" love he is not doing him the violence that Rousselot imagines. For there is a place in Augustine's thought not only for
"free love" and "pure love," a Gospel ethic distinct from anything
carnal, but even for actual "self-forgetfulness" in the contemplation
of God's goodness.[22]

And yet there are aspects of the ecstatic conception to which Augustine could never have subscribed. We may note two of them.
First, Abelard is representative of the tradition as a whole when he
takes his concern for "pure" love so far as to rule out even the
Augustinian *ipse praemium*, the doctrine that God himself is the reward
of the blessed:

> Perhaps you say that our reward will be God himself and not
> something else . . . so that when you serve him for the eternal
> blessedness you expect to receive from him, that is pure and true
> love, love of God for his own sake. . . . But if we really make
> God alone the object of our love, it must follow that we will love
> him just the same whatever he may do to us or to others, be-
> cause it cannot but be what is best. In him our love has an object
> that stabilises it; since he remains stable, always the same, good
> in himself and as such worthy of our love.[23]

Behind this divergence there lies a disagreement about the relation of
God to his creation. For Augustine to say that God is or that God is
good is to make a statement about the whole, of which creation is a part:
God is the source of being, God is the source of value. "God is" means
that we exist in and from his being; "God is good" means that he is *our*
good. For Abelard, on the other hand, God's being and God's goodness
have to be thought about independently, without any reference to the being and good of his creation. What God does is "best" simply because
he does it, and no inference can be drawn from this about its being best
for his creatures.

Again, Augustine could not easily have subscribed to the concept
of an intermediate ethic of practicality, contrasted with an ultimate ideal.

Mediaeval ecstatics, though not in this case their Reformation successors, make considerable use of the "stages" of love. This doctrine
can be seen in a highly developed form in the mystical ascent to the
love of God expounded by St. Bernard; but in a more vestigial form
we can see it in the commonplace distinction between slavish love
(based on fear), mercenary love (based on hope of reward), and filial
love, which is truly free.[24] Self-concern in different forms marks
and mars the first two of these; and yet we must begin our pilgrimage
with self-concern, for that is the reality of our present condition.
Abelard identifies this intermediate ethic with the requirement of the
law; it is the light load laid on an untrained mule, far from the perfect demand of the Gospel. "The fear of the Lord is the beginning of
wisdom," he quotes; for although fear is slavish, it would be foolish
to pretend we were in a position to begin anywhere else. It is the
starting point (*incohatio*) but not the completion (*perfectio*). Such an
account of ethical obligation presupposes an interest in ascetic theology
more characteristic of John Cassian than of his great contemporary.
The mature Augustine was not interested in spiritual and moral progress
as a matter for speculative theorizing. True, he began where the
ascetic theologians began, with the Platonic mystical ascent of the soul;
like them, he worked this out in Christian terms as a pilgrimage toward the purification of the soul and the vision of God; like them, he
believed that the Christian life was a protracted moral struggle. But
for him there was no ladder of progress by which the soul's movement
from one level of moral achievement to a higher one could be charted.
The struggle rather consisted in a series of recapitulations of Adam's
choice between good and evil.[25]

Rousselot detects within the ecstatic concept of progress to pure love
a failure to reckon with the possibility of love, for God and self, which
is natural but not fallen. "Between charity and cupidity there is an
absolute antithesis. As charity and grace are equivalent, and grace is
the opposite of nature, it was tempting to identify nature loosely with
cupidity, to regard the latter as the natural fruit of the former and to
draw only a very hazy distinction between natural and perverted love."

St. Bernard is quoted: *Natura semper in se curva est.*[26] Rousselot's
objections are founded on the entirely Augustinian premise of original
righteousness: There is all the difference in the world between fallen
and unfallen human nature; grace restores and, the Thomist will add,
perfects nature. In the ecstatic concept, however, the weight of the
contrast is between nature and grace as such. The irruption of the divine, as represented by demonic *amor*, summons nature to judgment
not for being fallen but simply for being natural, self-contained,
lacking the transcendent reference. The consequence for ethics must
be a sharp division between all "natural" ethics and the evangelical per-
cept of love. And when the latter is believed to be realizable only at
the end of a period of moral ascesis, there is implied a relative and temp-
orary authorization of the former. Here is the *iustitia minor* of which
Holl complained, an absurdity in the context of a theological ethic. But
it is not Augustine who can be charged with it.

A Rousselot finds it hard to see how a rational thinker could belong
to the ecstatic group, a Nygren how a Christian thinker could be among
the physicalists. In conspiring to class Augustine (as rational but only
half-Christian) among the ranks of St. Thomas's predecessors, they misrepresent him, for Augustine belongs to neither tradition. And yet he
anticipates both. There are clear premonitions of the ecstatic doctrine of
the stages in the passage from the *Tractates on 1 John* in which Augustine speaks of how we learn to love our enemies: "Extend your love
to your neighbour. . . . Extend it to those whom you do not know
but who have done you no wrong. Pass beyond them, and reach the
stage of loving your enemies."[27] As yet there is no suggestion that the
highest stage, the love of enemies, is to be left out of our ethical principles for practical purposes until an intermediate ascesis has brought us
to the point at which it is realistic. It is still a duty incumbent upon
every Christian. But here is the acorn from which that oak will grow.
There are premonitions of the physicalist treatment, on the other
hand, in the later books of the *De Trinitate*, where perfected self-love
is regarded as the correlate of perfected self-knowledge and is allowed
greater continuity than usual with the imperfect self-love which is

common to all. This is the beginning of the road which will end in the identification of love-of-God, love-of-self, and love-as-such as a single undifferentiated teleological force in nature. But again it is only the beginning.

However, Holl and Nygren could have omitted all mention of self-love and we would still have had to meet the most important part of their critique, their case against eudaemonism. To this larger issue we devote a few general observations in concluding.

EUDAEMONISM AND CHRISTIAN ETHICS

In order to discover the profoundest motivation of the critique, let us set up against it an imaginary defender of Augustine and of eudaemonism, who will owe something to contemporary philosophical fashions in the English-speaking world. He will be an empiricist and as such will find no difficulty in the idea of casting an ethic of self-sacrifice in a eudaemonist framework, always provided that it is no more than a framework. Holl's charges we have already said are directed against the formal aspects of classical eudaemonism. He does not credit Augustine with any thing so blatant as recommending vice instead of virtue. But what interest, our defender will ask, can a merely formal objection have for the theologian and moralist? If Christ had said that men should deny themselves, and some Christian eudaemonist then proposed that they should seek their own happiness instead, then the point at issue would be clear. The counsel of the disciple would differ substantially from the counsel of the Master. But the eudaemonist has not done this. He has translated the requirement of self-denial out of the language and concepts of "deontology" into the language and concepts of eudaemonism. If he has translated accurately, what matter? Holl wants to make a moral criticism of a "language of ethics," and that simply cannot be done.[28]

Clearly such a defense will be committed to taking a positivist interpretation of the classical *finis bonorum* tradition. The analysis of different moral options in terms of different views of the final good will be seen primarily as a formal framework for posing the questions and marking the disagreements. When Aristotle begins his *Nicomachaean Ethics* with the words, "Every art, every means, every activity and moral choice appear to aspire to some good," he is plainly not pretending (on this interpretation at least) to have identified a definite end, "some good," to which every activity really aspires; for although he says that "the good has been well defined as 'that to which things aspire,'" he must add, "on the other hand, it is plain that they aspire to different things." [29] But neither is he encouraging us to view all activity as activity of one special kind. He is not telling us that every art and every moral choice is, for example, acquisitive. Acquisitive acts are grasping, clinging, seizing; but Aristotle's discovery relates as much to giving, loving, renouncing. In truth there is the world of difference between Aristotle's thesis and, let us say, the Christian doctrine of original sin, which is prepared to contemplate at least as an ideal possibility the thought of an unselfish man in order to argue by contrast that all actual men are selfish. The whole point of Aristotle's thesis is that every conceivable variety of human behavior is included in it. It is a formal structure of analyzing human activity morally, in a way in which we can think of, describe, and compare the choices which confront the human agent as he acts.

Leaving aside for the moment the question of how the classical tradition should be interpreted, let us imagine how Augustine's critics would answer this defense on its own terms. Perhaps they would say something like this: Christ presents self-denial and the selfish pursuit of personal happiness as diametrically opposed; the eudaemonist presents them, certainly, as sharply contrasted, but yet as related under the formal concept of happiness. The critic is disturbed not because the eudaemonist has forgotten the difference between virtue and vice but because after he has made every allowance for the difference there remains a suggestion of residual similarity in that both are conceived to be pursuits of happiness. The defense drew a sharp distinction between the *language* of ethics, which is not susceptible of moral criticism, and the *content*, which is its legitimate object. But does a language not control the content of what is said in it? Certain moral "languages" might invite us to distort or misrepresent the Christian ethic. One way of speaking brings one issue to prominence, another brings another. The eudaemonist formulation of Christ's demand for self-denial robs it of its starkness. By saying the same thing in a less challenging way, it distorts it, so that in the end it is not quite the same thing that has been said. The ultimacy of the demand is lost in the shadow of a purely formal but nevertheless obtrusive idea of happiness.

The defense might well be able to accept a good deal of this case. The critique is directed less against the *morality* of eudaemonist concepts (an idea which it finds difficult to understand) than against their *epistemological efficiency* as a linguistic vehicle for Christian ethics. And by interpreting the critique in this way, the defense might succeed in limiting its scope, so that it does little damage to Augustine. If someone complains that eudaemonism is inefficient, he is bound to say what it is that it is inefficient at doing. Efficiency and inefficiency are measured in relation to a task, and there may be some tasks for which eudaemonist terms are the most efficient tool available. There are times, for example, when it is convenient to refer to a straight line as the circumference of a circle with infinite radius; and the effect of doing this is not to obscure the distinctiveness of a straight line but to illuminate it by showing that no quantifiable increase in radius could ever transform a circle into a straight line. To make a contrast a formal point of comparison is required, and the concept of happiness, by affording such a point, can be a valuable framework for making contrasts. When Augustine, in a famous section of *City of God* XIX, contrasts the Christian understanding of happiness with all the possibilities of classicism, it is clear that he intends not to elide the distinction between Christianity and classicism but to throw it into the sharpest relief. Such considerations should suffice to vindicate the Christian use of eudaemonist categories at least as an occasional possibility, and although a critic may object to an unguarded or unqualified eudaemonism, Augustine, a great deal of whose ethical reflection is in fact cast in a deontological form, cannot reasonably be accused of that.

But the critic is unlikely to consent to being brushed aside so light-
ly. The defense undertook to justify eudaemonism solely in terms
of its being a useful conceptual "tool," and now it has agreed to limit
it by the same criterion. Either way it has avoided any discussion
of the relation of eudaemonist language to reality. Yet how else can
a conceptual tool be "useful" except by its correspondence to
reality? True, if one is arguing against someone who believes that happiness is the supreme goal, one may say (but not without irony!),
"My happiness is to do my duty"; but once the disputant has gone his
way, there is no reason whatever to continue speaking in this way
unless there is a *real relation* between happiness and duty. The "useful-
ness" or "epistemological efficiency" of a "language of ethics" can
be evaluated only by its truthfulness. The critic finds great difficulty
with the distinction between the "justifying" and the "epistemological" role of happiness in moral theory to which we made a reference
in the Introduction. The man who says "Heaven is full of people who
are not particularly concerned with being there" seems to want
things both ways, to believe in an ethic of reward without encouraging
other people to believe in it. Why should he *not* be concerned with
getting to heaven if that is really the goal of human life? What grounds
can there be for discouraging such a "language" for understanding
our duties, unless it be that this "language" is telling us a lie?

In this way the critic makes it plain that his complaint against Augustine is a metaphysical one. He does not believe that a neutral
eudaemonist language is conceivable nor, indeed, that that was what
Augustine intended. Augustine's eudaemonism was meant to be a description of the universe, a characterization of man's moral life in
relation to the wider context of reality in which it was set. Nygren's
description of *agape* and *eros* as "fundamental motifs" plainly means
to suggest that he is criticizing something of the nature of "world-
views," structures of thought more deeply committed to a perception
of reality than mere linguistic convention could ever be.[30] And, of
course, in his assessment of Augustine's own intentions the critic is perfectly correct. As we have seen, the classical tradition is open to a

realist as well as a positivist interpretation, and Augustine's Neoplatonism inclined him to read it that way.[31] The "quest for happiness"
reflects (at least) the teleological thrust by which all creatures are oriented toward their supreme good. The quest is common to all humanity
not by definitional fiat but by virtue of man's status as creature. True,
it accounts for all varieties of human behavior and is not itself one
among other possible varieties; but that is not because it is a merely
formal category but because all human behavior really does take
place within this given metaphysical condition. It is this uncompro-
misingly metaphysical understanding of eudaemonism that the
critique intends to take issue with, and that on the ground that its
understanding of the nature of things is simply false.

However, once the critic has taken the battle onto the metaphysical
field, he is bound to accept the realist interpretation of what Augustine says about man's goal. And (as we observed in chapter one) he
needed the positivist interpretation in order to characterize his
teleology as "egocentric." The force of his charge was that every object
of desire was posited by the subject as desirable for himself; desire,
even of the supreme good, did not involve the subject in genuine confrontation by a reality greater than himself which simply laid claim
upon him. (That seems to be the force of Holl's jibe about divine grace
becoming no more than a "change of taste.") But once the realist
interpretation of the supreme good has been accepted, the charge appears to fall to the ground. Man's goal is an objective reality which
the subject has not chosen for himself and his orientation to which is a
necessity of his creation. Desire itself is understood not simply as an
affect of the subject but as a decisive confrontation between subject and
object. Where, then, is the egocentricity? This defense, common, with
modifications, to most of the scholars who have written on Augustine's
eudaemonism since Nygren, certainly puts the critic in an embarrassing
spot. If he accepts the positivist interpretation of the theory, he is
back on the empiricist's ground, struggling to show that his complaint
is important; if he accepts the realist interpretation, he is on Augustine's
ground, struggling to show that there is anything to find objectionable.

But if the critic is prepared to replace his charge of "egocentricity," a moral objection, with a charge of "anthropocentricity," a metaphysical one, then the fundamental nature of his quarrel with Augustine can emerge clearly. Augustine's picture of the universe shows us one who is the source and goal of being, value, and activity, himself in the center of the universe and at rest; and it shows us the remainder of the universe in constant movement, which, while it may tend toward or away from the center, is yet held in relation to it, so that all other beings lean, in a multiplicity of ways, toward the source and goal of being. But the force which draws these moving galaxies of souls is immanent to them, a kind of dynamic nostalgia rather than a transcendent summons from the center. Such a summons, of course, is presupposed; but it is reflected by this responsive movement which is other than itself, so that there is a real reciprocity between Creator and creature. In the last resort what is at issue is whether all movement in the universe is from the center to the circumference or whether there is also this responsive movement. Here is the nub of the *agape-eros* question for Nygren, who stands in a respectable Protestant theological tradition (though at an extreme point of it) rejecting immanent teleology as inconsistent with the doctrine of Creation.[32]

This issue can be arbitrated no further within the limits of this study. We can simply say that Augustine does believe in immanent teleology and that that is the metaphysical root of his eudaemonist ethics. We can also observe, as we have done, that his epistemological program, *credo ut intelligam*, acts as a barrier against his allowing too much to the immanent force and requires him constantly to invoke the initiating movement of revelation and grace as the immediate and not just the ultimate presupposition of the response. In this context we can allow some validity to the distinction, which was brought into question a moment ago, between the metaphysical justification for the ethical demand and the immediate epistemological access to it. Augustine does not allow that we could infer the whole of our Christian duty by consulting our self-interest, even though the whole of our Christian duty does serve our self-interest. Rather, we are to discover the meaning of self-interest by heeding the voice of authority as it tells us of our Christian duty. Augustine does not think we should be unconcerned with getting to Heaven; but he does not allow us to imagine that our natural ideas of what Heaven is like or how we might reach it will be of any service to us.

Yet even when so cautiously urged, the responsive movement, in the view of the critics, robs those categories which speak of the divine initiative of their force. Talk about God's "love" in particular seems hopelessly debilitated when it is followed in the same breath by talk about man's reciprocal love for God. Something quite different must mark the believer's attitude to God, something so very different indeed that many of Nygren's commentators have found it hard to tell whether he endorses the biblical command to love God at all.[33] It has sometimes been suggested that Nygren has no place for the doctrine of Creation, the ground on which Augustine would assert the continuity and stability of the created subject who is the object of God's grace.[34] It could perhaps be argued that the reverse is the case: He has no room for anything other than the doctrine of Creation, since every movement from the divine center has to be presuppositionless, *ex nihilo*, creative, bringing into existence something quite unprecedented. His rejection of "philosophic eros" is not so much the rejection of Creation as the refusal to presuppose it. Creation is existential, never to be taken as read, never to be regarded as the foundation for subsequent movements, both of initiative and response, which will be differently characterized. When man's conversion is described as a "new creation," the phrase is taken literally.

The heart of the quarrel between Augustine and his critics, then, is whether the creative work of God allows for teleology, and so for a movement within creation, which can presuppose the fact of creation a a given starting point, to a destiny which "fulfills" creation by redeeming it and by lifting it to a new level. It is the meaning of salvation that is at stake: is it "fulfillment," "recapitualtion"? If this is indeed the authentic Christian understanding of what God has done in Christ, then Augustine's critics will have to face this implication: Between that which is and that which will be there must be a line of connection, the redemptive purpose of God. We cannot simply say that *agape* has no presuppositions, for God presupposes that which he himself has already given in *agape*. However dramatic a transformation redemption may involve, however opaque to man's mind the continuity may be, we know, and whenever we repeat the Trinitarian creed with Saint Augustine we confess that our being-as-we-are and our being-as-we-shall-be are held together as works of the One God who is both our Creator and Redeemer.

NOTES

ABBREVIATIONS

For the full titles of works by Augustine and other ancient writers abbreviated in the Notes the reader is referred to the Index of Passages Cited. Apart from these the following abbreviations are used:

A.M.   *Augustinus Magister.* Congrès international augustinien. 3 vols. Paris, 1954.

B.A.   *Bibliothèque Augustinienne: Oeuvres de Saint Augustin.* Paris, 1933–.

C.C.C.M.   *Corpus Christianorum Continuatio Mediaevalis.* Turnhout, 1966–.

C.C.S.L.   *Corpus Christianorum Series Latina.* Turnhout, 1953–.

C.S.E.L.   *Corpus Scriptorum Ecclesiasticorum Latinorum.* Vienna, 1866–.

M.A.   *Miscellanea Agostiniana.* 2 vols. Rome, 1930–31.

P.G.   *Patrologiae Cursus Completus Series Graeca.* Edited by J.-P. Migne. Paris, 1857–.

P.L.   *Patrologiae Cursus Completus Series Latina.* Edited by J.-P. Migne. Paris, 1844–.

P.L.S.   *Patrologiae Cursus Completus Series Latina Supplementum.* Edited by A. Hamman. 4 vols. Paris, 1958–67.

R.A.   *Recherches Augustiniennes* 1– (1958–). Paris.

R.E.A.   *Révue des Etudes Augustiniennes* 1– (1955–). Paris.

R.G.G.   *Die Religion in Geschichte und Gegenwart.* 3rd. ed., 6 vols. & index. Tübingen, 1957–65.

S.C.   *Sources Chrétiennes.* Paris, 1942–.

NOTES TO INTRODUCTION

1. The two key scriptural texts: Mark 12:31 (= Matt. 19:19, 22: 39, Luke 10:27, Rom. 13:9, Gal. 5:14, James 2:8 in the New Testament; = Lev. 19:18,34 in the Old) and Mark 8:35 (= Matt. 16:25, Luke 9:24; cf. Matt. 10:39, Luke 17:33, John 12:25). Other texts in

the Bible relevant to the subject are 2 Tim. 3:2, "Men will be lovers of self, lovers of money" (on the usually negative word φίλαυτος see below), also such *sententiae* of the Wisdom books as Prov. 15:32, 19:8, Ecclus. 14:5. Vagaries of translation sometimes created spurious allusions to love and hate of one's own soul: see p. 44 below for Augustine's use of Ps. 10 (11):6 in this sense.

2. Thomas Aquinas, *Summa theologica* II–II.25.7: "Self-love is in one way common to all, in another way proper to good men, in another proper to evil men." John Calvin, *Institutes* III.7.4; Joseph Butler, *Works*, 2 vols., ed. W. E. Gladstone (Oxford, 1896), 2:26; Søren Kierkegaard, *Works of Love*, trans. Howard Hong and Edna Hong (New York, 1962), p. 39.

3. Three different evaluations of self-love in Augustine are correctly recognized by John Burnaby (*Amor Dei* [London, 1938], p. 117), Anders Nygren (*Agape and Eros*, rev. ed., trans. Philip S. Watson, p. 548), against Hannah Arendt (*Der Liebesbegriff bei Augustin* [Berlin, 1929], p. 25) and Gunnar Hultgren (*Le Commandement d'Amour chez Augustin* [Paris 1939], p. 157), who suppose tw

4. In what follows we are dependent on Irenée Hausherr, S. I., *Philautie, de la tendresse pour soi à la charité selon Saint Maxime le Confesseur*, Orientalia Christiana Analecta cxxxvii (Rome, 1952), pp. 1–41.

5. Cicero, *Ad Att. Ep.* XIII.13 (=Sh.-B. 321).1 is no exception to the rule that φιλαυτία is negative in tone, despite the ninth edition of Liddell & Scott's lexicon (1932B) and the translation of D. R. Shackleton-Bailey (*Cicero's Letters to Atticus*, 7 vols. [Cambridge, 1965–70], 5:203, who renders it "amour propre." For the use of the word in Philo, see Jean Daniélou, *Philon d'Alexandrie* (Paris, 1958), pp. 175–81.

6. Nor can the positive sense have been important even to Maximus, as Hausherr (*Philautie*, p. 49f.) has only one text to illustrate it (*P. G.* xc.260c). For other instances of the word before Maximus, see Hausherr, *Philautie*, pp. 25–41; also G. W. H. Lampe, *Patristic Greek Lexicon* (Oxford, 1961), p. 1476.

7. Plato, *Leges* 731e; Aristotle, *Eth. Eud.* 1240ab; *Eth. Nic.* 1168ab. It is noticeable that the author of the Pseudo-Aristotelian

Magna Moralia (1212b) is more jealous for common usage than the authentic Aristotle.

8. *Thesaurus Linguae Latinae* (Leipzig, 1900–) has a special entry for *se amare* (I.1954) and another for *amor sui* (1969) but makes no such provision for *se diligere* (but see V (1).1178) or *dilectio sui*. Neither this work nor the new *Oxford Latin Dictionary* (Oxford, 1968–) makes adequate use of Christian Latin.

9. Hence the epithet *caecus* at Horatius, *Carm.* I.18.14. Cicero *(De leg.* I.12.34) describes it as an apparently incredible but nevertheless possible feat to love others no less than one loves himself. Cf. also Cicero, *De har. resp. or.* 9.19.

10. Cicero, *Lael.* 21.80: "Ipse enim se quisque diligit, non ut aliquam a se ipse mercedem exigat caritatis suae, sed quod per se sibi quisque carus est. Quod nisi idem in amicitiam transferetur, verus amicus numquam reperietur: est enim is, qui est tamquam alter idem." 26.98: "Omnino est amans sui virtus: optime enim se ipsa novit quamque amabilis sit intelligit." For the view that Cicero draws on a lost work of Theophrastus see L. Laurand's introduction to the Budé text (Paris, 1942), pp. vff.

11. Cicero, *De fin.* III.18.59: "Ex quo intellegitur quoniam se ipsi omnes natura diligant, tam insipientem quam sapientem sumpturum quae secundum naturam sint reiecturumque contraria. Ita est quoddam commune officium sapientis et insipientis; ex quo efficitur versari in iis quae media dicamus." Seneca, *De benef.* IV.17.2: "Quemadmodum nemo in amorem sui cohortandus est, quem a momento, dum nascitur, trahit, ita ne ad hoc quidem, ut honesta per se petat . . ."; *Ep.* 82.15: "Mors inter illa est quae mala quidem non sunt, tamen habent mali speciem: sui amor est et permanendi conservandique se insita voluntas atque aspernatio dissolutionis . . . "; *Ep.* 109.16: "Hoc illis evenit quos amor sui excaecat quibusque dispectum utilitatis timor in periculis excutit." Cf. also *Dial.* IV.31.3, X.14.5; *Nat. quaest.* I.17.6; *Ep.* 36.8. Further comment in Armand Pittet, *Vocabulaire Philosophique de Sénèque*, vol. 1 [Paris, 1937], pp.89f., 156f.

12. Rufinus, *P. L.* ciii.540ab; Clement of Alexandria, *Quis dives* 29 (*P. G.* ix.633d); Origen, *In Cant.*, prooem. (*P. G.* xiii.70a); Gregory

of Nyssa, *In Cant. hom.* 4 (*P. G.* xlvi.845); *Ep. Barn.* 19.5 (*P. G.* ii. 777b). Note also Tertullian, *Adv. Iud.* 2.3f. (*C.C.S.L.* ii.1341f.), where the neighbor is apparently taken to be the self. Other Latin texts in H. Petré, *Caritas* (Louvain, 1948), pp. 141–60. The general lack of interest in the phrase "as yourself" is illustrated by Ambrosiaster, who comments on Romans 13:9 and Galatians 5:14 without remarking on it (*C.S.E.L.* lxxxi (1).424f., (3).56, 58). Cf. also Marius Victorinus, *Comm. in Ep. Paul. ad Gal.* 1191d–92a.

13. Recent proposals to abandon talk of self-love altogether have come from Karl Barth (*Church Dogmatics*, I/2, trans. G. T. Thomson and Harold Knight [Edinburgh, 1956], p. 387f.)—but ambiguously, as if unable to make up his mind whether self-love is nonsense or sin—and Paul Tillich (*Love, Power and Justice* [New York & London, 1954], p. 6).

14. See T. M. De Ferrari, *The Problem of Charity for Self, A Study of Thomistic and Modern Theological Discussion* (Washington, D. C., 1962).

15. See Percival M. Symonds, *Dynamic Psychology* (New York, 1949), pp. 339f.

16. See, for example, the approach of Irving Singer, *The Nature of Love, Plato to Luther* (New York, 1966).

17. Gérard Gilleman, *Le Primat de la Charité en Théologie Morale* (Brussels & Paris, 1952), p. 142.

18. Sigmund Freud, *The Complete Psychological Works*, trans. James Strachey, vol. 22 (London, 1964), p. 58: "The ego can take itself as an object, can treat itself like other objects, can observe itself, criticize itself, and do Heaven knows what with itself. In this, one part of the ego is setting itself over against the rest. So the ego can be split. . . ."

19. Percival M. Symonds, *The Ego and the Self* (New York, 1951), pp. 4, 74. Much of the recent theological writing on self-love has been prompted by the challenge of "dynamic psychology," especially by the undisguised hostility of Erich Fromm toward world-denying Christianity (see, for example, *Man for Himself* [London, 1949], pp. 119ff.). Responses range from a stout refusal to be impressed (e.g., Reinhold Niebuhr, *Faith and History* [London, 1949], p. 201) to a cautious acceptance (e.g., Tillich, *Love, Power and Justice*, p. 119),

and even to wholehearted appropriation of psychological categories into a Neo-Thomist framework (Paul E. Staes, C.I.C.M., *Positive Self-Regard and Authentic Morality* [Manila, 1972]).

20. Keith Ward, *Ethics and Christianity* (London & New York, 1970), p. 252. Compare the positions of Kenneth E. Kirk (*The Vision of God* [London & New York, 1931], p. 144) and Karl Barth (*Church Dogmatics*, IV/2, trans. G. W. Bromiley and T. F. Torrance [Edinburgh, 1958], p. 750). This position begins to look grotesque if it is suggested that the agent must necessarily forget, or even be unaware of, the fact that what is virtuous is also rewarding; but this exaggeration is not necessary.

21. It is one of the great virtues of the most adequate analysis of the idea of self-love to date, that of Gene Outka's recent study, *Agape* (New Haven & London, 1972), pp. 55–74, 221–29, 285–91, that the theological and the philosophical considerations are brought together and allowed to illuminate each other. Outka's distinction of four categories, however, is not entirely persuasive. His categories are: "wholly nefarious," "normal, reasonable, prudent," "justified derivatively," and "definite obligation." In criticism of this, two points can be made. First, "derivative justification" is a closer relation than Outka supposes to the view that self-love is "wholly nefarious," since, by confining the scope of proper self-concern entirely to the service of other-regard, it effectively discounts the significance of self-love as a principle of ethical guidance. Secondly, self-love as "normal, reasonable, prudent" is made to include far too wide a selection of views: At one end of the spectrum there is Bultmann's assertion that "it is the attitude of the natural man which must be overcome" (a candidate for the "wholly nefarious" group, despite Outka's palliating exegesis of it, p. 64); at the other is Niebuhr's acceptance of "epiphenomenal" self-love, the view that "self-giving is bound to contribute ultimately to self-realisation." This, as we have argued, is a special case of self-love as ultimate value; but Outka has not admitted a category of ultimate value other than "definite obligation." That the *summum bonum* is not exhaustively accounted for in terms of our obligations is, perhaps, one of the points Augustine might make to Gene Outka if he had the opportunity! Outka's task has certainly been made difficult for him by his sources, mainly twentieth-century

theologians, to whom he shows a staunch loyalty. Unfortunately one cannot assume that every theologian is attempting to be consistent in his use of this slippery phrase.

NOTES TO CHAPTER ONE

1. See Anders Nygren, *Agape and Eros*, pt. II, chap. 2, "The Caritas Synthesis," trans. Philip S. Watson, pp. 449–562. This work, originally published in two parts (1930, 1936, in Swedish), will be referred to in the revised edition of the English translation (London, 1953). The extraordinary influence of Nygren's interpretation of Augustine is due not only to the charm of his writing and the alluring simplicity of his thesis but to the real enjoyment of Augustine which communicates itself even to those who find his reading tendentious. His influence is detectable in the writing of Reinhold Niebuhr and Karl Barth as well as in numerous standard theological works. He has provoked a number of full-length refutations, some of them, such as that of John Burnaby (*Amor Dei* [London, 1938]), works of great distinction in their own right. The present state of critical reaction to Nygren's work may be judged from a recent volume, *The Philosophy and Theology of Anders Nygren*, ed. Charles W. Kegley (London & Amsterdam, 1970), in which articles by John M. Rist, John Burnaby, and Rudolf Johannesson are directly relevant to our theme.

2. Nygren, *Agape and Eros*, p. 557 and n. 3.

3. A refusal to adopt the "philological orientation" has been defended at length by Victor Paul Furnish (*The Love-Command in the New Testament* [London, 1973], pp. 219–31). But nobody could accuse the most valuable philological study which has appeared in this field, Hélène Petré's *Caritas* (Louvain, 1948), of making the mistake which we are anxious to avoid. Indeed, it is just because Petré's book is so thoroughly philological that it alerts us to all the extraneous influences which must enter the picture to confound an oversimple philosophical semantics. We are taught by her to ask, "What version of the Bible has our author been using?" "Does his usage in the matter of verbs correspond to his usage in the matter of nouns?" "How much is he affected by secular philosophical usage?" "What is vulgar and what is literary in the language of his day?" and so on.

4. *De div. quaest. 83* 35.2; *Enarr. in Psa.* 9.15; *In I Ep. Ioh. tract.* 8.5.

5. *De div. quaest. 83* 36.1; *Enarr. in Psa.* 31(2).5.

6. *De civ. Dei* XIV.7.2; *In Ioh. Ev. tract.* 123.5 In both instances Augustine is discussing scriptural usage.

7. *De div. quaest. 83* 36.1; *Enarr. in Psa.* 31(2).5; *De pat.* 17.14.

8. *De civ. Dei* XIV.7.2 This passage has been misunderstood by Nygren (*Agape and Eros*, p. 558) and others to mean that Augustine's use of *amor* is derived from philosophical usage. In fact Augustine mentions the philosophers merely to demonstrate that a favorable sense of *amor* is not a peculiarity of Christian Latin.

9. Nygren, *Agape and Eros*, pp. 34, 451f.

10. See, for example, M. C. D'Arcy, *The Mind and Heart of Love* (London, 1946), p. 73: "The two keep reappearing, but they are so interwoven that we have to use the greatest care in disentangling them. . . . To have issue they have to commingle."

11. This position is represented by Paul Ramsey (*Nine Modern Moralists* [Englewood Cliffs, 1962], p. 135): "Love is just love, the genuine article, for which perhaps one univocal word should be reserved."

12. Nygren, *Agape and Eros*, p. 210.

13. Gunnar Hultgren, *Le Commandement d'Amour chez Augustin* (Paris, 1939), pp. 49ff. Among Nygren's critics Hultgren has been put somewhat in the shade by the contemporary work of Burnaby and the later contribution of Ragnar Holte, and it is true that he has neither the warmth of the one nor the impressive classical scholarship of the other. But it is not a negligible achievement to have focussed the issues clearly (more clearly than Burnaby) and to have exercised sound judgment on them (sounder than Holte). Hultgren's claim on our gratitude is simply that he has been more often right than anybody else.

14. Rudolf Johannesson, *Person och Gemenskap* (Stockholm, 1947); Ragnar Holte, *Béatitude et Sagesse* (Paris & Worcester, Mass., 1962). Holte's contribution is deservedly celebrated for its resourceful use of scholarship in classical philosophy and for its sustained virtuosity in the presentation of a thesis about Augustine's teleological thought. This thesis, however, appears to me to be less and less

convincing the more it is compared with the text. Some detailed disagreements will emerge in the course of the discussion.

15. Holte, *Béatitude et Sagesse*, pp. 222ff. See also pp. 207ff.

16. *De civ. Dei* XI.16, translation adapted from that of Henry Bet-
tenson in *Augustine: City of God*, ed. David Knowles (Harmonds-
worth 1972). This passage invites comparison with Basil, *Contra
Eunomium* I.20, where we find a very similar distinction between
τάξις φυσική and τάξις κατ᾽ ἐπιτήδευσιν. The parallel is striking enough
to suggest dependence, particularly in view of Augustine's earlier in-
ability to formulate this dintinction.

17. The final sentence of XI.16 is very difficult to understand:
"Sed tantum valet in naturis rationalibus quoddam veluti pondus voluntatis et amoris, ut cum ordine naturae angeli hominibus, tamen lege
iustitiae boni homines malis angelis praeferantur." Is the "weight of will
and love" in the object, so that beings are carried, as it were, from
their original position upward or downward in the order of things? Or
is it in the observer, who may properly superimpose moral judgments,
the inclinations of his love, on top of his rational judgments about
natural worth?

18. *De mag.* 9.25; cf. *De div. quaest. 83* 30.

19. *De mus.* I.6.12; cf. *De mag.* 9.25, *De div. quaest. 83* 35.1.

20. We are not told in so many words that what so struck the young
Augustine when he read Cicero's *Hortensius* (*Conf.* III.4.7) was the
argument beginning with the eudaemonist premise "Beati certe omnes
esse volumus," about which we know from *De Trin.* XIII.4.7, but
the inference is irresistible. Cicero has a similar argument at *De finibus*
V.29.86 (where a small and probable textual emendation attributes
it to Theophrastus, probably the exordium of his περὶ εὐδαιμονίας;
see commentary of J. N. Madvig, 3d ed. (Hanover, 1876), ad loc.),
where the eudaemonist premise appears together with the claim
that the whole function of moral philosophy is to point to happiness
(cf. Augustine, *De civ. Dei* VIII.3, XIX.1.1., *Sermo* 241.6). Augustine held to the eudaemonist premise with complete firmness
throughout his writing career, from his first work to his last. The following list of references, doubtless incomplete, conveys an impression
of its importance: *C. Acad.* I.2.5; *De beat. vit.* 2.10; *De mor. eccl.*
3.4; *De lib. arb.* I.14.30, II.9.26, 10.28f.; *De mag.* 14.46; *Conf.* X.20.

29–23.33; *De Trin.* XIII.3.6–8.11, 20.25, XV.12.21; *De civ. Dei*
X.1.1.; *Ench.* 28.105; *Retr.* I.25.36; *C. Iul. op. imp.* VI. 26; *Ep.* 130.
4.9, 155.2.6; *Enarr. in Psa.* 32(2) .s2.15, 118.s1.1.

21. The ambiguity in classical eudaemonism can be well seen in
Cicero, *De finibus* II.27.86; "Quoniam igitur omnis summa philoso-
phiae ad beate vivendum refertur, idque unum expetentes homines se
ad hoc studium contulerunt, beate autem vivere alii in alio, vos in
voluptate ponitis, item contra miseriam omnem in dolore, id primum
videamus, beate vivere vestrum quale sit." There is no doubt that
there is one thing that everyone is searching for, and each school believes it can persuasively be characterized in a way that will support
its own identification. At the same time the different schools are
offering more than rival *theories*. The verb *ponere* does not simply
mean to "suppose." These are rival *programs* for happy living ("o
praeclaram beate vivendi . . . viam! I.18.58), each of which promises
its adherent the goal he seeks (V.29.87), and the disagreements
among them (such as the disagreement about the virtuous man in the
bull of Phalaris) are disagreements about what happiness is.

22. *De mor. eccl.* 3.4; cf. *De civ. Dei* XIX.4, *Ep.* 118.3.14ff.

23. In *Ep.* 118.3.13 Augustine defines the question "ubi sit finis
boni" in a realist way as "ubi constitutum sit, non prava opinione
atque temeraria sed certa atque inconcussa veritate, summum hominis
bonum." Again at *De Trin.* XIII.5.8 he rejects the positivist interpretation of the eudaemonist premise as a way of getting out of the
difficulty it posed about the opacity of the identification of the
happy life: "An forte illud est quod nos ab his angustiis possit eruere,
ut quoniam diximus ibi quosque possuisse beatam vitam quod eos
maxime delectavit, ut voluptas Epicurum, virtus Zenonem, sic alium
aliquid aliud, nihil dicamus esse beate vivere nisi vivere secundum
delectationem suam, et ideo falsum non esse quod omnes beate vivere
velint, quia omnes ita volunt ut quemque delectat?" But at *De civ.
Dei* X.3.2 God is a "finis appetitionis" that we are to *choose* ("hunc
eligentes"), and at XIX.1.1 the discussion of the ends of the two
cities is introduced with a purely formal definition of the *finis boni*
as "illud . . . propter quod appetenda sunt cetera, ipsum autem
propter seipsum" which will apply equally to the theories of all schools.

24. Augustine was always ready to move fairly easily between

saying that God himself was the blessed life and that it was a state of
the subject in relation to God (as for example at *Conf.* X.20.29, "cum
enim te . . . quaero, vitam beatam quaero" and 22.32, "est ipsa beata
vita, gaudere ad te, de te, propter te"). In writing *De Trinitate* he
found it necessary to distinguish rather more carefully the state of the
soul in blessedness from the source of the blessedness, as his theory
of the *imago Dei* depended on it. In *De civitate Dei* IV.23 he makes a
rather teasing use of the eudaemonist principle in arguing that the
Romans ought to have made Felicitas their sole goddess, but then,
somewhat anxiously perhaps, covers himself by insisting that happiness
is, after all, only a *gift* of the true God. In X.3.2 there is evidence
of confusion: "bonum nostrum" (!) is expressed in terms of a state,
"illi cohaerere," but then he proceeds as though he had just said
"Deus": "hoc bonum diligere in toto corde, in tota anima et in tota
virtute praecipimur." In the formal presentation of Christian teleology in XIX, however, the *finis* is always presented as a state of the
subject: "pax in vita aeterna" (11), "societas fruendi Deo" (17).

25. *Ep.* 137.5.17.
26. The saying τὸ ὅμοιον τῷ ὁμοίῳ ἀνάγκη ἀεὶ φίλον εἶναι was
already known to Plato from the cosmological writing of his
predecessors (*Lysis* 214b; cf. *Gorgias* 510b). Augustine has a version
of the saying at *Sermo* 15.2: "similis simili cohaeret, dissimilis
dissimilem refugit."
27. *De civ. Dei* XIX.12.
28. Ibid., XI.28.
29. *Conf.* XIII.9.10. Cf. *De Trin.* XI.11.18, also *Enarr. in Psa.* 29(2)
10, *Ep.* 55.10.18. A quotation from Vergil, *Ecl.* 2.65, "trahit sua
quemque voluptas" came conveniently to hand: God "draws" men to
himself by delighting them (*In Ioh. Ev. tract.* 26.4).
30. *Enarr. in Psa.* 121.1.
31. *De lib. arb.* III.1.2.
32. *Sermo* 336.1
33. Innumerable references to "rest in God" include Augustine's
most quoted saying at *Conf.* I.1.1. The soul's rest is connected often
with God's sabbath rest on the seventh day of creation; see, for
example, *De Gen. c. Man.* I.22.34, *De cat. rud.* 17.28, *De civ. Dei* XI.8,
Ep. 55.10.19.

34. *De pecc. mer. et rem.* I.10.11; *Enarr. in Psa.* 30(2) .sl.10. Cf.
De ord. II.18.48.

35. *De Gen. ad lit.* I.7.13, "egenus atque indigus amor"; *Sermo*
68.10, "amando sitis"; *De beat. vit.* 4.35, "sitiamus"; *Enarr. in Psa.*
29(1).5, "totum hoc medium tempus desiderio vestro longum."

36. Holte, *Béatitude et sagesse,* p. 199.

37. *De doctr. Christ.* I.36.40 (the essential meaning of Scripture);
Enarr. in Psa. 149.5, *Sermo* 68.13 (two wings); *Enarr. in Psa.* 33.s2.10
(two feet); *Quaest. Ev.* II.19, *Enarr. in Psa.* 125.15 (two pence); *De
doctr. Christ.* II.6.7, *Ep.* 149.1.4, *Sermo* 313B.3 (two lambs, cf. Cant.
4:2).

38. *Sermo* 65A, *Conf.* X.29.40; cf. *Enarr. in Psa.* 55.17, "illum
ergo sic diligamus, ut aliud praeter ipsum non diligatur." See Outka's
discussion of this question, *Agape,* pp. 214–20.

39. *Ep. ad Gal. exp.* 19.

40. *Sol.* I.2.7: "Et homines sunt, et eos amo, non eo quod ani-
malia, sed eo quod homines sunt; id est, ex eo quod rationales animas
habent." At *De mus.* VI.14.46 Augustine adapts the two-fold command
to suit this conception: "socias autem animas tamquam seipsam."
For "God and the soul," see also *De ord.* II.7.24, *Sol.* I.9.16, *De util.
cred.* 16.34, *De div. quaest. 83* 36.1.

41. At *Sol.* I.12.20 personified Reason forces Augustine to concede the possibility of irresoluble conflict between friendship and the
quest for God. Various phrases show Augustine attempting to unify
the two commands: love of neighbor is a "step" (*De mor. eccl.* 26.48,
C. Adim. 6) toward or a "cradle" for (*De mor. eccl.* 26.50) the love
of God. But perhaps nothing illustrates the difficulty so well as the
structure of *De moribus ecclesiae,* in which, after a lengthy demon-
stration that God is the sole *summum bonum* and alone to be
loved (3.4–14.24), Augustine suddenly and late in the day introduces
the neighbor as a second object of love (25.46–29.61), making no
attempt to show how this can be reconciled with the strictly theo-
centric orientation of the opening.

42. Augustine notes this problem in commenting on *De div. quaest.
83* 36.1 in *Retr.* I.25.37: " Quod si verum est, quomodo apostolus
ait: 'nemo umquam carnem suam odio habuit'?"

43. Holte's interpretation of Augustine's teleology, which has

no place for the positivist aspect, leads him to seek alternative understandings of *appetitus* (as a translation of Stoic ὁρμή cf. *De civ. Dei*
XIX.4.2, pp. 33, 201) and *habere* (as Platonic μέθεξις, pp. 216 ff.)
But the sense of these terms must be taken from their normal eudaemonist context, which is perfectly clear in such a passage as *De mor.
eccl.* 3.4: "Nam et qui appetit quod adipisci non potest, cruciatur; et
qui adeptus est quod appetendum non est, fallitur; et qui non appetit quod adipiscendum esset, aegrotat. . . . Quartum restat, ut video,
ubi beata vita inveniri queat, cum id quod est hominis optimum et
amatur et habetur."

44. There appears to be no classical example between Plato's *Lysis*
219c and Augustine's *De moribus ecclesiae* of the verb "to love"
being used in the context of the pursuit of ends and means. When he
says (*De div. quaest. 83* 35.1), "Nihil enim aliud est amare, quam
propter se ipsam rem aliquam appetere," his readers must have found
the combination of ideas as unsettling as we do. But he immediately
parallels it with something more familiar, the "cosmic" aspect of love
as motion: "Deinde cum amor motus quidam sit, neque ullus sit
motus nisi ad aliquid. . . ."

45. The idea is normally held to have had its genesis in Plato's
Republic, where there are distinguished three kinds of good, that
which we welcome for its own sake, that which we welcome both for
its own sake and for the sake of its consequences, and that which
we welcome for its consequences alone (357b). Plato regarded the
second of these as the highest kind of good, but Aristotle (*Eth. Nic.*
1094a) held the view that the highest good was that which we wish
for its own sake and not for anything consequent upon it, thus incor-
porating it into the psychological teleology that was to characterize
the Peripatetic tradition. In fact Aristotle's answer had been antici-
pated earlier by Plato (*Lysis* 219c), who, however, developed his
teleological thought in a different direction, toward the cosmic eros
of the *Symposium* and *Phaedrus*.

46. Cf. *De mus.* VI.14.46: "Tenet ordinem seipsa tota diligens
quod supra se est, id est Deum, socias autem animas tamquam seipsam. Hac quippe dilectionis virtute inferiora ordinat, nec ab infer-
ioribus sordidatur. . . . Quapropter quicumque de nostra quoque
poenali mortalitate numeri facti sunt, non eos abdicemus a fabricatione

divinae providentiae . . . neque amemus eos, ut quasi perfruendo tali-
bus beati efficiamur. His etenim, quoniam temporales sunt, tamquam
tabula in fluctibus, neque abiciendo quasi onerosos, neque amplec-
tendo quasi fundatos, sed bene utendo carebimus." *De mor. eccl.*
20.37: "Amandus igitur solus Deus est: omnis vero iste mundus, id est
omnia sensibilia contemnenda; utendum autem his ad huius vitae
necessitatem." *De lib. arb.* I.15.33: "Cum igitur eisdem rebus alius
male, alius bene utatur; et is quidem qui male, amore his inhaereat
atque implicatur, scilicet subditus eis rebus quas ei subditas esse
oportebat, et ea bona sibi constituens, quibus ordinandis beneque trac-
tandis ipse esse utique deberet bonum. . . ."

47. *De ver. rel.* 47.91: "Hic vir quamdiu est in hac vita, utitur
amico ad rependendam gratiam, utitur inimico ad patientiam, utitur
quibus potest ad beneficentiam, utitur omnibus ad benevolentiam.
Et quamquam temporalia non diligat, ipse recte utitur temporalibus,
et pro eorum sorte hominibus consulit. . . ."

48. The first appearance of the pair will either be *Enarr. in Psa.* 4.8
(dated 392 by S. Zarb; see *C. C. S. L.* xxxviii, pp. xv–xviii) or *De
div. quaest. 83* 30, perhaps written some time before the collection of
the questions in 394. Holte (p. 201) attaches too much weight to the
equivalence Augustine here claims with the Stoic pair *honestum–utile.*
Each term of the pair *usus–fruitio* had already achieved its sense
independently of the other before Augustine hit upon the idea of
using them together.

49. *De div. quaest. 83* 30: "Perfecta igitur hominis ratio quae
virtus vocatur, utitur primo se ipsa ad intelligendum Deum ut eo frua-
tur a quo etiam facta est. Utitur autem caeteris rationalibus animan-
tibus ad societatem, irrationalibus ad eminentiam."

50. See p. 41 below.

51. He often prefers to speak of a false choice of end as *wishing* to
enjoy something other than God (*De Gen. c. Man.* II.9.12, *De lib.
arb.* III.25.76) and of a choice of means to such an end as "abuse"
rather than "use" (*De div. quaest. 83* 30, *De doctr. Christ.* I.4.4).

52. Holte, *Béatitude et Sagesse*, p. 200.

53. The apparent exceptions to this are those that arise from the
wider sense of the verb "uti," which simply means "to have dealings
with" someone. Thus in *De Trin.* X.11.17 "to use" is simply to "bring

into the faculty of the will," and "enjoyment" is a special case of "use." But Augustine is quite clear that this is a different meaning of the two terms from that which they have in the pair, *usus–fruitio*. This is stated unambiguously at *De civ. Dei* XI.25. Until the recent edition of *Sermo* 65A by R. Etaix (*Révue Bénédictine* 86 (1976): 38–48) there was no comparable instance either of the verb "uti" expressing God's love for man. This sermon now affords the only parallel to *De doctr. Christ.* I on this point, and should accordingly be dated to 397 or 398. P. -P. Verbraken's arguments for a later date (Etaix, p. 40) are insubstantial.

54. Burnaby's remark has proved influential (*Amor Dei*, p. 18): "Eros and Agape are not the only Greek words for Love. The Philia in which Aristotle discovered the richest endowment of human personality is strange neither to the Old Testament nor to the New. It differs both from Eros and from Agape in being a mutual relation, a bond which links two centres of consciousness in one." In fact the Aristotelian tradition of discussing friendship, which reached Augustine through Cicero's *Laelius*, had two aspects, *iudicium* and *benevolentia* (Aristotle, *Eth. Nic.* 1155b, Cicero, *Lael.* 9.32). These two roughly correspond to the rational love and benevolent love which we trace in Augustine's thought.

55. *Sermo* 284.3.

56. *Sermo* 159.3. On *delectatio* see Burnaby, *Amor Dei*, pp. 219ff.

57. *De spir. et lit.* 36.64: "quanto maior notitia tanto erit maior dilectio."

58. *Ep.* 45.1.

59. *C. Faust.* XXII.78; *De nupt. et conc.* I.18.20; cf. *In Ioh. Ev. tract.* 32.2, *Sermo* 281.2.

60. *C. Faust.* XIX.24.

61. *Enarr. in Psa.* 138.28, 139.2.

62. *Sermo* 105A.2; cf. *In I Ep. Ioh. tract.* 7.11.

63. *Sol.* I.2.7.

64. *De serm. Dom. in mont.* I.15.41.

65. *Sermo* 335I.5; cf. *Ad Simp.* I.2.8.

66. Cf. *Ep.* 153.5.14, *Enarr. in Psa.* 47.4, *In Ioh. Ev. tract.* 65.2, *Sermo* 335I.5.

67. *C. mend.* 6.15; *De ver. rel.* 46.89.

68. See A. -M. la Bonnadière, "Le Cantique des Cantiques dans S. Augustin," *R. E. A.* 1 (1955): 225–37, who lists five occurrences of the text, to which two more must be added: *De civ. Dei* XX.21 and the then unpublished *Sermo* 65A. In 1955 la Bonnadière dated all occurrences to 410 and afterward, but her date for *Sermo* #37 has since been revised to 397 (P. -P. Verbraken, *Etudes Critiques sur les Sermons Authentiques de Saint Augustin* [Bruges & The Hague, 1976], p. 62) in keeping with Lambot's conjecture. On the date of *Sermo* 65A see n. 53 above.

69. *De civ. Dei* XV.22.

70. *Enarr. in Psa.* 43.16, *Conf.* IV.7.12; cf. *In I Ep. Ioh. tract.* 2.11. The text Matthew 10:37, "He who loves father or mother more than me . . ." is used in a comparable way at *Sermo* 344.2, 349.7.

71. *Enarr. in Psa.* 85.8, "tamquam Deum"; *De doctr. Christ.* I.27. 28, "in quantum peccator est . . . in quantum homo est."

72. *In Ioh. Ev. tract* 32.2. Here as often Augustine regards the desire to live as an expression of love for the soul, while licentiousness is an expression of love for the body. Cf. p. 51 below.

73. *De cat. rud.* 7.11: "sed et se ipsum et nos et quoscumque alios diligit amicos, in illo et propter illum diligat"; *Sermo* 336.2: "Ipsum amemus propter ipsum, et nos in ipso, tamen propter ipsum. Ille enim veraciter amat amicum, qui Deum amat in amico, aut quia est in illo, aut ut sit in illo."

74. *In Ioh. Ev. tract.* 6.1: "nam volumus amari a vobis, sed nolumus in nobis. Quia ergo in Christo vos amamus, in Christo nos redamate, et amor noster pro invicem gemat ad Deum." At *Sermo* 349.7 the phrase "secundum Christum amare" is explained, "non in eis nisi Christum diligatis, et oderitis in vestris si Christum habere noluerint." Cf. *Sermo* 229N.3. Christ's love for man is also said to be love of "God in us," *In Ioh. Ev. tract.* 65.2. On the classical ancestry of the idea of loving "God in" someone, i.e., the divine element, the mind, see Pierre Courcelle, *Connais-toi Toi-même* (Paris, 1974), pp. 28–38.

75. *Ep.* 130.6.13: "In his itaque omnibus incolumitas hominis et amicitia propter se ipsa appetuntur; sufficientia vero rerum necessariarum non propter se ipsam . . . 7.14. Deum igitur diligimus per se ipsum, et nos ac proximos propter ipsum."

76. *In I Ep. Ioh. tract.* 8.5.

77. *De ver. rel.* 47.91, e.g., quoted n. 47 above.

78. *De civ. Dei* XIX.14, XXI.26.4, *De serm. Dom. in mont.*
II.12.43, *De doctr. Christ.* I.22.21, *Sermo* 348.2.

79. *De Trin.* VIII.6.9 (cf. IX.6.11); *De cat. rud.* 27.55 (cf. *Ep.*
153.5.14).

80. *In Ioh. Ev. tract.* 83.3.

81. *De serm. Dom. in mont.* II.12.43.

82. *De Trin.* VIII.6.9; *Sermo* 336.2; *In Ioh. Ev. tract.* 65.2; cf.
De cat. rud. 25.49, 27.55.

NOTES TO CHAPTER TWO

1. *Ep.* 130.7.14.

2. *Sermo* 348.2. Cf. *De fid. et op.* 16.27, *Ep.* 177.10, *Enarr. in
Psa.* 118.s27.6, *In Ioh. Ev. tract.* 123.5, *Sermo* 35.2, 301A.6.

3. *Ep.* 155.4.15; cf. *Enarr. in Psa.* 118.s27.6.

4. *C. Adim.* 20.2, *De cat. rud.* 27.55, *De spir. et lit.* 25.42, *Enarr.
in Psa.* 26(1).8, 32(2).s2.16, 34.sl.12, 43.16, 53.10, 55.17, 72.32,
118.s11.6, 134.11, *Sermo* 2.4, 19.5, 165.4, 331.5.4.

5. *Sermo* 142.3, 34.7f.

6. *Sermo* 34.8, *De civ. Dei* X.5.

7. *De civ. Dei* X.5, *Sermo* 56.4.5f., 57.4, *Enarr. in Psa.* 102.4. For
the use of Psalm 15 (16):2, cf. *De doctr. Christ.* I.31.34, *Conf.* VII.
11.17, *Enarr. in Psa.* 69.7, *In Ioh. Ev. tract.* 11.5, *Ep.* 102.3.17,
138.1.6f.

8. *De doctr. Christ.* I.25.26, *Sermo* 90.6, 96.2, *Ep.* 155.4.13.

9. *De civ. Dei* X.3.2, *Sermo* 128.3.5.

10. Cicero, *De officiis* III.4.19: "quicquid honestum est, idem
utile videtur nec utile quicquam, quod non honestum . . . 5.21: Si
enim sic erimus adfecti, ut propter suum quisque emolumentum
spoliet aut vilet alterum, disrumpi necesse est eam, quae maxime est
secundum naturam, humani generis societatem." Cf. Ambrose, *De
off. min.* (*P. L.* xvi) I.9.27f., II.6.22ff. Proclus, *Commentarius in Al-
cibiadem*, p. 316 (Creuzer): διότι τό συμφέρον οὐχ ὁρῶσιν ἔνδον ἐν
αὐτῇ τῇ ψυχῇ μονίμως ἐστηκός, ἀλλ᾽ ἐν τοῖς ἔξω κείμενον ἐσπαρ-
μένοις πράγμασιν, καὶ ἀναγκαίοις μᾶλλον ἢ ἀγαθοῖς.

11. If we could trust the Maurist text, *De Trin.* VIII.8.12 would

afford a very clear statement (a) asserting the coextensiveness of love-of-God and love-of-self/neighbor and rejecting proportional assignment, (b) subordinating the one to the other teleologically: "Nec illa iam quaestio moveat, quantum fratri caritatis debeamus impendere, quantum Deo: incomparabiliter plus quam nobis Deo, fratri autem quantum nobis ipsis: nos autem ipsos tanto magis diligimus, quanto magis diligimus Deum. Ex una igitur eademque caritate Deum prox-imumque diligimus: sed Deum propter Deum, nos autem et proximum propter Deum." The Mountain-Glorie Text (*C.C.S.L.* 1) omits the words "incomparabiliter plus quam nobis Deo."

   12. *De civ. Dei* XIX.14, *Ep.* 155.4.15; cf. *De mor. eccl.* 26.48.

   13. *De doctr. Christ.* I.26.27; cf. I.23.22, *Sermo* 179A.4. The modification whereby there are four proper objects of love, self and self's body being counted separately, is peculiar to *De doctrina Christiana* I. The argument as a whole has Stoic antecedents, cf. Seneca, *De beneficiis* IV.17.2.

   14. Cf. Hultgren, p. 3: "En réalité, la manière d'envisager les choses qui caractérise la conception religieuse d'Augustin se manifeste précisément dans sa conception du rapport existant entre *auctoritas* et *ratio* et dans la manière dont il applique cette conception, quand il traite des problèmes théologiques. . . . On peut même dire qu'elle est évoquée dans tous ses écrits du premier au dernier." The validity of *credo ut intelligam* for the early Cassiciacan dialogues has been challenged (R. J. O'Connell, *St. Augustine's Early Theory of Man* [Cambridge, Mass., 1968], pp. 227–57) but its validity for the mature Augustine could hardly be put in doubt. On *ratio* and *auctoritas* in Augustinian ethics see also Gösta Hök, "Augustin und die Antike Tu-gendlehre," *Kerygma und Dogma* 6 (1960): 104–30.

   15. *Sermo de disc. Christ.* 4.4, *Sermo* 90.6, 34.8, *Enarr. in Psa.* 140.2.

   16. Plato, *Gorgias* 509b: μέγιστον τῶν κακῶν ἐστιν ἡ ἀδικία τῷ ἀδικοῦντι. Plotinus, *Enn.* III.2.4: ἴσχουσι δὲ ἀδικοῦντες δίκας κακυνόμενοι ταῖς ψυχαῖς ἐνεργείαις κακαῖς. IV.3.16: καὶ τὸ ἄδικον δὴ τὸ παρ' ἄλλου εἰς ἄλλον αὐτῷ μὲν τῷ ποιήσαντι ἄδικον. Ambrose, *De off. min.* I.12.46 (*P. L.* xvi.37): "Ergo impius ipse sibi poena est." Cf. Augustine, *De mus.* IV.4.5, *Enarr. in Psa.* 36.s2.10. For the use of the theme in Chrysostom, see Eric Osborn, *Ethical*

Patterns in Early Christian Thought (Cambridge, 1976), pp. 119–21.

17. *Enarr. in Psa.* 140.2.

18. *De doctr. Christ.* I.23.23.

19. *De Trin.* XIV.14.18.

20. *De doctr. Christ.* I,24.24.

21. *De doctr. Christ.* I.25.26.

22. *De civ. Dei* XXI.27.2, X.6, *Ench.* 20.76. Similar uses of Ecclus. 30:24 are found at *De bapt.* IV.14.21, *Ep.* 173.1, 247.2, *Sermo* 106.4, 161.6. The same motif, but without the text, at: *Conf.* I.13.21, *C. Gaud.* I.11.12, *Ep.* 106, *Sermo* 109.3, 299D.6. Cf. Ambrose, *De ob. Theod.* (*C.S.E.L.* lxxiii) 16: "Bonum est misericors homo, qui, dum aliis subvenit, sibi consulit. . . ." On the balancing of duties to self and neighbor see also pp. 112–20 below.

23. *Sermo* 106.4, *Enarr. in Psa.* 35.5; cf. *De serm. Dom. in mont.* II.12.43.

24. *Ench.* 20.77.

25. *Sermo* 161.6.

26. *Enarr. in Psa.* 140.14, *In Ioh. Ev. tract.* 51.10.

27. *De div. quaest. 83* 36.1, *De mor. eccl.* 5.7.

28. *Enarr. in Psa.* 140.16. For the comparison of wife and body, cf. *De civ. Dei* XV.7.2, *De Trin.* XII passim. Although Julian used Ephesians 5:29 against Augustine, and Augustine used Galatians 5:17 against Julian, this was not simply a repeat of the debate with the Manichees, Augustine having taken the other side! See p. 51 below.

29. *De doctr. Christ.* I.23.22–26.27; *De Trin.* X.8.11, XIV.6.9, 10.13, 14.18; *Sermo* 179A.4, 330.3.

30. *De civ. Dei* XIX.4.5.

31. Cicero, *De finibus* III.5.16, 2d. ed., trans. H. Rackham (London & Cambridge, Mass., 1931), p. 233. Cf. III.6.20: "Initiis igitur ita constitutis ut ea quae secundum naturam sunt ipsa propter se sumenda sint contrariaque item reicienda, primum est officium (id enim appello καθῆκον) ut se conservet in naturae statu, deinceps ut ea teneat quae secundum naturam sint pellatque contraria. . . ." Cf. also Diogenes Laertius VII.85, quoting Chrysippus on *oikeiosis*. See especially S. G. Pembroke, "Oikeiosis," in *Problems in Stoicism*, ed. A. A. Long (London, 1971), pp. 114–49 and G. B. Kerferd,

"The Search for Personal Identity in Stoic Thought," *Bulletin of the John Rylands Library* 55 (1972-73): 177-96.

32. *De doctr. Christ.* I.25.26.

33. *Sermo* 299.8; cf. *Ep.* 140.6.16, *De civ. Dei* XIX.4.4, XIII.20.

34. *De cur. pro mort. ger.* 18.22; cf. *Sermo de util. iei.* 4.4, *Ep.* 130.6.13.

35. *Conf.* I.20.31.

36. Cf. *Ep.* 140.6.16: "tantam habet vim carnis et animae dulce consortium"; *De civ. Dei* XIX.14: "pacem qua conciliantur anima et corpus."

37. *Sermo* 331.1; *In Ioh. Ev. tract.* 32.2; *Ep.* 140.2.3.

38. The use of Ephesians 5:29, though obviously called forth by the controversy with Manichaeism, begins surprisingly late, in 396, with *De continentia* (where it is used throughout) and *De doctr. Christ.* I.24.24f. Thereafter it is pitted against the Manichaean use of Galatians 5:17 at *C. Faust.* XXI.5.7 and *Sermo de util. iei.* 4.4. The pair appear with an ironically different point at *C. litt. Pet.* II.69.154, and, come the debate with Julian, there they are again, with Augustine now defending Gal. 5:17 against Eph. 5:29: *C. Iul.* VI.14.41, 15.47.

39. *De lib. arb.* III.7.21.

40. *De ver. rel.* 46.86f.

41. *De doctr. Christ.* I.23.22.

42. Ibid., I.23.23-24.24.

43. Ibid., I.24.24-25.26.

44. Ibid., I.25.26: "Modus ergo diligendi praecipiendus est homini, id est quomodo se diligat ut prosit sibi. . . ."

45. Ibid., I.26.27: "Cum enim praecurrat dilectio Dei eiusque dilectionis modus praescriptus appareat, ita ut cetera in illum confluant, de dilectione tua nihil dictum videtur. Sed cum dictum est: 'Diliges proximum tuum tamquam te ipsum,' simul et tui abs te dilectio non praetermissa est."

46. Cf. Cicero, *De fin.* III.6.21.

47. Compare, for example, *De mor. eccl.* 3.4 with *De Trin.* XIII.3.6-8.11 and *De civ. Dei* XIX.4. For a background to this argument, cf. Cicero, *De fin.* II.27.86f.

48. See J. Mausbach, *Die Ethik des Heiligen Augustinus*, vol. 1,

p. 257; H. Arendt, *Der Liebesbegriff bei Augustin*, p. 19; Nygren,
Agape and Eros, pp. 532, 538; Burnaby, *Amor Dei*, p. 118; Hultgren,
Le Commandement d'Amour, p. 158; T. J. Bigham and A. T. Mollegen, "The Christian Ethic," in *A Companion to the Study of St.
Augustine*, ed. R. W. Battenhouse (New York, 1955), pp. 378f.; A.
Becker, *De l'Instinct du Bonheur à l'Extase de la Béatitude* (Paris,
1967), p. 63. Holte (*Béatitude et Sagesse*, pp. 221ff.) attributes his
dissenting opinion to Rudolf Johannesson, but I can find nothing
in Johannesson's discussion to support this.

49. Augustine insists very explicitly on the self-evidence of the
principle: "neque quisquam est in hominum genere, qui non huic
sententiae, antequam plene sit emissa, consentiat," *De mor. eccl.* 3.4;
"quod si quaeratur a duobus, utrum militare velint, fieri possit, ut
alter eorum velle se, alter nolle respondeat: si autem ab eis quaeratur,
utrum esse beati velint, uterque se statim sine ulla dubitatione dicat
optare," *Conf.* X.21.31. Holte's interpretation of these passages as
descriptions of a kind of Platonic *maieutike*, calling forth an *anam-
nesis* of submerged knowledge, is implausible in the extreme (p. 226).
One could only be astonished at the perfection to which Augustine
thought he had brought the Socratic science of midwifery, if he really
believed he could be certain of immediate and total success with
every member of the human race. One further passage seems proof
against Holte's understanding: "Atque ego rursus exordiens, 'Beatos
esse nos volumus?' inquam. Vix hoc effuderam, occurrerunt una
voce consentientes," *De beat. vit.* 2.10. The chorus of assent is evidently a literary convention for marking what is *manifestum*, or
self-evident. It has occurred in the previous chapters with this function and now marks the absolutely safe and unchallengeable foundation from which the "new beginning" to the argument can proceed.
And we may observe that mass midwifery would hardly be appropriate for such a disparate group, including as it did Augustine's mother,
who had already "captured the very citadel of philosophy." We
may note, too, *De lib. arb.* II.10.28, where Evodius says that Augustine could see the truth of the eudaemonist principle, even though
he, Evodius, might not want him to, and *De Trin.* XIII.4.7, where the
principle is so obvious that even the skeptic Cicero thought it beyond
challenge.

50. Holte, *Béatitude et Sagesse*, p. 256.

51. *De civ. Dei* X.3.2: "Ut enim homo se diligere nosset, constit-
utus est ei finis, quo referret omnia quae ageret, ut beatus esset;
non enim qui se diligit aliud vult esse quam beatus." *Sermo de disc.
Christ.* 6.6: "Quaerere habes quomodo diligas te ipsum: et audire
habes, 'Diligere Dominum Deum tuum ex toto corde tuo et ex tota
mente tua et ex tota anima tua.' Homo enim quomodo a se fieri non
potuit, sic nec beatus fieri a se potest."

52. *Conf.* X.21.31.

53. Cf. *De lib. arb.* I.14.30, *Conf.* X.20.29–23.33, *De Trin.* XIII.
4.7–9.11. Augustine constantly had difficulty understanding how
some men could fail to love God while they continued to desire the
happy life. In his early writing he experimented with the answer
that all men do love God after a fashion (*Sol.* I.1.2, *De serm. Dom.
in mont.* II.14.48, cf. *Retr.* I.18.8) but abandoned this in favor
of the view, presented in different forms, that the desire could be
frustrated by moral weakness and unbelief. At the same time, as
we have observed, he slowly withdrew from the absolute identification of God and the happy life, preferring to say that the happy
life was lived "with God" and "in God," thus allowing for a certain
opacity between the two which made the blindness of the unbe-
liever more comprehensible.

NOTES TO CHAPTER THREE

1. See M. Schmaus, *Die Psychologische Trinitätslehre des Hl.
Augustinus*, 2d ed. (Munster, 1967), pp. 376f. This principle has important implications for the doctrine of the Double Procession of
the Holy Spirit.

2. See p. 30 above.

3. *Enarr. in Psa.* 18 (2).14; *In Ioh. Ev. tract.* 12.13; *Enarr. in Psa.*
44.18.

4. *In Ioh. Ev. tract.* 87.4; *Enarr. in Psa.* 128.4; 32(2).s2.16;
Sermo 330.1; *Ep. ad Rom. inc. exp.* 9: "Ea enim demum est humanae
iustitiae disciplina non in se amare nisi quod Dei est, et odisse quod
proprium est. . . ."

5. *Sermo* 216.8; *Enarr. in Psa.* 38.9; *De ver. rel.* 48.93; *Sermo* 9.10; 336.2.

6. *Enarr. in Psa.* 140.14.

7. Cf. Plotinus, *Enn.* V.1.1.

8. *C. Acad.* I.1.1; *Enarr. in Psa.* 32(2).s2.16; *Sermo* 216.2 .

9. *Ep.* 143.2.

10. *C. Iul.* IV.3.28.

11. *De civ. Dei* XIV.28.

12. The parallelism, of course, is purely rhetorical. The "self-despite" which accompanies love-of-God is quite compatible with right self-love, whereas the "despite of God" implied by wrong self-love is not compatible with love-of-God.

13. *Sermo* 96.2: "Si enim se non amaret et Deum sibi praeponeret. . ."; 330.3: "Quisquis enim dimisso Deo amaverit se. . ."; 142.3: "Quae si se ipsum amaret neglecto a quo facta est. . . ."

14. *De ver. rel.* 48.93: "Et haec est perfecta iustitia, qua potius potiora, et minus minora diligimus."

15. *In Ioh. Ev. tract.* 25.16.

16. *De Trin.* IX.4.4. On Augustine's dichotomous anthropology see Schmaus, *Die Psychologische Trinitätslehre*, pp. 310f. *Spiritus* and *mens* are aspects of *anima* and do not presuppose a three-fold division of man.

17. *In Ioh. Ev. tract.* 32.2.

18. *Sermo* 90.6.

19. *De Trin.* X.5.7–7.9, trans. John Burnaby (*Augustine: Later Works* [Library of Christian Classics, London & Philadelphia, 1954], pp. 80ff.).

20. Cf. *De Trin.* IX.2.2: "Quid est autem amare se, nisi sibi praesto esse velle ad fruendum se? Et cum tantum se vult esse, quantum est, par menti voluntas est, et amanti amor aequalis. Et si aliqua substantia est amor, non est utique corpus sed spiritus: nec mens corpus sed spiritus est. Neque tamen amor et mens duo spiritus, sed unus spiritus; nec essentiae duae sed una: et tamen duo quaedam unum sunt, amans et amor; sive sic dicas, quod amatur et amor."

21. Holte's interpretation places great weight upon the differentiation of the parts of the soul and the coexistence of the active

and contemplative life. "L'amour est une tendance; or la tendance se trouve en toutes les parties de l'âme; donc l'amour chrétien de Dieu est psychologiquement possible. Mais, nous l'avons vu, *appetitus* désigne le mouvement (*tendere esse*) qui traverse toute l'existence, tel qu'il se présente chez les êtres animés. Dans cette portion du cosmos que constitue l'âme humaine, cet *appetitus* est un dynamisme unifiant l'âme et pourtant différencié, qui s'exprime de différentes façons dans les différentes parties de l'âme: dans la vie contemplative, c'est un désir naturel et une recherche du divin, de la béatitude et de la sagesse; dans la vie active, c'est un effort pour conserver et développer le moi raisonnable (amour de soi) ainsi qu'une tendance à la communauté sociale extérieure (amour du prochain); dans la vie sensible, c'est le souci du corps (instinct de conservation) et la tendance instinctive à s'unir à d'autres corps (instinct sexuel)," p. 256. This reading of *De doctrina Christiana* I is arguable, though to me finally unconvincing. With the later books of *De Trinitate* it is quite clearly incompatible. To anticipate our exposition in only one point: In *De Trin.* XIII the desire for happiness is assigned to the active not to the contemplative aspect of the soul.

22. *De Trin.* X.4.6. See P. Agaësse, "La Connaissance de l'Ame par elle-meme," *B. A.*, vol. 16, pp. 603 ff.

23. Proclus, *S. T.* 10: τί γὰρ ἐστιν ἄλλο τὸ αὐταρκες ἢ τὸ παρ' ἑαυτοῦ καὶ ἐν ἑαυτῷ τὸ ἀγαθὸν κεκτημένον;

24. Porphyry, *Sent.* 33 (35).4: εἰ τὸ μὲν ἐν τόπῳ καὶ ἔξω ἑαυτοῦ, ὅτι εἰς ὄγκον προελήλυθε, τὸ δὲ νοητὸν οὔτε ἐν τόπῳ καὶ ἐν ἑαυτῷ, ὅτι οὐκ εἰς ὄγκον προελήλυθεν, εἰ τὸ μὲν εἰκὼν τὸ δὲ ἀρχέτυπον, τὸ μὲν πρὸς τὸ νοητὸν κέκτηται τὸ εἶναι, τὸ δὲ ἐν ἑαυτῷ. Cf. Proclus, *Comm. in Alc.*, p. 92 (Creuzer): οὐκ ἐξιστάμενα τῆς ἑαυτῶν ἕδρης, ἀλλ' ἐν ἑαυτοῖς μένοντα καὶ προϊέναι φανταζόμενα.

25. Plotinus, *Enn.* II.9.1: ὥστε ἐν τῷ πρώτως νοεῖν ἔχοι ἂν καὶ τὸ νοεῖν ὅτι νοεῖ ὡς ἒν ὄν. καὶ οὐδὲ τῇ ἐπινοίᾳ ἐκεῖ διπλοῦν; III.2.1 (of the intellectual cosmos): ἡ πᾶσα ζωὴ αὐτοῦ καὶ πᾶς νοῦς ἐν ἑνὶ ζῶσα καὶ νοοῦσα ὁμοῦ καὶ τὸ μέρος παρέχεται ὅλον καὶ πᾶν αὐτῷ φίλον οὐ χωρισθὲν ἄλλο ἀπ' ἄλλου οὐδὲ ἕτερον γεγεννημένον μόνον καὶ τῶν ἄλλων ἀπεξενωμένον.

26. Marius Victorinus, *Ad Cand.* 15 (*C.S.E.L.* lxxxiii.33): "semper in semet manens." See Pierre Hadot, *Porphyre et Victorinus,*

vol. 1 (Paris, 1968), pp. 283ff., 317f. on the self-relationships of the
Godhead in Victorinus's thought.

27. Plotinus, *Enn.* I.4.12: αὐτὸς αὐτῷ πάρεστι; I.6.5: ἑαυτοῖς
συνεῖναι ποθεῖτε; I.8.2: σύνεστιν αὐτῷ συνών. Cf. Porphyry, *Sent.*
40 (41).4: καὶ ἔστης ἐν αὐτῷ παρὼν παρόντι, τότε πάρει καὶ τῷ
ὄντι πανταχοῦ ὄντι. ὅταν δ᾽ ἀφῇς αὐτόν, ἀπέστης κἀκείνου. τοιαύτην
γὰρ ἀξίαν εἴληφε, παρεῖναι τῷ αὐτῷ παρόντι καὶ ἀπεῖναι τῷ αὐτοῦ
ἔκσταντι.

28. Plotinus, *Enn.* I.2.5: συνάγουσαν πρὸς ἑαυτήν; I.6.5: συλλεξ-
άμενοι αὐτοὺς ἀπὸ τῶν σωμάτων; III.5.9: τὸ γὰρ ἐν νῷ συνεσπει-
ραμένον. Porphyry, *Sent.* 32 (34).9: συνάγειν αὐτὸν ἀπὸ τοῦ σώματος.
Cf. Plato, *Phaedo* 67c: αὐτὴν καθ᾽ αὐτὴν πανταχόθεν ἐκ τοῦ σώματος
συναγείρεσθαί τε καὶ ἀθροίζεσθαι.

29. *De civ. Dei* X.29.2.

30. See Werner Beierwaltes, *Proklos: Grundzüge seiner Metaphysik* (Frankfurt, 1965), pp. 161ff. on the three senses of ἐπιστροφή,
the first of which is the most significant for our study: (*a*) man's
return to his soul from the world of sense, (*b*) the self-reflection of
the thinking mind, (*c*) the return of the caused to the Primal Cause.

31. Plotinus, *Enn.* I.2.7: τὸ δὲ πρὸς αὐτὸν ἡ σωφροσύνη; III.5.1:
οἰκειότητος ἄλογον σύνεσιν. Proclus, *S. T.* 42: πᾶν τὸ αὐθυπόστατον
πρὸς ἑαυτό ἐστιν ἐπιστρεπτικόν; 83: πᾶν τὸ ἑαυτοῦ γνωστικὸν πρὸς
ἑαυτὸ παντῇ ἐπιστρεπτικόν ἐστιν; *Comm. in Alc.*, p. 14: ἐπιστρέψει
πρὸς ἑαυτὸν ἕκαστον ἡμῶν; p. 26: τὸ γὰρ εἰς ἑαυτὸν ἐπιστρέφειν
τὸν ἐρώμενον καὶ ἀνακαλεῖσθαι καὶ συλλέγειν, οἰκεῖόν ἐστιν τοῖς
ἐν θεοῖς ἐρασταῖς.

32. Ambrose, *Hex.* VI.7.42 (*C.S.E.L.* xxxii (1).233): "'Adtende' inquit 'tibi soli' (Deut. 4:9). Aliud enim sumus nos, aliud sunt
nostra, alia quae circa nos sunt. Nos sumus, hoc est anima et mens,
nostra sunt corporis membra et sensus eius, circa nos autem pecunia
est, servi sunt et vitae istius adparatus. Tibi igitur adtende, te ipsum
scito." On the possibility that Augustine may have heard this sermon
preached, see Pierre Courcelle, *Recherches sur les Confessions de
Saint Augustin* (Paris, 1950), p. 138.

33. Ambrose, *Ep.* VII.22. On this theme in Ambrose's writing see
Pierre Courcelle, *Recherches sur Saint Ambroise* (Paris, 1973),
pp. 25–33.

34. Ambrose, *Hex.* III.12.49 (*C. S. E. L.* xxxii (1).91 f.): "In te ipso suavitas tuae gratiae est, ex te pullulat, in te manet, intus tibi inest, in te ipso quaerenda iocunditas tuae est conscientiae." *De off. min.* (*P. L.* xvi) I.12.44: "Ideo non secundum forensem abundantiam aestimandam beatitudinem singulorum; sed secundum interiorem conscientiam."

35. On what follows cf. Aimé Becker, *De l'Instinct du Bonheur à l'Extase de la Béatitude* (Paris, 1967), pp. 150–64.

36. *Conf.* VII.10.16, *C. Acad.* II.2.5.

37. *De quant. an.* 28.55. Cf., with many other examples, *C. Acad.* III.19.42, *De ver. rel.* 39.72, *De lib. arb.* II.16.41, *Enarr. in Psa.* 38.9, 55.10, *Sermo* 341A.3.

38. *De Trin.* XI.5.9: "id amare alienari est." See R. A. Markus, "*Alienatio*: Philosophy and Eschatology in the Development of an Augustinian Idea," in *Studia Patristica* ix, ed. F. L. Cross (Texte und Untersuchungen xciv), pp. 431–50.

39. *De civ. Dei* XI.28, *Retr.* I.7.3, *Sermo* 96.2, 179A.4, 330.3.

40. *Sermo* 34.7, *Ep. ad Gal. exp.* 59, *Sermo* 163B.5, 348.2, *Quaest. Ev.* II.13.

41. *De ord.* II.6.19, *De quant. an.* 30.61.

42. *Adnot. in Iob* 9:35, *Conf.* VII.7.11, *De Gen. c. Man.* II.12.16.

43. *Conf.* VII.11.17, quoting Sap. 7:27.

44. *Conf.* IX.10.24, *Sermo* 187.1. Cf . *De Gen. ad lit.* I.5.10: "principium manens in se incommutabiliter." Augustine's Christology is compared to that of Cyril of Alexandria by E. Portalié, *A Guide to the Thought of Saint Augustine* (London, 1960), p. 156. For a more cautious conclusion see T. J. van Bavel, *Recherches sur la Christologie de Saint Augustin* (Fribourg, 1954), pp. 176 ff.

45. *De Gen. ad lit.* IV.15.26.

46. *De ver. rel.* 39.72.

47. *Conf.* VII.10.16. On the relation between this and Plotinus *Enn.* I.6 see Courcelle, *Recherches sur les Confessions*, p. 167. R. J. O'Connell (*St. Augustine's Early Theory of Man*, pp. 31–64) finds the two treatises *Enn.* VI.4,5 to be the source of Augustine's conception of divine omnipresence and transcendence, and sees no serious departure from Plotinus in this passage (p. 59).

48. *Sermo* 330.3.

49. It is not a phrase generally used by Neoplatonist philosophers, though Plotinus has αὐτοῦ ἔρως (in a good sense) at *Enn.* VI.8.15.

50. *De Trin.* XV.6.10, translation adapted from that of Burnaby in *Augustine: Later Works,* pp. 136 f.

51. See F. Cayré's note, "Mysticisme et theologie trinitaire," *B. A.,* vol. 16, p. 574.

52. *De Trin.* VIII. pro. 1.

53. VIII.3.4.

54. "Quo se sutem convertat ut fiat bonus animus nisi ad bonum, cum hoc amat et appetit et adipiscitur?" (3.4). With P. Agaësse I take the *cum*-clause to refer to the natural activity of the soul before conversion: "Vers quoi donc se tournera-t-elle pour devenir une âme bonne, sinon vers le bien, puisque c'est lui qu'elle aime, qu'elle désire, qu'elle atteint?" (*B. A.*, vol. 16, p. 35), and not to its converted activity, as does Burnaby: ". . . but to *the* Good, loving, pursuing, attaining it," *Augustine: Later Works*, p. 42.

55. "Inde enim approbatur factus ubi videtur fuisse faciendus. Haec est veritas et simplex bonum" (3.5). The second sentence follows directly from the first, as in Agaësse's translation: "car nous ne la trouvons digne d'éloges, une fois créée, que parce que nous référons à l'idéal qui a présidé à sa création. Voilà la vérité, le bien sans mélange . . ." (p. 37).

56. 3.4,5. On Augustine's use of Acts 17:27f. see R. J. O'Connell, *St. Augustine's Early Theory of Man,* pp. 103 ff.

57. See P. Henry, *St. Augustine on Personality* (New York, 1960), p. 15.

58. "Qui ergo amat homines, aut quia iusti sunt aut ut iusti sint amare debet. Sic enim et se ipsum amare debet aut quia iustus est aut ut iustus sit; sic enim diligit 'proximum tamquam se ipsum' sine ullo periculo. Qui enim aliter se diligit iniuste se diligit quoniam se ad hoc diligit ut sit iniustus, ad hoc ergo ut sit malus, ac per hoc iam non se diligit: 'Qui' enim 'diligit iniquitatem odit animam suam.'" The best defense that can be offered for the strange claim that the evil man loves himself "to this end, that he may be unrighteous," is that the distinction between *ut finale* and *ut consecutivum* is weak, and that this syntactical ambiguity has tripped Augustine, already giddy from a series of leaps between *quia* and *ut* clauses.

59. Augustine uses 1 John 4:16: "God is love."

60. But see below, p. 83, and n. 62.

61. X.3.5. Cf. XIV.6.8ff.

62. The former view is maintained by M. Schmaus, *Die Psychologische Trinitätslehre*, pp. 277f., the latter by J. Moingt, "L'analogie de la conscience de soi," *B. A.*, vol. 16, pp. 608ff.).

63. Etienne Gilson (*The Christian Philosophy of St. Augustine* [London, 1961], pp. 27–111, esp. p. 56) represents sense-knowledge as the *fourth* step on an ascent which began with faith and proceeded through the acceptance of rationality to the certainty of personal existence and life and to belief in the evidence of the senses. This is to conflate the polemic against the Academics with the Plotinian ascent. It is perfectly true that when Augustine is countering Academic skepticism, sense-perception is demonstrated to be reliable only by a train of argument which begins with a priori certainties about reason and life. But this is a different enterprise altogether from the Plotinian journey, which starts from reliance on the senses as characteristic of all unreflective humankind. To string the two enterprises together has the unfortunate effect of concealing the mystical elements in the Plotinian–Augustinian program and representing it as a merely propositional sequence. It also ignores the strong disapproval with which Augustine views those who live by the senses, for on Gilson's reconstruction they are halfway up while in Augustine's eyes they have not yet started.

64. It is explained at XIV.15.21 that there is no recollection of beatitude in the human race; so presumably, despite the agreement on its content, it is not obvious to the wicked that they are forfeiting it.

65. XIV.14.18, quoting Vergil, *Georg.* III.513f.

NOTES TO CHAPTER FOUR

1. *De civ. Dei* XIV.28.

2. On balance *Enarr. in Psa.* 44.9,17, tentatively dated to 403 (S. Zarb, *C. C. S. L.* xxxviii p. xv) has it over *De Gen. ad lit.* XI.15.20, which was probably written near the end of the period 401–14. Other examples of perverse *amor sui*: *Sermo* 34.7f. (undated,

C.C.S.L. xli.423); *Sermo* 96.2 (416–17); *Sermo* 142.3 (undated);
Sermo 145.4 (397 popularly after Lambot); *Sermo* 330.3 (397
popularly after Lambot); *Sermo* 336.2 (undated); *Sermo* 348.2 (425–
30). I abandon Lambot's date for *Sermo* 330 without hesitation,
resting as it does upon a conjectural identification. *Sermo* 145 is more
troublesome, though Lambot's date is still far from certain. For
dates of Sermons consult first P. -P. Verbraken, *Etudes Critiques sur
les Sermons Authentiques de Saint Augustin* (Bruges & The Hague,
1976).

   3. *Regula ad Monachos* 154, *P. L.* ciii.540.

   4. Porphyry, *Sent.* 40 (41).4 (expounding Plotinus).

   5. Plotinus, *Enn.* IV.4.3, V.1.1, 4th ed., trans. S. MacKenna and
B. S. Page (London, 1976).

   6. *De Gen. ad lit.* XI.15.19; cf. *De Trin.* XII.9.14.

   7. *De civ. Dei* XIV.13.1, XIII.21. XIV.28.

   8. *De Gen. c. Man.* II.9.12, 15.22.

   9. *De lib. arb.* III.24.72, 25.76.

  10. *Ep.* 118.3.15, *Sermo* 96.2.

  11. *Conf.* I.13.21, *De pat.* 17.14, *In I Ep. Ioh. tract.* 2.8f., *Sermo*
121.1 (*amor mundi*); *Enarr. in Psa.* 64.2, *Sermo* 125.7, 344.1 (*amor
saecli*).

  12. *De ver. rel.* 13.26, 48.93.

  13. *C. Sec.* 17.

  14. *Sermo* 330.3, 142.3 *De civ. Dei* XIV.28.

  15. *Enarr. in Psa.* 44.9. "Sibi placere" and "se amare" are declared
to be synonymous at *Enarr. in Psa.* 106.14.

  16. *De doctr. Christ.* III.10.16. See pp. 26–29 above.

  17. *Sermo* 336.2.

  18. *Sermo* 348.2, *Conf.* X.36.59, *In Ioh. Ev. tract.* 6.1.

  19. *Ep.* 140.37.85, *Sermo* 145.4.

  20. The use of 1 Cor. 4:7 is a good example of how an idea present quite early in Augustine's thought could be brought into prominence by apologetic need. Of the 100 or so occasions on which he
used the text, 5 may be confidently dated to the years before 400,
another 7 or 8 with some probability to the first decade of the
new century. The Pelagian storm appeared on the horizon in 411, and
there are 7 uses probably datable to that year alone. Cyprian's

comment on the text (*Test.* III.4) attracted Augustine's attention only
later in his life: *C. ep. ii Pel.* IV.9.25, *Retr.* II.27.3, *De praed. sanct.*
3.7, *De don. pers.* 14.36.

21. *Sermo* 67.6. For the treatment of the Pharisee and the Pub-
lican (Luke 18:9–14) see e.g., *De pecc. mer. et rem.* II.5.6.

22. *De civ. Dei* XIV.13.1, *De doctr. Christ.* I.22.21.

23. *Enarr. in Psa.* 41.12.

24. *De Gen. c. Man.* II.16.24.

25. *Sermo* 21.3, *Enarr. in Psa.* 50.15. Cf. also *De Trin.* IX.8.13,
XII.11.16.

26. *De Gen. c. Man.* II.9.12, *De civ. Dei* XIV.13.1.

27. *De Trin.* XII.9.14.

28. *Sermo* 96.2, 179A.4.

29. *De Trin.* XII.9.14: "totumque illud ubi aliquid proprium
contra leges quibus universitas administratur nititur per corpus proprium gerit quod partiliter possidet. . . ."

30. *Enarr. in Psa.* 103.s2.11, 105.34.

31. *Enarr. in Psa.* 103.s2.11, *Sermo* 8.5, *Enarr. in Psa.* 91.6. Augustine did know a text of St. John which read *cum* instead of *qui* at
8:44 (*In Ioh. Ev. tract.* 42.12f.).

32. Curiously the substantival form *amor sui* is never used in anything but this radically evil sense, while the verbal form *amare se*
is used in both good and evil senses. The synonymous *dilectio sui*,
diligere se, is used in both good and evil senses in both substantival
and verbal forms. With both words the verbal forms are considerably more frequent in Augustine's pages than the substantival.

33. We reject Hultgren's comment (p. 161): "Lequel de ces amours
est-il *naturel*? Celui qui aboutit à l'amour de Dieu ou celui qui fait
un Dieu de notre 'moi'? Au point de vue de l'idéal c'est sans doute le
premier de ces amours qui est naturel comme prenant sa source
dans l'ordre méme de la création, mais au point de vue de la réalité
c'est l'orgueil qui après la chute constitue l'attitude naturelle de
l'homme. Il n'est point besoin de commander à l'homme de s'aimer
soi-même ou d'aimer son corps." Hultgren's failure to distinguish
the natural from the radically evil sense of self-love leads him to suppose that the latter is universal and that the former is evil. But in
the very passage of *De doctr. Christ.* which he cites natural self-love

is said to be a trace of original righteousness. Augustine's remark that a command to love oneself was not necessary is not to be taken *ironically*!

34. *Conf.* VII.18.24, *Enarr. in Psa.* 131.6.

35. *Ep.* 125.2, 211.12, *De doctr. Christ.* IV.27.59, *Sermo* 46.2, *In Ioh. Ev. tract.* 6.18, *De bapt.* IV.10.15.

36. *Enarr. in Psa.* 115.1, *In Ioh. Ev. tract.* 46.5.

37. *In Ioh. Ev. tract.* 123.5. But 1 Cor. 13:5 is also used in the earliest "two loves" passage, *De Gen. ad lit.* XI.15.19.

38. *De serm. Dom. in mont.* II.15.50.

39. The incidence of the two interpretations can be usefully studied if the references are set out in groups:

A. Complementary interpretation assumed:

De serm. Dom. in mont. II.15.50	394
De doctr. Christ. III.16.24	396
Ep. 243.5	?
Sermo 330.2	397 popularly after Lambot
Sermo 313D.1 f.	?

B. Two possibilities considered:

In Ioh. Ev. tract. 51:10	413 (S. Zarb, *C.C.S.L.* xxxvi. 439) or 414 (M. Berrouard, *R. A.* 7:439)
Sermo 331.1	?
Sermo 313C.1	396–97 popularly after Morin

C. Antithetical interpretation assumed:

Sermo 305.2	before 417

D. Ambiguous:

Enarr. in Psa. 102.3	412 (S. Zarb, *C.C.S.L.* xxxviii)

It makes an attractive hypothesis to say that the complementary interpretation was abandoned by Augustine when he expounded St.
John's Gospel systematically. Thus his round declaration in favor of
the antithetical interpretation in the 51st Tractate would announce
his change of mind. We would then date the two sermons that review the options inconclusively a little before 413–14 (abandoning
Morin's weak date for 313C, as Kunzelmann, *M. A.*, vol. 2, pp.
491 f., encourages us to do). Sermo 330 would be a little earlier again,
its use of *amor sui* forbidding us to date it very many years before
410 (Lambot's earlier date must be abandoned; see n. 2 above). This
hypothesis may be sound, but to dampen our enthusiasm for it
there is not only a comparative lack of evidence that the antithetical
interpretation was Augustine's normal understanding in later life
but also the thought that the complementary interpretation is characteristic of martyr-sermons; it would be not untypical of the man
to use an interpretation he thought less probable in order to exhort
his flock to lay down their lives. Underlining this doubt we find
the complementary interpretation applied to Matt. 10:38f. at *Sermo*
344.6, which can be dated with some confidence to the end of
Augustine's life.

40. *Sermo* 96.2, 305.2, 330.2, *In Ioh. Ev. tract.* 123.5.

41. *De Trin.* VIII.6.9, *In Ioh. Ev. tract.* 87.4.

42. *Sermo* 330.3: "Nemo enim est qui non se amet; sed rectus
amor est quaerendus, perversus cavendus. Quisquis enim dimisso Deo
amaverit se, Deumque dimiserit amando se, non remanet nec in se,
sed exit et a se. . . . Ergo quia contempsit Deum ut amaret se, amando
foris quod non est ipse, contempsit et se. Videte et audite Apos-
tolum . . . etc."

43. *De doctr. Christ.* I.23.23.

44. *De Trin.* XIV.14.18.

NOTES TO CHAPTER FIVE

1. When Augustine uses the words "your neighbour as yourself"
he usually does not specify which of the nine biblical texts (see Introduction, n. 1) he has in mind. Nevertheless, each of them is mentioned

specifically at some point, though the two occurrences in Lev. 19 are
not distinguished. By contrast Augustine makes rather little use of
the "Golden Rule" in its classic form (Matt. 7:12).

2. *Conf.* IV.12.18, *Enarr. in Psa.* 118.s28.3. Cf. *De doctr. Christ.*
I.29.30, *Enarr. in Psa.* 33.s2.6, 53.10, 72.34.

3. *Sermo de disc. Christ.* 3.3.

4. *De ver. rel.* 46.86 ff.

5. *De doctr. Christ.* I.22.20.

6. *De ver. rel.* 46.87, *Enarr. in Psa.* 39.4.

7. Cf. Cicero, *Lael.* 23.88.

8. *De civ. Dei* XIX.1.3. Cf. Hultgren, p. 32: "Ces déclarations ne
laissent, par conséquent, aucun doute sur la haute valeur et sur le
caractère de nécessité qu'Augustin attribue à l'amour du prochain
pour parvenir à l'amour de Dieu et par là à la béatitude et au sou-
verain bien. Cependant il faut bien admettre qu'il s'agit en l'occurrence plutôt d'un postulat de l' *auctoritas* que d'une représentation
de la *ratio*."

9. *De civ. Dei* X.3.2: "Ut enim homo se diligere nosset, constitu-
tus est ei finis, quo referret omnia quae ageret, ut beatus esset; non
enim qui se diligit aliud vult esse quam beatus. Hic autem finis est ad-
haerere Deo. Iam igitur scienti diligere se ipsum, quid aliud mandatur,
nisi ut ei, quantum potest, commendet diligendum Deum?"

10. Karl Holl, "Augustins Innere Entwicklung," in *Gesammelte
Aussätze zur Kirchengeschichte*, vol. 3 (Tübingen, 1928), p. 87.

11. See pp. 56–59. Right self-love, as coextensive with the love of
God, will always be equivalent to pursuit of the "summum bonum,"
when that is correctly identified.

12. Søren Kierkegaard, *Works of Love*, trans. Howard Hong and
Edna Hong (New York, 1962), p. 34.

13. *Sol.* I.3.8: "Illam enim legem amicitiae iustissimam arbitror,
qua praescribitur, ut sicut non minus, ita nec plus quisque amicum
quam se ipsum diligat." I suppose the source of this "law" to be
the principle of which Cicero does not quite approve, "ut eodem modo
erga amicos affecti simus quo erga nosmet ipsos" (*Lael.* 16.56). The
influence of the Ciceronian tradition constantly makes itself felt in
this area of Augustine's thought; although Augustine does not use the
term *amicitia* very widely, whenever his thoughts turn to the friend-

ships of his youth, the word and the cluster of Ciceronian thoughts attached to it make an appearance. At *C. Acad.* III.6.13 he quotes *Lael.* 6.20 directly; note also the quotation of *De invent.* II.55.166 at *De div. quaest. 83* 31.3.

14. *De mend.* 6.9.

15. *Sermo* 319.4, *De civ. Dei* X.6, *De fid. et op.* 15.25.

16. See Outka, *Agape*, pp. 207-20, on Barth's defense of "mutuality."

17. Petré's section "Frère et Prochain" (*Caritas*, pp. 105-60) is of considerable importance and has been freely used in what follows.

18. *Adv. Iud.* 2.3f. (*C. C. S. L.* ii.1341f.).

19. *De div. quaest. 83* 53.4, *De serm. Dom. in mont.* I.19.59, *Sermo* 359.9, 299D.1.

20. Petré, *Caritas*, p. 156. Cf. *Ep.* 130.6.13, *Enarr. in Psa.* 25(2).2.

21. *Enarr. in Psa.* 25(2).2: "Proximus tuus ille est, qui tecum natus est ex Adam et Eva. Omnes proximi sumus conditione terrenae nativitatis; sed aliter fratres illa spe caelestis hereditatis." At *Sermo de disc. Christ.* 3.3 the universal sense of "brother" is mentioned but the restricted sense preferred.

22. See Outka, *Agape*, pp. 268-74.

23. *De ver. rel.* 46.88, *Retr.* I.12.12.

24. *De civ. Dei* XIX.14, *In I Ep. Ioh. tract.* 8.4. Cf. *De doctr. Christ.* I.28.29.

25. It is clear that for other purposes Augustine did recognize specific differences in types of relationship, for example in his thinking about marriage.

26. *Enarr. in Psa.* 25(2).2.

27. *C. mend.* 6.15, *De cat. rud.* 27.55, *Sermo* 306.9.8.

28. *In I Ep. Ioh. tract.* 8.11; cf. *De mor. eccl.* 27.52, *Ep.* 153.5.14.

29. *De doctr. Christ.* I.29.30: "Ad quem [God] si conversi fuerint, et illum tamquam beatificum bonum et nos tamquam socios tanti boni necesse est ut diligant." *In I Ep. Ioh. tract.* 1.9: "Quae est perfectio dilectionis? Et inimicos diligere, et ad hoc diligere, ut sint fratres"; 8.10: "Si ergo hoc optas, diligendo inimicum, ut sit frater tuus, cum eum diligis, fratrem diligis. . . . Adtende quare te monuit Christus ut diligas inimicos."

30. *Conf.* II.8.16, III.3.6, V.13.23.

31. *Ep.* 130.6.13; cf. *De fid. rer. invis.* 2.4.

32. 4.7.

33. Cf. *Lael.* 14.49 (*redamare*), 20.71 ff. (inferior and superior).

34. *In I Ep. Ioh. tract.* 8.4.

35. See Burnaby's memorable chapter, *Amor Dei*, pp. 43–82. The development by which Augustine came to see the doctrine of the "two lives" as an eschatological doctrine does not seem to have touched his rationalization of the monastic secular lives as "higher" and "lower."

36. See further, p. 150 below.

37. *Enarr. in Psa.* 36.s3.19. Cf. *C. litt. Pet.* III.3.4.

38. *De serm. Dom. in mont.* II.12.43.

39. *Conf.* VI.16.26 (friends), *Enarr. in Psa.* 53.10, 55.17 (man and wife).

40. Cicero, *De invent.* 55.166, quoted at *De div. quaest. 83* 31.3.

41. *De Trin.* VI.5.7.

42. *De Trin.* VI.10.11. It is generally considered that this interpretation of Hilary erred on the side of creativity. Cf. Schmaus, *Die Psychologische Trinitätslehre*, p. 387.

43. *De Trin.* VIII.10.14.

44. *De div. quaest. 83* 35.1.

45. Augustine's Latin Bible furnished him with the phrase "diligere invicem" at Rom 13:8, 1 John. 3:23, and John. 13:34f.

46. *De spir. et lit.* 32.56: "Caritas quippe Dei dicta est diffundi in cordibus nostris, non qua nos ipse diligit, sed qua nos facit dilectores suos: sicut iustitia Dei, qua iusti eius munere efficimur, et Domini salus, qua nos salvos facit, et fides Iesu Christi, qua nos fideles facit." See Burnaby, *Amor Dei*, p. 99.

47. We must notice how often the genitive *Dei* is interchanged with the adjective *divina*, which preserves the ambiguity between subjective and objective more effectively. Even "your self-love," "dilectio tui," is on occasion rephrased as "your self's love," "dilectio tua"! See *De doctr. Christ.* I.26.27, *Sermo* 179A.4.

48. *Conf.* IV.6.11, cf. *Retr.* II.32.4.

49. *Conf.* X.3.3: "conexos sibimet unum facit"; *De cat. rud.* 12.17: "habitemus in invicem"; *Enarr. in Psa.* 30(2).s2.1: "Caritas autem compagem facit, compages complectitur unitatem."

50. *Sermo* 136B, *Enarr. in Psa.* 62.17, *De bapt.* II.13.18 and many other uses of "vinculum," a favorite metaphor. Acts 4.32 is quoted at *In Ioh. Ev. tract.* 14.19, 18.4, 39.5 etc.

51. *In Ioh. Ev. tract.* 83.3. Augustine is generally careful to make his sense clear when he uses "se diligere" and equivalents to mean "each other." The use of "se frui" at *De doctr. Christ.* I.22.20 is not analogous: it means "mankind (as a class) loving mankind (as a class)."

52. *In I Ep. Ioh. tract.* 10.3.

53. *De div. quaest.* 83 79.1.

54. *Enarr. in Psa.* 103.s2.11.

55. Cf. *Ep.* 110.4: "Ego autem quando laudor a germanissimo et familiarissimo animae meae, velut a me ipso lauder sic habeo."

56. *In I Ep. Ioh. tract.* 8.4, p. 126 above.

57. G. B. Kerferd, "The Search for Personal Identity in Stoic Thought," *Bulletin of the John Rylands Library* 55 (1972–73): 177–96, distinguishes the "inward-looking" aspect of *oikeiosis* as self-protection from the "outward-looking" aspect as relation-forming.

58. *De civ. Dei* XIX.4.4.

59. My conclusion on the meaning of "commune bonum" will be seen to differ from that of R. Johannesson ("Gemeinschaft: IV, In Christentum," *R. G. G.,* 3d ed., vol. 2, cols. 1357–63), who denies this collectivism to Augustine.

60. *In Ioh. Ev. tract.* 18.4.

61. *De fid. et sym.* 9.19, *De Trin.* XV.17.27. Cf. *C. Max.* I.14, II.24, *De Trin.* XV.6.10.

62. *De Trin.* XV.18.32 (cf. Schmaus, *Die Psychologische Trinitätslehre,* p. 392), VIII.7.10ff.

63. *De Trin.* VI.5.7: "cum illo autem unus spiritus quia agglutinatur anima nostra post eum." See R. J. O'Connell, *St. Augustine's Early Theory of Man,* pp. 121–31.

NOTES TO CHAPTER SIX

1. In keeping with philosophical convention, I use the term *eudaemonism* to mean the theory which accounts for moral obligation in terms of the quest for one's *own* happiness, as distinct from "utilitarianism," which accounts for it in terms of the quest for some

happiness, whether one's own or others'. Many of the issues are common to both theories, and the energetic attention which English-speaking philosophers have given to the thought of J. S. Mill can be of use also to students of Augustine.

2. Holl, "Augustines Innere Entwicklung" (1922) (=*Gesammelte Aussätze zur Kirchengeschichte*, vol. 3 [Tübingen, 1928], pp. 54–116), in reply to Adolf von Harnack, "Die Höhepunkte in Augustins Konfessionen" (=*Reden und Aufsätze*, vol. 3 [Giessen, 1916], pp. 67–99).

3. Holl, p. 85.

4. Ibid., p. 87.

5. Ibid., pp. 94 f. On Augustine's handling of Romans 5:5 see p. 130 above.

6. Ibid., pp. 107 f. The reference is to *De spir. et lit.* 36.65. A glance at the context suggests that Holl is rather cavalier with his quotation. Augustine has been stressing the very Pauline point that only when we see God perfectly will we love him perfectly. "Hoc primum praeceptum iustitiae . . . in illa vita implebimus, cum videbimus facie ad faciem. Sed ideo nobis *hoc etiam nunc praeceptum est*, ut admoneremur quid fide exposcere, quo spem praemittere, et . . . in quae anteriora nos extendere debeamus." In other words it is not the demand that is lower here but simply the achievement. I can only suppose that Holl has confused this rather uncontroversial doctrine either with Augustine's theory of monasticism, which really does retain the idea of a "double standard," or with his theory of political action, in which it is not the demand that is less than the ideal but the circumstances in which the demand has to be implemented (see, for example, *Ep.* 187.5). Thus misinterpreted, *iustitia minor* has been seen as the root of the mediaeval doctrine of the "stages of love," discussed below, p. 150.

7. See chap. 1, n. 1. Nygren does rather scant justice to Holl (p. 533), and I cannot accept his claim that his own position is substantially different from that of his predecessor. Holl does not believe, any more than Nygren does, that Augustine's "entire outlook" is "pure eudaemonism." Nygren's contribution was to expand and document the position described in outline by Holl.

8. Nygren, *Agape and Eros*, p. 532.

9. Ibid., p. 533.

10. Ibid., pp. 543 ff.

11. Outka, *Agape*, p. 24.

12. Nygren, p. 210.

13. Outka, p. 278.

14. *The Christian Philosophy of Saint Augustine* [London, 1961], pp. 137f.

15. See pp. 56–59 above.

16. Rousselot's work, originally published in 1908, is cited from the 2d ed. (Paris, 1933). For a recent assessment of his thesis, see H. De Lavalette's contribution to the memorial issue of *Recherches de Science Religieuse* 53 (1965): 462–94.

17. *In Ev. hom.* 17.1 (*P. L.* lxxvi.1139): "minus quam inter duos caritas haberi non potest. Nemo enim proprie ad semet ipsum habere caritatem dicitur, sed dilectio in alterum tendit, ut caritas esse possit."

18. See pp. 127–36 above.

19. See p. 181, n.53, also pp. 48–52.

20. To be precise, the argument does occur in Augustine's *pages*, in the Maurist editors' *Sermo* 368; but its occurrence there (at 4) constitutes a strong supporting argument for the verdict of inauthenticity against this sermon, which occurs also in the corpus of Caesarius of Arles (*C.C.S.L.* civ) as *Sermo* 173. Morin's hypothesis that Caesarius reworked a genuine sermon of Augustine does not take note of the radically un-Augustinian thought of the fourth section. The authentic Augustine never argued for the universality of self-love on the grounds that to love any object is to love oneself as its possessor.

21. Cf. *De civ. Dei* XII.7: "Nemo igitur quaerat efficientem causam malae voluntatis: non enim est efficiens sed deficiens."

22. Abelard, *Comm. ad Rom.* III ad 7:13 (*C. C. C. M.* xi.200 ff.).

23. *C. C. C. M.* xi.203.

24. Bernard, *De diligendo Deo* 8.23–10.29, also (from an earlier treatise) 15.39 (*P. L.* clxxxii), traces the ascent in four stages: first, one loves himself for his own sake; second, he loves God for his own, not God's sake; third, he begins to love God for God's own sake while continuing to love himself for his own sake; fourth, he loves himself only for God's sake, a kind of ecstatic condition described as "laying oneself out from the whole of one's soul and crossing over to God." Al-

though a kind of self-love is left in place at the summit of this ascent, it bears little resemblance to the self-love with which the aspirant began.

25. Cf. Cassian, *De inst. coen.* IV.39–43 (*S. C.* cix) on the ascent of the soul, and *Coll.* XI.7, 8, 12 (*C.S.E.L.*\| xiii, *S. C.* liv) on the three stages of slavish, mercenary, and filial love. Once again it is the presence of such a concept of progress in the Maurist editors' *Sermo* 385 (= Caesarius, *Sermo* 21, *C.C.S.L.* ciii) that marks it as inauthentic. The remarks of F. Edward Cranz deserve attention: "Gradually . . . Augustine's thinking comes to center on the absolute contrast between the sinners and the saved, and in consequence he begins to abandon the whole idea of a series of steps or stages on the way to salvation," "The Development of Augustine's Ideas on Society before the Donatist Controversy," in *Augustine: A Collection of Critical Essays,* ed. R. A. Markus (Garden City, N.Y., 1972), p. 355). To this we need only add that Augustine's use of the stages had never given him a theory of moral progress *within* the Christian life but only a theory of *entry* to it.

26. Rousselot, *Pour l'histoire du Problème de l'amour au Moyen Age,* p. 88.

27. *In I Ep. Ioh. tract.* 8.4. See p. 126 above.

28. For the purposes of this argument I ignore the important consideration that the ethics of Christ are not exclusively deontological but include appeals to the notions of reward and happiness, entirely as one would expect in the tradition not only of Mosaic but also of Solomonic *torah.* The embarrassment caused by these elements in the Gospels makes an interesting comparison with that caused by Augustinian eudaemonism. In recent literature see, for example, Gunther Bornkamm, "Die Lohngedanke im Neuen Testament," in *Studien zu Antike und Urchristentum: Gesammelte Aufsätze,* vol. 2 (Munich, 1959), pp. 69–92; Bo Reicke, "The New Testament Conception of Reward," in *Aux Sources de la Tradition Chrétienne,* Festschrift M. Goguel (Neuchatel & Paris, 1950).

29. Aristotle, *Eth. Nic.* 1094a.

30. Nygren, *Agape and Eros,* p. 42: "A fundamental motif is that which forms the answer given by some particular outlook to a ques-

tion of such a fundamental nature that it can be described in a categorical sense as a fundamental question."

31. See p. 16f. above.

32. See, for example, T. F. Torrance, *Theological Science* (Oxford, 1969), pp. 55–75.

33. Burnaby, *Amor Dei*, p. 6: "The non-mystic constantly betrays a more or less embarrassed consciousness that the words [*love of God*] cannot for him retain their normal significance." Nygren shows an inclination to replace the idea of love for God with that of faith (pp. 123–27 e.g.).

34. This criticism is presumed throughout the engaging theological autobiography of Nygren's fellow Swede Gustaf Wingren (*Creation and Gospel: The New Situation in European Theology* [Toronto, 1979]). See especially pp. 3–17.

BIBLIOGRAPHY

Augustinian bibliography is excellently served. Carl Andresen's *Bibliographia Augustiniana* (Darmstadt, 1973) provides a compendious survey; more extensive studies of recent writing have been provided by T. J. van Bavel, *Repertoire Bibliographique de Saint Augustin 1950-1960*, Instrumenta Patristica iii (Bruges & The Hague, 1963), and Rudolf Lorenz, "Zwölf Jahre Augustinusforschung (1959-1970)," *Theologische Rundschau* 38-40 (1974-75). There is also an annual "Bulletin" in *Révue des Etudes Augustiniennes*. In view of this largesse, it has seemed appropriate to make the following list a restricted and personal one. Not every work included in the Notes appears here.

✓Adam, K. *St. Augustine, The Odyssey of his Soul.* Translated by J. McCann. London, 1932.

Arendt, H. *Der Liebesbegriff bei Augustin, Versuch einer philosophischen Interpretation.* Berlin, 1929.

✓Armstrong, A. H. *St. Augustine and Christian Platonism.* Villanova, 1967. Reprinted in *Augustine: A Collection of Critical Essays*, edited by R. A. Markus, pp. 3-37. Garden City, N.Y., 1972.

Austin, J. "Pleasure and Happiness." *Philosophy* 43 (1968): 51-62. Reprinted in *Mill: A Collection of Critical Essays*, edited by J. B. Schneewind, pp. 234-50. London & Melbourne, 1969.

Barth, K. *Church Dogmatics* IV/2, Sect. 68, "The Holy Spirit and Christian Love." Translated by G. W. Bromiley and T. F. Torrance. Edinburgh, 1958.

van Bavel, T. J. *Recherches sur la Christologie de Saint Augustin.* Fribourg, 1954.

Becker, A. *De l'Instinct du Bonheur à l'Extase de la Béatitude, Théologie et Pédagogie du Bonheur dans la Prédication de Saint
Augustin.* Paris, 1967.

Beierwaltes, W. *Proklos: Grundzüge seiner Metaphysik.* Philoso-
phische Abhandlungen xxiv. Frankfurt, 1965.

Berrouard, M.-F. "La date des Tractatus I–LIV in Iohannis Evangelium
de Saint Augustin." *R.A.* 7 (1972): 105–68.

Bigham, T. J., and Mollegen, A. T. "The Christian Ethic." In *A
Companion to the Study of St. Augustine,* edited by R. W. Battenhouse, pp. 371–97. New York, 1955.

Bornkamm, G. "Die Lohngedanke im Neuen Testament." In *Studien
zu Antike und Urchristentum, Gesammelte Aufsätze,* vol. 2, pp.
69–92. Munich, 1959.

Brown, P. R. L. *Augustine of Hippo, a Biography.* London, 1967.

Burnaby, J. *Amor Dei, A Study of the Religion of St. Augustine.* London, 1938.

——. "The *Retractationes* of St. Augustine: Self-Criticism or Apologia?
A.M., vol. 1, pp. 85–92. Paris, 1954.

——. "Amor in St. Augustine." In *The Philosophy and Theology of
Anders Nygren,* edited by C. W. Kegley, pp. 174–86. Carbondale &
Edwardsville, Ill., London & Amsterdam, 1970.

Chadwick, O. *John Cassian.* Cambridge, 1950.

Courcelle, P. *Recherches sur les Confessions de Saint Augustin.* Paris,
1950.

——. *Recherches sur Saint Ambroise: "Vies" Anciennes, Culture,
Iconographie.* Paris, 1973.

——. *Connais-toi Toi-même, de Socrate à Saint Bernard,* vol. 1. Paris,
1974.

Cranz, F. E. "The Development of Augustine's Ideas on Society
before the Donatist Controversy." *Harvard Theological Review* 47
(1954): 255–316. Reprinted in *Augustine: A Collection of Critical
Essays,* edited by R. A. Markus, pp. 336–403. Garden City, N.Y.
1972.

D'Arcy, M. C. *The Mind and Heart of Love.* London, 1946.

De Ferrari, T. M. *The Problem of Charity for Self: A Study of Thomistic and Modern Theological Discussion.* Washington, 1962.

De Lavalette, H. "Le Théoricien de l'Amour." *Memorial Pierre Rousselot S.J., Recherches de Science Religieuse* 53 (1965): 462-94.

Folliet, G. " 'Deificari in Otio,' Augustin Epistula X.2." *R.A.* 2 (1962): 225-36.

Furnish, V. P. *The Love-Command in the New Testament.* London, 1973.

Gilleman, G. *Le Primat de la Charité en Théologie Morale, Essai Méthodologique.* Brussels & Paris, 1952.

Gilson, E. *The Christian Philosophy of St. Augustine.* Translated by L. E. M. Lynch. London, 1961.

———. *Philosophie et Incarnation selon Saint Augustin.* Montreal, 1947.

Hadot, P. *Porphyre et Victorinus.* 2 vols. Paris, 1968.

von Harnack, A. "Die Höhepunkte in Augustins Konfessionen." In *Reden und Aufsätze,* vol. 3, pp. 67-99. Giessen, 1916.

Hassel, D. J. "Conversion-Theory and Scientia in the De Trinitate." *R.A.* 2 (1962): 383-401.

Hausherr, I. *Philautie, de la tendresse pour soi à la charité selon Saint Maxime le Confesseur.* Orientalia Christiana Analecta cxxxvii. Rome, 1952.

Henry, P. *St. Augustine on Personality.* New York, 1960.

Hök, G. "Augustin und die Antike Tugendlehre." *Kerygma und Dogma* 6 (1960): 104-30.

Holl, K. "Der Neubau der Sittlichkeit." In *Gesammelte Aussätze zur Kirchengeschichte,* vol. 1, pp. 155-287. Tübingen, 1927.

———. "Augustins Innere Entwicklung." *Gesammelte Aussätze zur Kirchengeschichte,* vol. 3, pp. 54-116. Tübingen, 1928.

Holte, R. *Béatitude et Sagesse: Saint Augustin et le problème de la fin de l'homme dans la philosophie ancienne.* Paris & Worcestèr, Mass., 1962.

Hultgren, G. *Le Commandement d'Amour chez Augustin: Interpretation Philosophique et Théologique d'après les Ecrits de la Période 386-400.* Paris, 1939.

Johann, R. *The Meaning of Love.* Glen Rock, N.J., 1966.

Johannesson, R. *Person och Gemenskap, enligt Romersk-Katolst och Luthersk Grundaskadning.* Stockholm, 1947.

———. "Gemeinschaft: IV, In Christentum." *R.G.G.*, 3d ed., vol. 2, cols. 1357-63. Tübingen, 1958.

———. "Caritas in Augustine and Mediaeval Theology." In *The Philosophy and Theology of Anders Nygren*, edited by C. W. Kegley, pp. 187-202. Carbondale & Edwardsville, Ill., London & Amsterdam, 1970.

Kenny, A. J. P. "Happiness." *Proceedings of the Aristotelian Society* 66 (1966): 93-102. Also in *Moral Concepts*, edited by J. Feinberg, pp. 43-52. Oxford, 1969.

Kerferd, G. B. "The Search for Personal Identity in Stoic Thought." *Bulletin of the John Rylands Library* 55 (1972-73): 177-96.

Legrand, L. *La Notion Philosophique de la Trinité chez Saint Augustin.* Paris, 1930.

Lorenz, R. "Fruitio Dei bei Augustin." *Zeitschrift für Kirchengeschichte* 63 (1950-51): 75-132.

———. "Die Herkunft des augustinischen Frui Deo." *Zeitschrift für Kirchengeschichte* 64 (1952-53): 34-60.

Louth, A. "Bernard and Affective Mysticism." In *The Influence of St. Bernard*, edited by Sr. Benedicta Ward, S.L.G., pp. 1-10. Oxford, 1976.

Maclagan, W. G. "Self and Others: A Defence of Altruism." *Philosophical Quarterly* 4 (1954): 109-27.

———. "Respect for Persons as a Moral Principle." *Philosophy* 35 (1960): 193-217, 289-305.

Macnamara, M. A. *Friendship in St. Augustine.* Fribourg, 1958.

Mandouze, A. *Saint Augustin, L'Aventure de la Raison et la Grâce.* Paris, 1968.

Markus, R. A. "The Dialectic of Eros in Plato's Symposium." *Downside Review* 73 (1955): 219-30. Also in *Plato II—Ethics, Politics and Philosophy of Art and Religion*, edited by G. Vlastos, pp. 132-43. Garden City, N.Y., 1971.

——. "*Alienatio:* Philosophy and Eschatology in the Development of an Augustinian Idea." In *Studia Patristica* ix, edited by F. L. Cross (Texte und Untersuchungen xciv), pp. 431–50. Berlin, 1966.

——. *Saeculum: History and Society in the Theology of St. Augustine.* Cambridge, 1970.

——. "St. Augustine on Signs." *Phronesis* 2 (1957): 60–83. Also in *Augustine; A Collection of Critical Essays,* edited by R. A. Markus, pp. 61–91. Garden City, N.Y., 1972.

Marrou, H.-I. *Saint Augustin et la fin de la Culture Antique.* Paris, 1938. Vol. 2, *Retractatio.* Paris, 1949.

Mausbach, J. *Die Ethik des Heiligen Augustinus.* 2 vols. 2d ed. Fribourg, 1929.

Munz, P. "John Cassian." *Journal of Ecclesiastical History* 11 (1960): 1–22.

Nygren, A. *Agape and Eros, Part I—A Study of the Christian Idea of Love* (1930). *Part II—The History of the Christian Idea of Love* (1936). Rev. ed. Translated by P. S. Watson. London, 1953.

——. *Augustin und Luther.* Berlin, 1958.

——. "Reply to Interpreters and Critics." In *The Philosophy and Theology of Anders Nygren,* edited by C. W. Kegley, pp. 347–75. Carbondale & Edwardsville, Ill., London & Amsterdam, 1970.

O'Connell, R. J. *St. Augustine's Early Theory of Man, A.D. 386–391.* Cambridge, Mass., 1968.

——. "Action and Contemplation." In *Augustine: A Collection of Critical Essays,* edited by R. A. Markus, pp. 38–58. Garden City, N.Y., 1972.

O'Daly, G. J. P. *Plotinus' Philosophy of the Self.* Shannon, 1973.

O'Meara, J. J. *The Young Augustine, The Growth of St. Augustine's Mind up to his Conversion.* London, New York & Toronto, 1954.

——. "'Arripui, aperui et legi.'" *A.M.*, vol. 1, pp. 59–66. Paris, 1954.

——. "Augustine and Neo-Platonism." *R.A.* 1 (1958): 91–111.

Oppenheimer, H. "Christian Flourishing." *Religious Studies* 5 (1969): 163–71.

Outka, G. H. *Agape, an Ethical Analysis.* New Haven & London, 1972.

van Oyen, H. "Selbstbehauptung," "Selbstverleugnung," *R.G.G.*, 3d ed., vol. 5, cols. 1668–72, 1679–82. Tübingen, 1961.

Pembroke, S. G. "Oikeiosis." In *Problems in Stoicism*, edited by A. A. Long, pp. 114–49. London, 1971.

Petré, H. *Caritas, Etude sur le Vocabulaire Latin de la Charité Chrétienne.* Louvain, 1948.

Portalié, E. *A Guide to the Thought of St. Augustine.* Translated by R. J. Bastian from *Dictionnaire de Theologie Catholique*, s.v. "Augustin" (Paris, 1903).

Rahner, K. "Experience of Self and Experience of God." In *Theological Investigations*, vol. 13, translated by D. Bourke, pp. 122–32. London, 1975.

Reicke, B. "The New Testament Conception of Reward." In *Aux Sources de la Tradition Chrétienne*, Festschrift M. Goguel, pp. 195–206. Neuchatel & Paris, 1950.

Rist, J. M. *Plotinus: The Road to Reality.* Cambridge, 1967.

——. *Stoic Philosophy.* Cambridge, 1969.

——. "Some Interpretations of Agape and Eros." In *The Philosophy and Theology of Anders Nygren*, edited by C. W. Kegley, pp. 153–73. Carbondale & Edwardsville, Ill., London & Amsterdam, 1970.

Rousselot, P. *Pour l'histoire du Problème de l'amour au Moyen Age.* 1908. 2d ed., Paris, 1933.

Schindler, A. *Wort und Analogie in Augustins Trinitätslehre.* Tübingen, 1965.

Schmaus, M. *Die Psychologische Trinitätslehre des heiligen Augustinus.* 1927. Reprint Münster Westfalen, 1967.

Sciacca, M. F. "Trinité et Unité de l'ésprit." *A.M.*, vol. 1, pp. 521–33. Paris, 1954.

Singer, I. *The Nature of Love, Plato to Luther.* New York, 1966.

Staes, P. E. *Positive Self-Regard and Authentic Morality.* Manila, 1972.

TeSelle, E. *Augustine the Theologian.* London, 1970.

Verbeke, G. "Connaissance de soi et connaissance de Dieu." *Augustiniana* 4 (1954): 495–515.

Verbraken, P.-P. *Etudes Critiques sur les Sermons Authentiques de Saint Augustin.* Instrumenta Patristica xii. Bruges & The Hague, 1976.

Williams, B. "Egoism and Altruism." In *Problems of the Self*, pp. 250–65. Cambridge, 1973.

INDEX OF PASSAGES CITED

1. Works of St. Augustine
2. Other Ancient and Mediaeval Christian Writers
3. Ancient Pagan Writers
4. Scripture

1. WORKS OF ST. AUGUSTINE

Works referred to in the text or notes are listed here in alphabetical order, together with the principal source for the text, with editor and date of text where appropriate.

Adnotationes in Iob (*C.S.E.L.* xxviii
 (2), J. Zycha, 1895)
 9:35: 185
Ad Simplicianum de diversis quaest-
 ionibus (*C.C.S.L.* xliv, A. Mut-
 zenbecher, 1970)
 I.2.8: 174

Confessiones (*B.A.* xiii, xiv, M.
 Skutella, 1934)
 I.1.1: 170
 13.21: 178, 188
 20.31: 50
 II.8.16: 193
 III.3.6: 193
 4.7: 168
 IV.6.11: 194
 7.12: 175
 12.18: 192
 V.13.23: 193
 VI.16.26: 194
 VII–IX: 77
 VII.7.11: 185
 10.16: 73f., 185

 11.17: 176, 185
 18.24: 190
 IX.10.24: 185
 X: 77
 X.3.3: 194
 20.29ff.: 168f., 170, 181
 21.31: 180, 181
 22.32: 170
 29.40: 171
 36.59: 188
 XIII.9.10: 170
Contra Academicos (*C.C.S.L.* xxix,
 W. M. Green, 1970)
 I.1.1: 182
 2.5: 168
 II.2.5: 185
 III.6.13: 193
 19.42: 185
Contra Adimantum (*C.S.E.L.* xxv,
 J. Zycha, 1891)
 6: 171
 20.2: 176
Contra epistulas duas Pelagianorum
 (*C.S.E.L.* 1x, *B.A.* xxiii, C. F.

209

2. OTHER ANCIENT AND MEDIAEVAL CHRISTIAN WRITERS

3. ANCIENT PAGAN WRITERS

GENERAL INDEX

Entries for ancient writers, Christian or pagan, are intended only to supplement entries in the Index of Passages Cited, which should therefore be consulted in conjunction with this Index.